Jean Monnet and the United States of Europe

Jean Monnet and the

MERRY AND SERGE BROMBERGER

United States of Europe

TRANSLATED BY ELAINE P. HALPERIN

Coward-McCann, Inc.   New York

Contents

5

Jean Monnet and the United States of Europe

I

*Traveling Salesman
in the Far West*

JEAN MONNET is better known in England and in the United States than in his own country. To the majority of Frenchmen he is practically unknown. Yet he is the greatest political innovator of the postwar period, the creator of the European Coal and Steel Community, and the father of the Common Market. As the moving spirit of the campaign for a United States of Europe associated with the United States of America, he inspired the opposition to the European Europe of General de Gaulle.

René Pleven, former French premier, a collaborator and disciple of Jean Monnet, has said: "Like de Gaulle, Jean Monnet is a historical figure who towers above his time. In this he resembles the Big Four. It was inevitable that de Gaulle and Jean Monnet should clash, that each should aspire to refashion Europe. They conceived of Europe differently, although ultimately they reached similar conclusions. Above all, they envisaged opposite means and tactics. It was therefore inevitable that Monnet would be anti-de Gaulle, just as de Gaulle would be anti-Monnet."

The twenty years of unremitting, behind-the-scenes battle that the two great French Europeanists waged against each other produced merely a muffled echo. Jean Monnet cannot abide the footlights. His triumphs, even his failures, would be a source of pride to any international political figure, but his career as a statesman has been cloaked in anonymity.

Monnet was one of the organizers of victory in the First World War, and he subsequently became Deputy Secretary-General of the League of Nations. Later, as an international financier, he played a

9

role in America's economic recovery by revealing one of the mechanisms that caused the crisis of 1929. On the eve of World War II, he initiated the manufacture of the American planes and engines that were to save England. He inspired Churchill to suggest a union of Great Britain and France, and attempted to establish a French government in exile. He became the most active of Churchill's representatives to the United States, and Roosevelt's adviser in preparing the arsenal of the free world. In Algiers, he helped to oust General Giraud in order to place de Gaulle at the head of the provisional French government. He hit upon the plan that put France back on her feet, and discovered the mechanisms that were to make possible the functioning of the European communities. The Schuman Plan was actually the Monnet Plan; the Treaty of Rome, the Monnet Treaty.

Paul Delouvrier, one of de Gaulle's right-hand men who also collaborated with Monnet, has said, "His most astonishing feat is to have remained incognito in spite of everything he accomplished." How could this man achieve so much and yet remain anonymous? How was he able to exert so much influence? A hundred questions arise at the sound of his name.

Physically, he is an invisible man, the embodiment of impersonality: ageless, of an unremarkable build, on the small side, average nose and forehead, gray hair, and a little gray mustache. He dresses inconspicuously and is the epitome of an amiable, colorless bourgeois. He comes and goes to palaces, chancelleries, and national banks, without attracting attention. No news releases allude to his visits to Downing Street, to the White House, Bonn, Brussels, or Rome.

Professionally, he is indefinable. For half a century he has been at the center of events, but he is not a politician. He never sought a mandate from the people. Nor is he a technocrat. He has no particular expertise in any given field. Although he was Deputy Secretary-General of the League of Nations, he is not a diplomat. He is listed as an economist and has spent a large part of his life reconstructing ruined countries, bolstering currencies, and drafting international agreements. But he is no theoretician. His memory for figures is deplorable. He has confused millions of tons of production with millions of tons of exports, and mixed up rates and coefficients. Yet the experts have a reverential affection for him.

Intellectually, he is no less surprising—a genius by fits and starts.

10

At important meetings, politicians and high officials confess their astonishment at this awe-inspiring "pontiff." He searches for a phrase, seems to lose his train of thought, and refrains, for what seems an eternity, from uttering a word, while everyone waits anxiously. But at times, like lightning, an idea strikes him that changes the course of history, or he has the kind of inspiration that an ultrasensitive medium might conjure to convince a doubting Thomas—an argument like a bull's-eye, a key word.

Jean Monnet is from the Charente. He was born in Cognac on November 9, 1888. His family were winegrowers, slow-speaking, miserly with words, practical, realists like all peasants, yet with something secretive and mystical about them. Such men are sturdy, indestructible. His grandfather died at the age of one hundred and three, and his father lived to be eighty-eight. Jean Monnet at eighty looks no more than an alert sixty. He has two daughters and a wife who is an artist. Unable to live in a big city, he has always made his home in open country, in Seine-et-Oise or in China, on the outskirts of London or of New York. Each day he spends several hours in the woods or meadows, reflecting. In Luxembourg, where he served as president of the High Authority of the Coal and Steel Community —the most difficult period of his life because he was condemned to the hard labor of administration—he held court in the forest, awakening his associates at five in the morning to clarify a neglected point or to explain some new inspiration.

He is a Euro-American, as much at home in Washington as in Brussels, yet at heart he has remained a rustic. From Paris or from the other end of the world, he will telephone daily to Charente for news of the Monnet cognac and of his sister, a devout Christian, who has not given up trying to convert him.

He, too, is a mystic in his own fashion, dedicated to achieving understanding among his fellowmen, to a quest for the mechanisms of international integration. Yet there is nothing of the visionary about him. He does not think that progress improves human nature. But he thinks that when all men are in the same boat, they can be made to pull together instead of fighting. "Whenever nations and men accept the same rules," he says, "their conduct toward one another changes. This is the process of civilization."

His father, Jean-Gabriel Monnet, was a member and director of a small winegrowers' trade union that had established a winemaking

11

plant. But the association broke up. The British brandy barons who, ever since the time of Eleanor of Aquitaine and the Hundred Years War, have dominated this branch of trade, often paid more for the harvest than did the trade union, and they paid in cash. Jean-Gabriel Monnet held onto his wine casks. He bought up the shares of all those who were quitting. Having acquired a controlling interest, he proceeded to launch the family cognac.

Meanwhile, his son was not doing especially well at school. Since reading held little fascination for him, he had difficulty expressing himself. Even today he changes his mind ten times before dictating the final copy of a letter. Every paragraph of a given statement is redrafted thirty times, with the help of his collaborators. Like the Anglo-Saxons, he uses only the simplest words and phrases. But his written texts, repeatedly worked over, are technically precise, strikingly full and clear, although they seem to consist of generalities. One academician has referred to them as "sumptuous fare."

At the age of eighteen, Jean Monnet gave up the idea of studying for the second part of his *baccalauréat* examination. He wanted to see action, life. Nothing frightened him. His classmates said, "He has the nerve of a commissar." He wanted to go into business. From his father he obtained permission to depart for the virgin territories of Canada. Off he went, wearing his first bowler hat and taking with him a trunkful of brandy samples.

At that time Canada represented the Far West. The railway to Vancouver was being built, and towns made of wooden planks were springing up along its entire length. They were dismal, devoid of women, crowded with immigrants joining the gold rush. Calgary, the capital of the Indian cowboys, counted 200,000 horsemen for 800 women. It offered no attraction save the saloon, no diversion but brawls. The young Frenchman was happy in this atmosphere of classless pioneers who knew no law beyond that of Canada's red-coated mounted police. He was an appealing young man and people responded to him. When Monnet sought a carriage, a stranger currying his horse in front of a saloon offered him his mount. From every stagecoach he collected customers. The suitcase filled with samples was soon emptied, yet he continued to take orders for brandy.

Success awaited him in the Northwest Territories on the counters of the Hudson's Bay Company, which bought skins from the Indian trappers. No firewater was supposed to be sold to the Indians. Natu-

12

rally, it was what they wanted most. And naturally, too, the Hudson's Bay Company purchased large quantities of cognac from young Monnet for its fur buyers.

From Canada he went to the United States. In those days there were no identification papers, no import licenses, no quotas. From a clientele of saloonkeepers he soon moved on to the wholesalers and the big importers. In Canada he had learned to speak the English of the masses; in the United States he mastered the American as well as the British-American idiom, acquiring a New England accent in the process. This experience provided Monnet with a passport valid anywhere in the world.

Brandy took him next to Egypt, then to Scandinavia. In Sweden he became friendly with the heads of the alcohol monopoly, peerless experts in the matter of wine and spirits. These men maintained the world's first wine cellars in the hotels they controlled. For a commission, Monnet became their buyer in France.

If we attempt to explain the success of Monnet's career we will discover that these early travels played an important role. With his imagination, his bold self-confidence and disarming optimism, it was a stroke of good fortune for him to have been a mediocre student eager to see the world. He grew accustomed to a continent devoid of frontiers, eluded the traditional pattern of French bourgeois education, and was spared the respect for historical tradition and the cultivated skepticism that is the hallmark of Europeans. His graduate school was the Canadian saloon in the Far West and the rough familiarity of the pioneers he encountered along the entire length of the Canadian Pacific Railroad. His friend André Fontaine has observed: "His education, far from being classical, was personal and pragmatic. He knows more English words than he does French."

Monnet is a self-made man. His experience in the burgeoning towns of the American West taught him to approach problems directly. For him, speech is not intended to voice complaints but to convince: writing is a means of making and consummating a deal; to think is to create something new.

Much later he said, "I was daring because I knew no taboos. I was unaware of the importance of official functions. Like Americans, I was trained to think that if something needs to be changed every man has the right to point this out. I felt very self-confident because I was not asking anything for myself."

13

II

Programmer of Victories

BY July, 1914, Jean Monnet at twenty-six had become something of a dandy: he sported a little mustache, his suits were tailored in London. He was a familiar figure at palaces and international meetings. He now drove a car and had a sizable bank account. Thanks to him, his father's business was booming.

He was in Canada when the first rumors of war sent him scurrying back to Europe. Heading for England aboard a ship that was to take eight interminable days to reach port, it occurred to him that naval transport would play an important role in the looming conflict. His fellow passengers were worried about the German submarines. And indeed the ship was in constant danger of U-boat attacks. As he tried to control his impatience, Monnet turned his thoughts to the practical solution of pressing problems. With France and England at war, perhaps invaded, naval transport would be essential for procuring raw materials and supplies. It would have to be given top priority.

Finally he arrived in London. Trafalgar Square was the scene of endless parades and fanfare, but there was apparently little awareness of wartime needs. His friends gave him the latest news: The British army was to fight alongside the French across the Channel. No unified command had been organized for the two armies or their governments. In the city, tempers were at the boil. French orders for iron, coal, wheat, and copper were raising prices throughout the world, and the two allied countries were quarreling over the cargoes and outbidding each other for supplies.

14

When he landed in France, he saw the same chaos. British ships arrived with their holds filled and left with them empty. French cargo boats were heading for England and returning with empty holds. In Paris panic prevailed. The Germans were swooping down on the capital. Trains and highways were crowded with convoys of refugees. The government was packing up and going to Bordeaux. There was no special wartime organization to serve as liaison between Paris and London, only the usual diplomatic machinery of the Entente Cordiale.

Monnet arrived at Cognac. His brother, a reserve officer, had already assembled his regiment of hussars. Monnet, himself, had been excused from military service because of nephritis, the occupational disease of those who trade in wines and spirits.

"I must see the Premier immediately," he told his father.

"Are you mad? You want to see Viviani, *you*? He's got enough to do!"

"But you have no idea what's going on. France is at war. The British army is coming over to fight on our soil. But England is going to war on her own; there's no unified command, no joint services for supplies. I've got to tell the head of the government that supplies, maritime transport, and war production will all have to be coordinated."

"You? You're going to advise Viviani? You don't know what you're talking about. You'd do better to join the army."

But one of his father's friends, Benon, a lawyer from Cognac, was a friend of the Premier's. They had pleaded their first cases together. He agreed to introduce the young man to Viviani. Together they took the train to Bordeaux, where the government had been set up. Viviani received Benon and Monnet shortly after the Battle of the Marne, in which he had lost his two sons.

"You're right," Viviani said to Monnet. "England and France must coordinate their production and purchases, their entire war effort. You're going to tell this to Millerand for me."

Alexandre Millerand was the War Minister. He referred the young brandy salesman to Mauclair, the controller general in charge of supplies. Mauclair and Monnet went to London together. Monnet was to serve Mauclair as adviser and interpreter, and he was soon to appreciate the talents of this remarkable officer. Together they suggested to the English that joint purchasing agencies be set up in order to prevent the two allies from outbidding each other for steel, oil, coal, and supplies from America and Scandinavia. Their plan was

15

without precedent. The British ministers and heads of office were startled—and noncommittal.

"France and England will lose the war by going bankrupt," the financiers predicted. "They are paying gold to foreign countries for their provisions and the gold supply won't last three months."

Monnet appealed to his friends of the Hudson's Bay Company. They agreed to lend the Bank of France a billion in gold to pay for Canadian wheat. "What we need is not only joint purchasing agencies," he pleaded with Mauclair, "we also need a joint organization for supplies and maritime transport. We must requisition both the French and the British merchant marines and set up some sort of pool under a unified command."

This proposal produced consternation in London. The heads of the big shipping and armaments companies, among whom Monnet was later to enjoy a position of trust, gave their answer: "Unthinkable."

"We'll have to requisition French ships that are making a fortune in the Far East while our cargo boats carrying gasoline and vital supplies in the North Sea and in the Atlantic are being sunk by the German submarines," Monnet explained in 1915 to Étienne Clémentel, the Minister of Commerce. Clémentel accepted Monnet's idea and made him a member of his staff. But the suggestion caused such a commotion that the minister, de Monzie, resigned in protest.

Meanwhile, German submarines were wreaking havoc on the convoys. Torpedoes were winning the war for William II. Steps had to be taken. Clémentel, who had become a personal friend of Monnet's, sent him to London to negotiate with Lord Runciman about forming a maritime pool. The opposition was immovable. But necessity pleaded Monnet's cause. After three months of vacillation, the merchant marines on both sides of the Channel were requisitioned; by 1916 they were operating under a unified command.

But further difficulties had arisen before this victory. Agricultural production had declined dramatically. The great northern plains that produced the wheat and sugar of France were occupied by the enemy. The peasants had been mobilized.

"Why don't you requisition French wheat?" Jean Monnet asked Chapsal, the Minister of Food. "You'll soon be forced to ration food and hand out coupons for bread."

"How would you like to work in the food ministry?" was Chapsal's answer.

16

"We'll have to draw up a list of common needs for the French, British, and Italians," Monnet told London. "So much wheat, coal, and oil for each country. The cargoes will have to be distributed as they arrive. But we'll also have to be prepared for the torpedoing of some ships and parcel out whatever is in short supply. We must have an overall plan. . . ."

From 1916 on, Monnet's suggestions were accepted one by one on both sides of the Channel. Anglo-French purchasing agencies were organized and food rationing was established. The maritime pool was about to become a reality.

At the age of twenty-eight, Jean Monnet became France's representative on the Allied executive committees for the distribution of common resources. After 1917 America joined the organizations. At these committee meetings Monnet met influential Englishmen and Americans. He rubbed elbows with ministers, business tycoons, lawyers, government advisers, and big American industrialists. His imagination, his talent for organization and international integration, his impartiality—these won him the trust and respect that put him in a position of leadership. When the war was over he was awarded the Grand Cross of the Order of the British Empire which entitles Englishmen to be addressed as "Sir."

In France, where he acted on behalf of various ministries, he carefully refrained from claiming any personal credit for his ideas and victories. He remained unknown, his true worth appreciated by only a handful of people in high places.

In 1917 Georges Clemenceau, who had just assumed power, went to London, where his attention was drawn to Monnet. "Who is this civilian?" he thundered when he met the young initiator of the joint committees. "Good legs, good eyes, and working in an office? Off to the army with him, and the quicker the better!"

Clemenceau's orders were not obeyed immediately. But a few months later the Minister of Munitions, Louis Loucheur, who was also visiting London, repeated the order, instructing Monnet to sign up at an infantry recruiting depot. There he remained for a week, just long enough for the British and French authorities to get him back. He had become indispensable.

It is surprising that a young man who was not a general, an elected representative, a newspaper editor, or a high official, but merely a traveling salesman, should have made his voice heard by two govern-

17

ments and imposed decisions that altered the course of the war. In London or Paris, he was able to deal on an equal footing with ministers, generals, admirals, and business tycoons. Monnet himself later explained this:

"My strength was the naïveté of a young man. I had no idea what a premier really was. He was just a man like any other to me. In fact, it's taken years to bring myself to say 'Mr. President' or 'your Honor.' I've no feeling for the importance of offices. I've never wanted one for myself. Besides, I arrived on the scene at a time when the men in power were at a loss, when they didn't know which way to turn. You can suggest anything, you can get any idea accepted if it is well conceived and if it solves a problem.

"It must also be said that after pondering an idea for dozens, hundreds of hours, I'm very careful to wait for the right moment and to knock at the right door—that of the ministry involved or the administrator in charge.

"Another source of strength is that I never ask anything for myself. So I'm not competing with politicians or high officials. If I'm given a job that I didn't ask for, I'm not stepping on anybody's toes."

Monnet's boldness was reinforced by his personal independence. He did not need money. He had plenty of time to think as he tramped through the countryside for hours at dawn or during half the night. Monnet always managed to be free of immediate material concerns so that he had time for reflection—the rarest, most precious thing in the world.

"As soon as Anglo-French cooperation was established, I was struck by the ease with which foreigners were able to work together," says Monnet. In the supply bureaus after 1917, Frenchmen, Englishmen, Italians, and then Americans forgot about their nationality. They had a problem to tackle and they all worked on it together. The British, who take a long time to reach a decision and are tough negotiators, proved remarkably fair in their dealings on executive committees."

Monnet put a great deal of effort into gaining the confidence of his colleagues. He did nothing that might lead anyone to think that he was placing the interests of France above those of her allies, an attitude that was to win him lasting respect.

As the negotiations of the purchasing commission proceeded, he learned about the mechanisms of industry and finance. By 1918, when

18

victory was achieved, Monnet had become an economist—not a theoretician but a practical worker familiar with international banking procedures, an official spokesman among leading financiers.

In 1919 the Treaty of Versailles established the League of Nations, an organization ultimately crippled by the United States' refusal to join. An Englishman, Sir Eric Drummond, was named Secretary-General. The British and French gave Monnet, who had had experience in such matters, the post of Deputy Secretary-General. Although he had somehow managed to retain his anonymity, he was nevertheless an international figure at the age of thirty-one.

Behind the scenes he helped to arrange the appointment of the French Socialist Albert Thomas as head of the International Labor Office. "I've always voted Socialist, except on one occasion," Monnet said. (In the 1965 presidential elections he publicly backed Jean Lecanuet, the champion of an integrated Europe.) "Socialism to me means nationalization of the public services and the major means of production, but not the nationalization of enterprises in which private initiative has a daily role to play."

Of his work with the League, Monnet says: "I believed that the League of Nations, which made it illegal to wage war and proclaimed the advent of justice and international brotherhood, could establish true cooperation among peoples. In actuality, it did stimulate some useful things; through its special agencies it helped countries like Austria to get back on their feet. But the Treaty of Versailles was based on inequality, on a spirit of superiority and vindictiveness toward the vanquished. It couldn't last.

"In Geneva I was impressed with the power of a nation that can say no to an international body that has no supranational power. Goodwill between men, between nations, is not enough. One must also have international laws and institutions. Except for certain practical but limited activities in which I participated, the League of Nations was a disappointment."

Monnet was responsible for the League's economic agencies which, under his direction, were especially effective in Vienna and Upper Silesia. He remained in Geneva for three years. Functioning on a global scale, he learned the duties of both a foreign minister and a minister of economics. In the process, he also acquired a host of friends all over the world.

Suddenly, in 1923, he resigned. His sisters had called for help.

The family business was tottering. Monnet returned to Cognac where he had to cope with bills, cellars, salesmen, tariff complications, and the overwhelming competition of such firms as Hennessy and Martel. Within two years he had put the business back on its feet, recruited personnel capable of taking over from him and, after a series of trips, made sure that the business would have all the foreign outlets it needed. Soon prohibition was instituted in the United States—a boon to the Monnet distilleries. "The rum route," the great highway for contraband, was to stretch all the way to Charente.

In 1925 Monnet received an offer from America. The Blair Foreign Corporation, a New York bank that issued stock, invited him to become a member of the firm. Blair was well known for having negotiated loans during the war for various countries allied to the United States, notably France. It had specialized in loans to governments and national banks that were seeking to stabilize their currencies. In the United States it bought up industries, incorporated them, and sold their shares in the stock market. This was the golden age of Wall Street.

Blair's new partner was not a financial expert. Jean Monnet refuses to become a specialist in any field. But he has a passion for teamwork and the gift of leadership. He surrounded himself with teams of specialists. While they worked, he thought. He was always one step ahead of the technicians. "Some people can perceive only concrete, day-to-day problems. I am always seeking the long-range view," he said.

As a private financier, Jean Monnet faced the same problems that had confronted him when he was an international official. Under the aegis of Blair, he went to Warsaw to study the Polish economy and, with the help of American capital, to put it on a sound footing. He was called to Bucharest to stabilize the Rumanian currency.

The American economy was at that time experiencing an unprecedented phase. Industries were asking the government for huge loans. Blair transferred its assets to Transamerica, a holding company in San Francisco, and Monnet became its vice-president. Transamerica owned the Bank of America, a small savings and deposit bank that was soon to grow substantially.

Monnet had become an authority on Wall Street. One Friday in 1929—Black Friday—the New York stock market crashed. Within a few hours Monnet had lost a million dollars, or so it was rumored. (He does not remember the precise figure.) No one understood what was happening. President Hoover, hoping to remedy the situation by instituting austerity measures, persuaded the heads of large businesses to cut costs and prices. Like Pierre Laval's policy of deflation in 1935, this served merely to exacerbate the depression.

Trying to save what he could from the disaster, Jean Monnet reappraised Transamerica's assets. He suggested to the heads of the company that the operations of the Bank of America be split. A savings bank, he explained, should not issue stock. For a banker, the temptation to use his customers' deposits to issue stock was too great. This, he claimed, was at the root of the crisis. When the stock market began to go down, the financiers who were speculating tried to cash in on their mortgages. But since everything was going down, they could not find any buyers. Nor could they reimburse their depositors, all of whom were anxious to withdraw their funds. And it was these depositors who caused the panic to spread.

But the members of Transamerica were not willing to submit to such discipline. Monnet, who represented a minority, withdrew and returned to Europe. But Monnet's advice to his partners was later accepted by Roosevelt. When he became President of the United States, it was enacted into law. It served as a basis for reform and recovery: savings banks were forbidden to issue stock. The government guaranteed savings accounts. Hopefully, the 1929 crisis would never recur.

Shortly after his return to France, Monnet was called to Sweden. The "match king," Ivar Krueger, had committed suicide, leaving a financial and industrial empire in ruins. With the concurrence of the Swedish government and the national bank, Monnet was asked to supervise the liquidation process. He audited Krueger's books, placed the business on a new footing, and completely reorganized the match industry.

Even when he was preoccupied with ordinary business affairs, Monnet did more than an ordinary businessman. His great talent was his ability to come to the rescue of private enterprises without sacrificing the public interest. This won him friends in governments and central banks. His presence inspired confidence and facilitated the adoption of shrewd solutions that served governments as well as individual stockholders.

Monnet's private life had also assumed an international aspect. At a dinner party in Paris he had met the beautiful Madame Silvia de Bondini, a painter. Her husband, an Italian diplomat, was planning to found a bank in New York and invited Monnet to become a partner. But Monnet was more susceptible to the beauty of Madame de Bondini than to the offer of half of her husband's bank. Leaving the bank to be organized without his assistance, he went off to China, taking along Silvia and her paint brushes. It was impossible to obtain an Italian divorce. A few years later Monnet found a place in Moscow where the impossible divorce could be granted immediately. He married Silvia right afterward.

He was then to spend two years in China. Having formed a partnership with the American firm John Murnee, Monnet sought to do something about China's economy and her railroads. In 1933 China, behind the façade of Shanghai's foreign concessions, was in a state of chaos. It was the China of Malraux, of the great warlords, of the Kuomintang. Monnet quickly realized that any attempt to restore the Chinese economy would be a hopeless undertaking. The Chinese conducted business, lived or starved, in a state of utter confusion. It might be possible, however, at least to put the railroads back on their feet.

The Chinese government—if one could so designate it—had no money. In London and in New York, no financier would risk a shilling or a penny in that cutthroat place. The Chinese bankers of Shanghai, however, were draining the savings of millions of shopkeepers. Their compatriots, dispersed throughout the Far East, had immense amounts of capital at their disposal.

Monnet, "the mechanic" of cooperation, hit upon a solution. The railroads could be restored and made profitable if the Chinese financiers put money into them, if Western and Chinese stockholders shared identical interests when they lined up in front of the station ticket window. Then, regardless of which general happened to be in power, the trains would continue to run. To the Shanghai millionaires Monnet proposed the establishment of a bank, the China Financial Development Corporation. The Chinese would be on an equal footing with the English, American, and French financiers who put money into it. Wall Street, the City, and the Bourse could all rest easy.

But all Monnet's suggestions to the Chinese came to nothing. "I tried to understand them but I gave up. The Chinese were far too subtle, far too intelligent for me. All I could do was make my own position clear and try to gain their confidence."

22

The negotiations went on interminably. Finally a day came when Monnet brought the president of the Bank of China an agreement to sign. After an elaborate exchange of compliments, Chang-Cha-Nao declined the honor. Monnet was deeply disappointed. He had been in China for nearly two years. Just when he thought he was accomplishing his mission he found that he had failed.

"You didn't understand," one of his Chinese friends explained. "Chang-Cha-Nao would have offended you greatly had he signed at once. To avoid being rude to you, he will not sign your agreement until you have presented it to him three times. This is his way of honoring you, of demonstrating that you have finally overcome very stubborn resistance and proposed a deal that does honor to foreigners. . . ."

"Monnet. What an extraordinary man," the Chinese ambassador to Paris said somewhat later. "The British and Americans have delivered huge quantities of matériel to China but have never been able to collect anything in return. Monnet received sizable honorariums from us for merely selling his ideas."

"Monnet, there's something surprisingly Chinese about you," General Chiang Kai-shek observed.

In 1938 the danger of war was apparent to all. Monnet, who had been free of his international financial preoccupations for some time, was filled with anguish. It looked as if 1914 were happening all over again. France and England were about to confront Hitler as allies but had made no preparations for a coordinated war effort. Monnet had maintained his highly placed connections in London. And in Paris his friends kept him well informed. Against Goering's *Luftwaffe,* the Royal Air Force and the French air force combined would prove unavailing. Addressing the National Defense Committee in March, 1938, General Vuillemin, commander of the French air force, predicted, "If war comes, our air force will be wiped out within two weeks."

Only American industrial power, thought Monnet, could offset Germany's production capability. American industry could operate in total security, safe from aerial bombardment should hostilities suddenly break out. He sought information from his American friends. Aeronautical firms in the United States were constructing new planes whose design was as yet top secret. But production was limited. The Glenn-Martin pursuit planes were being turned out at the rate of a thousand a year. Pratt and Whitney could equip them with excellent engines. But if the United States were to arm both France and Great Britain, it would have to build more factories. And that would take many long months. Monnet relayed this information to the ministers concerned.

In September, 1938, Premier Édouard Daladier returned in low spirits from Munich. He asked Monnet, Paul Reynaud, the Finance Minister, and Guy La Chambre, the Air Minister, to dine with him at the war ministry. La Chambre, unable to attend, sent in his place his chief of staff. William Bullitt, the United States ambassador, also attended.

"War is inevitable," said Daladier, still dazed at having been acclaimed when his plane landed at Le Bourget. (He had expected to be greeted with stones and rotten eggs for having forced Czechoslovakia to abandon the Sudetenland to Hitler.) "Munich is only a temporary truce. We need time to arm. What can the United States do for us?"

"President Roosevelt's hands are tied by the Neutrality Act which forbids the sale of munitions to foreign countries," Bullitt replied. "But he will certainly do as much as he can to aid France and England against the Nazi threat."

"Could Americans manufacture planes in Canada?"

"That would probably take years. For the moment, it is difficult to see how planes could be built secretly outside our borders."

"To insure mastery of the air for the Allies, we must have five thousand planes," Monnet said.

"Five thousand? What would we do with them?" General Vuillemin said a little later. The French air force had only a few hundred pilots.

Daladier immediately instructed Monnet to place an order for 200 Curtis pursuit planes. He was also to investigate the possibility of placing a much larger order that would hopefully lead to the construction of new airplane plants in the United States. He was to draw up a statement indicating present French and British manufacturing plans and prepare a schedule of additional orders to be placed in the United States.

In England Monnet sounded the same cries of alarm. "Twenty-five million pounds sterling?" the Minister of Finance exclaimed. "But that's much too expensive!"

On December 5, 1938, at a meeting of the National Defense

Council in Paris, the same financial anxiety was expressed. General Gamelin recorded the proceedings in his book *Prologue du Drame.*

Daladier said: "We can have one thousand American planes before next summer. The order will cost two thousand five hundred million francs."

"That might be possible if we used the one thousand seven hundred million francs earmarked in the budget for all the ministries," observed Finance Minister Reynaud.

"We could pay in installments if we could get certain Americans to agree," Daladier added.

Monnet was assigned the task of launching the arsenal of democracy on the other side of the Atlantic. His mission to the United States was to have historical importance: it initiated the manufacture of armaments in the U.S. French and British orders, paid for in cash, would triple America's capacity to produce airplanes. In the States this was called the opening of the American arsenal. The French and British rendered the United States an incalculable service. This was fully realized only at the time of the attack on Pearl Harbor.

Monnet was the guest of Franklin Roosevelt at the President's Hyde Park residence. Roosevelt was resolutely anti-Nazi. He, too, believed that war was inevitable. But, in order to arm England and France, he would have to overcome the tremendous obstacle of isolationism. Strategic items could not be sold to foreigners, who were also denied access to factories manufacturing products included in the Secret List, especially the new Glenn-Martin P 32 and P 40 pursuit planes. He promised, however, that he would do everything he could. He himself would receive Monnet's representative, René Pleven, and a group of French aviators. Roosevelt would allow them to visit factories that were closed to the public. They could even test planes that were still top secret. Roosevelt involved the United States morally in the war. He also promised to bend all his efforts to secure the abrogation of the Neutrality Act.

On December 16, 1938, and again on Christmas day, René Pleven was Roosevelt's guest. Traveling incognito, Colonel Jacquin and Commander Stelhin were ushered into the Douglas, Glenn-Martin and Lockheed plants where they tested the famous P 40's.

An official mission headed by René Mayer and Emmanuel Monick was to come to Washington to discuss the financial arrangements. Meanwhile, on January 25, 1939, General Vuillemin informed the

25

National Defense Council that France would buy only 600 planes instead of 1,000.

Since the start of his mission, Monnet had pestered the ministries in Paris and London to obtain an overall plan for the manufacture of airplanes. It took him six months to get it. Ministries do not like to be disturbed. "We simply have to know how many planes will be built in 1939 and 1940 and how many the *Luftwaffe* is going to have," Monnet insisted. "How many dive bombers and pursuit planes must we order from the United States to be on a par with the Germans?"

Some people found Monnet's persistence extremely irritating. Others said he was an agent for American firms. "Since you are neither a specialist nor a politician, how do you explain your complete understanding of the French and British armaments needs?" he was asked. "It seems amazing that had it not been for you the orders for American planes might not have been placed."

Monnet said later, "I wasn't in the political game so I had a chance to think. Bureaucrats and ministers are constantly preoccupied with official papers, their time is monopolized by the telephone. I had no personal ax to grind. But I was right. And I could foresee that I would be recalled to the same jobs I had performed in London during World War I."

Meanwhile, a frantic race had begun between Goering and the American factories. The outcome of Hitler's blitzkrieg would depend on the number of planes each side possessed. Two hundred and fifty Glenn-Martin pursuit planes, 100 Douglas aircraft, and 40 dive bombers were shipped from the United States to Casablanca in late April and early May, 1940. Hitler was unleashing his offensive. Monnet's planes arrived a few days too late to rescue French skies from the Stukas.

When war was declared in September, 1939, Monnet said to Daladier, "Let's not make the mistake of 1914 all over again. Let's not wage two wars, one English and the other French. We must immediately set up a joint agency for supplies." He made the same suggestion to the British. Acting simultaneously, the two governments appointed him to serve as head of the Anglo-French Coordinating Committee in the Allied war effort.

"Do you realize that you are violating the sovereignty of this ministry?" Robinson, the Permanent Undersecretary for Supplies, asked Monnet.

26

Churchill and Daladier finally decided to order a large number of planes from the United States. The new factories were operating at maximum capacity. The pursuit planes, and especially the engines earmarked for the British, arrived just in time for the Battle of Britain which the *Luftwaffe* unleashed in July, 1940. The planes ordered by France were ceded by de Gaulle to Churchill on June 18, just in time to replace the Spitfires destroyed in aerial combat.

"It must be said," Pleven has remarked, "that Jean Monnet, by his initiative, made an important contribution to the victorious outcome of the Battle of Britain and consequently to the winning of the war."

In May, 1940, the German offensive overwhelmed France. Premier Paul Reynaud told Churchill, who had gone to see him at Briare, that France might have to conclude a separate peace.

Now Monnet had a remarkable inspiration, stimulated by conversations with Pleven and Monick: to create a union of France and Great Britain, with French ministers included in a joint war cabinet. Dual citizenship, a customs union, a single currency, and a pooling of all resources, plus the sharing of war reparations, figured in Monnet's plan. This proposal, those close to him thought, would rouse French public opinion, put an end to panic, and keep France in the war. This daring scheme, later vindicated by events, was presented by Monnet to Sir Robert Vansittart, the Permanent Undersecretary for Foreign Affairs, and to Lord Halifax, the Foreign Minister. The latter presented it to Churchill, who was amazed but seduced by the scheme.

De Gaulle, who had just been named Undersecretary of State for War—Pétain was the minister—reached London at dawn on June 16. He had come to ask the English for enough ships to transport to North Africa and England those French units that could still be shipped out of the country. But a telephone call from Reynaud to Churchill had preceded de Gaulle's arrival. The idea of an armistice was gaining favor everywhere. England was requested to free France from her promises as an ally.

De Gaulle saw Eden, then went to the office of the Anglo-French Coordinating Committee where Monnet, with the assistance of Pleven, represented France. Without revealing the fact that he himself was the initiator, Monnet explained to de Gaulle, who remained rather skeptical, the sensational proposal that the Foreign Office was mulling over.

27

"You alone can obtain Churchill's acquiescence," said Monnet. De Gaulle telephoned Reynaud to warn him that something very important which would help France was being considered in London.

"I will delay the meeting of the Council of Ministers until five o'clock," Reynaud replied, "but it will take a gesture of considerable impact to put an end to all thought of negotiation."

Sir Robert Vansittart showed the text of the British declaration to General de Gaulle, who recorded in his *Memoirs:* "All that was grandiose about this text precluded any quick result. But the offer was of a kind to contribute a powerful argument to Paul Reynaud in the ultimate crisis in which he found himself."

Churchill and de Gaulle discussed the matter at lunch. The cabinet met immediately at 10 Downing Street. At 4:30 P.M., over the telephone, de Gaulle read Reynaud the text adopted by the British cabinet.

"What? Did Churchill really give you this document?" Reynaud asked.

"You can take my word," de Gaulle replied.

Then Churchill came to the phone. "Reynaud, de Gaulle is right, our proposal could have important consequences. You must hold out. Let us meet tomorrow at Concarneau. I will come there with Attlee, the First Lord of the Admiralty and our army chief of staff. Bring equally important advisers."

Monnet and Pleven were to go along. But later that evening the trip to Concarneau was called off. De Gaulle, who had rushed to Bordeaux, telephoned Monnet: Reynaud had been requested by his ministers to resign. Marshal Pétain was now head of the government.

On the following day, June 17, Pétain announced at noon that he had asked "the enemy" to name his conditions. But Monnet told Sir Robert Vansittart that this did not mean the Pétain government would necessarily accept any conditions. This was also the opinion of Reynaud. "Faced with Hitler's demands, the marshal will resign within forty-eight hours," said Reynaud. Then, he hoped, he would be called back to power.

Monnet and Pleven suggested that Vansittart send a telegram to Pétain offering him enough convoys to evacuate the government as well as all the troops and matériel that could be transported to North Africa. Protected by the French and British fleets and by American planes, North Africa could be defended. This might encourage Pétain to resist Hitler and the French defeatists.

Churchill refused to comply with the request. But two days later he was willing to send Lord Lloyd, a member of the war cabinet, to Bordeaux with a brief message for the President of the Republic, Albert Lebrun, and for Marshal Pétain, offering France all the ships she might need.

"It's probably too late," said de Gaulle, who had returned to London in the interim. The Germans were at Angoulême, two hours away from Bordeaux. A wave of anti-British feeling had swept official circles and public opinion after Dunkirk. Some claimed that the British wanted to make France one of their dominions. "We would rather have Hitler than be the slaves of England," people shouted in the halls of the prefecture of Bordeaux, the temporary seat of the government.

Meanwhile, Monnet had procured a huge Sunderland seaplane to take him to Bordeaux where he hoped to explain the spirit of the English proposal to the French ministers. He wanted, above all, to take the President of the Republic and all or part of the cabinet to North Africa. He hoped to bring one or two ministers to London afterward, if that were at all possible. He wanted to install representatives of French sovereignty far from German pressure, just as the crowned heads of Holland, Norway, and Luxembourg had left their invaded countries, leaving only *de facto* authority to those who remained behind.

Accompanied by his collaborators, Pleven, Robert Marjolin, the financial attaché, Monick, and Colonel Bonavita, Monnet was empowered by de Gaulle to tell the government and the army's general staff the number of ships the British authorities were offering for the evacuation of French personnel. The seaplane landed in the Biscarosse swamps, and by noon its passengers were in Bordeaux. Monnet and Pleven went to see Foreign Minister Paul Baudoin. The latter had declared on the radio that France would not accept dishonorable terms or any arrangements that would deprive her of independence. It was Baudoin himself who had urged the government to make the decision to send President Lebrun, the presidents of the assemblies, and some of the ministers to North Africa. But in spite of his visitors' pleas, Baudoin refused to leave France. Marshal Pétain, too, was determined to remain.

29

Twice Monnet and Pleven went to see Édouard Herriot, President of the Chamber of Deputies, to urge him to leave with them. Shocked by defeat and loyal to the alliance with England, the President of the Senate, Jean-Marcel Jeanneney, was resolved to go to North Africa with President Lebrun. Now he refused to leave France unless it was aboard a French vessel. Herriot took the same position. "I have no right to desert the chief of state," he said. "I would represent nothing, I could speak freely only under our own flag."

None of the officials Monnet saw that night or the following day was willing to leave with him. Jeanneney, a man of great patriotism, was preparing to embark on the *Massilia* with Lebrun, whom he would not abandon. Monnet and Pleven were unable to reach Lebrun. They approached Georges Mandel, Clemenceau's former collaborator. "I can't leave with you," he said, "I have luggage. . . ."

Luggage. Monnet and Pleven thought he was referring to his official records. At the time it did not occur to them that Mandel was thinking of his lifelong companion, the Comédie Française actress, Béatrix Bretty, and their daughter. The two men said no more. Georges Mandel's delicate reserve, and also, of course, his desire not to appear to be running away (he had been denounced as a personal and racial enemy of Nazi Germany) impelled him to acquiesce to the tragic fate of which he surely had some foreboding.

"We don't want to be emigrants," was the answer of several high officials. Monnet's efforts to persuade them to take advantage of the Anglo-French union's extraordinary offer and to continue the struggle from North Africa fell on deaf ears.

"England cannot hold out for long," these men said. "If Great Britain accepts Hitler's peace terms, she will emerge virtually unscathed. According to *Mein Kampf,* Hitler wants to destroy France. All he asks of England is to refrain from interfering on the Continent."

Nobody showed any interest in the offer of ships. A large-scale evacuation was considered impossible. Nor was anyone interested in a seat on the Sunderland: French sovereignty would be represented on board the *Massilia* sailing for North Africa. Monnet, however, was not at all surprised by the turn of events. Meanwhile, Marshal Pétain was sacrificing his prestige in an attempt to maintain some semblance of government that might offer protection to its people.

Monnet was unable to exert any influence on the crumbling Third Republic since he was not a political figure. As he and Pleven

30

munched sandwiches on a park bench in Bordeaux, he decided to return to London the following morning. Instead of flying the members of the French government to North Africa, he loaded the Sunderland with refugees.

"If a union between England and France had been proclaimed at Concarneau by Churchill and Reynaud there would never have been a National Committee in exile in London," Monnet said. "Instead, we would have had a working French government whose members would have participated in a joint war cabinet. French deputies would have been representing their constituents. Our entire history would have been different."

A cabinet based on dual nationality would have been an exciting if somewhat difficult venture. An integrated Europe would have emerged from the war, if only to resolve the complications of a union that made Frenchmen subjects of His Royal British Majesty and Englishmen citizens of the French Republic. The union's initiator would automatically have been called upon to play a significant role. He would have become the symbol of this dual nationality.

Much later de Gaulle was to ridicule Monnet's plan which would have "integrated" King George VI with President Lebrun, the Garde Républicaine with the Horse Guards. In any event, the plan had one unexpected result: It gave Paul Henri Spaak, who was living in exile in London, the idea of Benelux, which materialized when the war was over.

Monnet returned to London to find General de Gaulle waiting for him. De Gaulle had arrived the night before. At that time no politician had any inkling of, or inclination for, the historic role toward which he, in collaboration with General Spears, was moving.

"What are you going to do, General?" Monnet inquired.

"Save the honor of France!"

Could the two great personalities who represented France in exile work in harmony? It has been rumored that they clashed violently, that Monnet emerged from the encounter saying, "London is too small for both of us. I'm going to America." The rumor is false. Monnet said nothing of the kind. The two did not get along because they looked at things very differently. Each man assumed his own responsibilities; their respective missions did not entail direct collaboration.

"We must organize a French government," de Gaulle declared.

31

"We must win the war," replied the head of the Anglo-French Coordinating Committee. "A joint victory is all that matters. And victory means American machines and planes."

De Gaulle had other, more nationalistic, concerns: to keep France in the war through her overseas possessions, to maintain French sovereignty on her own soil, and to galvanize the Resistance by becoming its spirit incarnate. Monnet envisaged an integrated struggle in keeping with his plan to merge the French and English governments, whereas the general remained the champion of a separate French identity.

General Spears claims that Monnet went to see Lord Halifax to ask him not to permit the general to address the French people every day on the BBC as he planned to do. Both Halifax and Monnet were afraid, wrote Spears, that violent attacks against the Bordeaux government would ruin any chance of bringing the French leaders on board the *Massilia* back into the fight. But Monnet denies the truth of these allegations.

"What are you planning to do?" Churchill asked him. "The Anglo-French Coordinating Committee no longer exists. Will you join de Gaulle? He has only a few thousand soldiers to contribute to the fight. Stay with us. Take care of our armaments. We need you."

Churchill put Monnet on the British Supply Council to head the armaments program. He was to be Great Britain's representative to the American authorities. In the company of Lord Halifax, John Dillon, head of the army staff, and Purvis, the Canadian, he left for Washington. All that remained of the defunct union was Churchill's gesture invalidating Monnet's French passport by signing it.

"General de Gaulle disapproved of a Frenchman assuming a mission that should have been the responsibility of a high British official," Pleven recalls. "British agent! American agent!" charged those in the general's entourage.

For his part, Monnet was opposed to de Gaulle's emphasis on national grandeur. In his opinion, the general sounded like a dictator. "I had no further contact with him until 1943 in Algiers," he noted.

In Washington the "Franglais" who landed with the British dignitaries soon found old friends in the financial circles from which the White House recruits its personnel. They hailed him as the man who had given the impetus to American war production and who had involved the United States in hostilities before it declared war. Monnet took advantage of the warm reception to underscore the victory program. As a consequence of the large orders placed in 1939, American airplane production had tripled. Now production had to be stepped up again to surpass the prewar rate by 400 percent because, so argued Monnet, sooner or later the United States would enter the war.

It was Monnet who gave Roosevelt the slogan that he was later to use in one of his fireside chats: "America will be the great arsenal of democracy." It is also said that Monnet initiated the lend-lease law that enabled Roosevelt, after Pearl Harbor, to "lend" American armaments to Great Britain (so that she would not have to repay the cost) and deliver them to her ports in American ships. Thus the rule of "cash and carry," which would have required English cash and transport, was circumvented.

"No," says Monnet, "it was Roosevelt who thought up the lend-lease system." But behind the scenes Monnet played an important role in the negotiations that prepared the ground for lend-lease, which was so vital to England because her gold reserves and currency were dwindling.

Monnet worked hard to get the President and his advisers to implement the Victory Program which was to make America and England virtual partners in the war effort. He insisted that priority be given to planes rather than tanks. In Roosevelt's state of the union message in 1941, he announced that within twelve months the United States would turn out 50,000 planes. This was a great personal victory for Monnet.

Monnet was above all a public relations man. He was particularly close to Harry Hopkins, Roosevelt's right-hand man. Through Hopkins he became the President's personal adviser on Europe.

De Gaulle's clashes with Roosevelt were to have repercussions throughout the war. The President maintained diplomatic relations with Vichy and refused to recognize the Free French, whom Churchill supported. Also, he was exasperated by the complications created by de Gaulle, who was determined to control French territories overseas. He could not abide "that general who thinks he's Joan of Arc," who claimed to represent France although he had no such authorization.

The antipathy was mutual. De Gaulle reproached Roosevelt for his absolutist ideas, for his desire to intervene at the close of hosti-

33

lities as the liberator of France. Of course Roosevelt would eventually bestow upon the general expressions of his personal gratitude, but not before he had put an end to the French colonial empire. Preparations for the landings in North Africa were made by the American consul in Algiers, Robert Murphy. Murphy paid no attention to the Free French fighting in North Africa and made no contact with the French National Committee in London.

Was Monnet in part responsible for the lack of enthusiasm for General de Gaulle? His friends claim that he took no part in the Washington intrigues. He was acting on behalf of the British government and consequently remained aloof from the cliques that caused quarrels among the French refugees.

"Monnet and de Gaulle have nothing in common," his friends said. "Monnet deplores some of de Gaulle's attitudes. He especially dislikes the way the general virtually ended America's control of Saint Pierre and Miquelon in the strategic zone of Newfoundland."

Yet in Algeria Monnet was to lend the general his support when de Gaulle least expected it.

III

Monnet Goes to the
Aid of the General

THE United States' entry into the war, the arrival of Americans in England, the complete coordination of the Anglo-American war effort, the unified command—all this considerably lessened the role of Monnet in Washington. He was free. Soon he was to assume a new mission, that of an expert in cooperation.

In November, 1942, the Allies landed in North Africa. French troops loyal to Pétain's Vichy government greeted Eisenhower's army with artillery fire in Algeria and Morocco. After five days of fighting, Admiral Darlan, commander of all Vichy armed forces, concluded an armistice. French authority was vested in General Giraud and the proconsuls of Rabat, Algiers, and Tunis. Vichy disavowed Darlan and allowed German troops to enter Tunisia. The Resistance in France, not to mention de Gaulle in London, was indignant. De Gaulle had had no part in the landings. The French National Committee had been ignored, and it was the Vichy traitors, acting supposedly in the name of Pétain, to whom Roosevelt allocated authority.

No one seemed to know exactly what was going on. Giraud set up a directorate composed of the proconsuls. He supported the Vichy regime, perpetrated the "white terror," and opposed the Gaullists when, under Leclerc and Koenig, they were covering themselves with glory in the desert.

When he learned of the African landings, Monnet asked his friend Harry Hopkins to persuade Roosevelt to send him to Algiers on a

35

mission of conciliation. He foresaw the danger of a split between the Free French and the Allies. He was not going to back de Gaulle or Giraud; he merely hoped to unify France, to unite all Frenchmen who were willing to resume the fight against the enemy.

Hopkins talked to Roosevelt, cautioning him that Giraud was in dire need of a political adviser to give his regime some semblance of a democratic air and to establish an understanding with the Free French. Monnet was the man to send. He could be given the responsibility for equipping the French army with American matériel. Roosevelt consulted Secretary of State Cordell Hull, something he rarely did, according to the memoirs of Robert Murphy. Hull was opposed to sending Monnet to Algiers.

"He's far more attached to de Gaulle than he would lead you to believe," Hull asserted.

Meanwhile, on January 17, 1943, from Anfa in Morocco, where Churchill was conferring with Roosevelt, Churchill sent de Gaulle an invitation to join them. He would arrange a meeting with Giraud, he told de Gaulle. The general refused to attend any meeting unless he were granted free access to Algiers, which Roosevelt had denied him. De Gaulle's refusal caused a sensation in the world press.

Churchill urged him to accept his invitation and that of the President of the United States. On January 22 de Gaulle landed in Anfa and agreed to shake hands with Giraud in the presence of photographers, but he refused to submit to Giraud's political authority. He was not willing, he said, to accept the authority of a military regime based on foreign occupation of Algeria. In his opinion there was but one solution: that he himself establish a provisional government in Algiers and give Giraud command of the armed forces. Then he returned to London via Brazzaville.

But in the Atlantic ports the French sailors abandoned their Vichy ships and joined the Free French. In North Africa Giraud's officers and soldiers deserted their units to join the Gaullist fighters. In occupied France the National Council of the Resistance declared that it did not and never would accept any authority save that of de Gaulle.

Monnet was mobilizing friends and influence in Washington. All of France was about to stand firm against its future liberators. And who would profit from this? The U.S.S.R., the Communists. Hopkins again pleaded Monnet's cause. With the President's more or less tacit consent, he put Monnet on a plane and gave him letters to Eisenhower and Murphy asking, in the name of Roosevelt, that he be given aid and assistance. Officially, his mission was to make sure that the French troops would be adequately armed.

"I haven't come here to serve Giraud," Monnet told Robert Murphy and Harold Macmillan, Churchill's representative in Algiers. "I have come to seek some way to unite all fighting Frenchmen."

"But that's precisely our objective," they told him.

Eisenhower was relieved to see the former head of the British Supply Council. Here, at last, was a Frenchman who thought in terms of the Allies and who spoke an English that smacked of Washington. He requisitioned a villa for Monnet and assigned him a French-speaking sergeant. Monnet then vanished, or so it seemed. Actually, as was his habit, he had chosen a suburban villa, at Tipasa, 33 miles from Algiers, close to some Roman ruins that delighted his wife. He had several confidential conversations with Giraud, who made him financial and political adviser. He also talked with many other leading figures. Thanks to his influence, the portraits of Pétain disappeared from the offices of civil servants, certain Vichy regulations were abolished, and the word "democracy" was pronounced by Giraud.

"Monnet was exasperated by Giraud's incompetence," Murphy was to write later. "He stares at you with his porcelain-blue eyes, a sure sign that he doesn't understand a thing," Monnet said of him. Nevertheless, he went out of his way to gain Giraud's confidence. He was no less critical of de Gaulle. "Monnet was probably too eager to serve France to concern himself with personalities," Murphy wrote.

One day, Murphy recounts, he discovered that Monnet knew almost everything contained in the American official records, both military and civilian. He was even informed about top-secret negotiations. The sergeant assigned to Monnet finally confessed. Fascinated by Roosevelt's envoy, he had brought him all the confidential reports. There were few French-speaking sergeants in Algiers, so the culprit was merely demoted to the rank of corporal.

Monnet soon became indispensable to Giraud because of his American contacts, his economic expertise, and his political and international experience. Gradually he converted Giraud into a military and civilian leader, influencing him so much that he finally condemned Vichy and contemplated cooperating with the Free French. Giraud suggested to de Gaulle that a triumvirate be formed consisting of himself, de Gaulle, and General Georges, who had escaped from Paris. The French National Committee vigorously rejected the proposal despite the pleas of Churchill and Macmillan's threat that "If de Gaulle refuses the proffered hand, America and England will abandon him. He'll become a nonentity. . . ."

The triumvirate was to serve as a council for France's overseas territories. It would take the place of a French government until the war's end. The answer of the French National Committee in London was that such an arrangement would grant the commander in chief, Giraud—in other words, the Allied high command—unrestricted political authority.

There is a little-known incident that bears on all this. The victim of American and British ultimatums, de Gaulle allegedly turned in desperation to the U.S.S.R. and asked Stalin if he would grant hospitality to the French National Committee. Whether or not de Gaulle actually made the request is not known, but he deliberately spread the report that he had done so. Churchill heard that de Gaulle was about to settle down in Moscow. This would have been most embarrassing. The general personified the resistance of subject peoples to Nazism. If he broke with the Western Allies, the repercussions would be disastrous. Furthermore, the Communists in France were especially active in the Resistance. Should de Gaulle go to Moscow and the Resistance be taken over by the Communists, the prospects of liberation would be most dismal indeed.

After an interview with Churchill, de Gaulle announced, "I am quite ready to take a plane to Algiers but I will accept no conditions."

There was a furor at the White House. Free France must submit to General Giraud.

But in London de Gaulle was assured that whenever he chose to leave, a plane would be available to take him to Algiers. The big hurdle was to obtain the consent of the Americans. This was to be Monnet's task. Very discreetly, he approached the Gaullists, particularly Louis Joxe, former professor of history. Joxe had left the Lycée of Metz to become a journalist, and had been assigned to the diplomatic circles of Aristide Briand, Joseph Paul-Boncour, Herriot, and Henry de Jouvenel. In 1940 Joxe had won the support of the Algerians and the teaching profession. With General Astier and 500 other Gaullists, he prepared the way for the Allied landings. He took the radio by storm. Arrested in Constantine after having eluded

38

Giraud's grasp, he was accused of having plotted to assassinate Giraud. A few words saved him: "We did what we could in that epic event."

"Epic? Very well," Giraud replied, "but I'm relieved to know that you're in Constantine."

Monnet brought Joxe back to Algiers, where everything was in a state of confusion. He charged Joxe with the responsibility of organizing the first assembly line for American trucks and vehicles to be delivered to the French army.

"The truth," according to one witness, "was that Monnet, who really doesn't know how to express himself well either orally or in writing, needed a Gaullist spokesman to exchange ideas with him and draft the telegrams he sent to London."

At five o'clock one morning, Monnet awakened Joxe and asked him to come to Tipasa. With a knapsack on his back, Monnet took his visitor to the Roman ruins for a walk in the sun. He was silent. Joxe, too, said nothing. At noon Monnet, still silent, halted under a fig tree, pulled a tin of corned beef and a bottle of beer from his knapsack and began to make sandwiches. He looked very somber.

"This can't go on. Giraud is really too. . . . De Gaulle has to come here," he said at last.

Gradually Monnet unburdened himself. Giraud understood nothing about politics. The only solution was to bring de Gaulle to Algiers, in spite of local and American opposition, and to facilitate little by little his seizure of power. Joxe was more than willing. They drafted a telegram to de Gaulle that they would ask Giraud to sign. It called for the opening of negotiations. One telegram followed another. Finally, General Catroux arrived from London. He was the negotiator whose skill would be decisive.

But while Monnet was successfully influencing Giraud, the Americans remained ferociously opposed to bringing the leader of the Free French to Algiers. Monnet returned to Washington hoping to persuade Roosevelt's advisers, especially his friend Hopkins, and finally the President himself, to bow to the inevitable: to allow Churchill to unleash de Gaulle on Algiers. At the White House Monnet was coolly received. He returned to North Africa, determined to act. On April 27, 1943, he drafted a letter to de Gaulle and persuaded Giraud to sign it. The letter invited de Gaulle to come to Algiers and stated that Giraud was renouncing his claim to leadership.

Then suddenly everything seemed possible. Events occurred in rapid succession. The German army, which had been attacking the Allies in Tunisia, was encircled at Cape Bon. On May 11 General D. J. von Arnim capitulated with 250,000 of his men. The Free French hero Leclerc was acclaimed in Tunisia and General de Gaulle in Algiers.

On May 17, going a step further at Monnet's instigation, Giraud asked de Gaulle to come to Algiers to help organize a French government. His arrival in Algiers on May 30 aroused wild enthusiasm. A governmental committee was formed. But de Gaulle, surrounded by Catroux, André Philip, and René de Massigli, refused to be seated with the Vichyite proconsuls who, with Giraud, constituted the Directorate of Algiers. De Gaulle demanded their eviction. The meeting broke up before any agreement had been reached. Although he may not have noticed it, Giraud had on his side only a minority of the committee.

The following day the tanks were in the streets and the troops were confined to their barracks. The atmosphere of a coup d'état prevailed. The Americans had forbidden Giraud to allow himself to be maneuvered or to consent to the establishment of a provisional government that would supersede his authority. "General Giraud must remain in charge," Eisenhower proclaimed, on orders from Washington.

All Algiers thought that de Gaulle would be arrested.

On June 3 he came out of another meeting as joint president with Giraud of a government that issued the following communiqué: "General de Gaulle and General Giraud have ordered the establishment of a French National Liberation Committee that will serve as France's sovereign body." The two generals were copresidents of the committee. Giraud remained commander in chief but was subject to the authority of the civilian committee. The office of proconsul was liquidated.

This wording was de Gaulle's. Giraud's acquiescence can be attributed to Monnet. Giraud accepted the dual regime because he remained commander in chief in North Africa, whereas de Gaulle became the head of French forces dispersed all over the world. De Gaulle was willing to accept the situation because he had a majority in the council and thus acquired the power to make political decisions.

The Americans were dumbfounded. This was exactly what President Roosevelt did not want. The end of the story was too easy to guess. De Gaulle would gobble up Giraud. To put Giraud back in the saddle, Roosevelt invited him to come to Washington to sign some official agreements on arms for the French divisions. But at six o'clock in the morning Murphy was awakened by Veret, Giraud's orderly. "Here are the decrees that the commander in chief agreed to sign yesterday, after a few minutes' conversation with Mr. Monnet. He is transferring all his powers to de Gaulle."

"That means you're abdicating," Murphy said a little later to Giraud. "As commander in chief you agree to submit to the French Liberation Committee, in other words to de Gaulle. All you've been promised is that you'll be commander in chief, if some day such a position is available, which is unlikely." Giraud read the documents as if he were seeing them for the first time, Murphy recounts.

"Nobody told me anything about this," Giraud said. He shrugged his shoulders. . . . The idea of abdicating politically was far from unpleasant; he merely hoped to preserve his military command. "All this has to do with French affairs. I don't have to consult the British or Americans about it."

Murphy and Macmillan appealed to Monnet. "We have complete confidence in you," they said.

Monnet listened coolly to their remarks. "It is not up to me to keep you informed about purely internal French affairs. René Massigli, our career diplomat, is in charge of the foreign policy of the French Liberation Committee. You should talk to him."

"In this way Monnet very politely made it plain that France would be entirely independent in Algeria," Murphy concluded. He added, without a trace of bitterness, "Influenced by Hopkins, Roosevelt gave Monnet letters of credit that raised him almost to the status of a personal envoy of the United States to North Africa. He used those documents to put de Gaulle in power—the very opposite of Roosevelt's plan for the French empire. Such political shrewdness increased Roosevelt's distrust of de Gaulle and his followers. He refused to recognize the French Liberation Committee. Monnet's diplomatic skill has certainly served his country well for a half century, but never as effectively as in Algiers."

That same month, August, 1943, de Gaulle appointed Monnet Commissioner of Food and Supplies. He also charged him with the task of negotiating for lend-lease agreements with the Allies to procure arms, services, and supplies. "Calling into full play his talent for making use of friends and contacts, Monnet tried in Washington to get the Americans to give France as much help as possible, while there was still time," de Gaulle wrote. But he was never quite reconciled to Monnet's Anglo-Saxon friendships.

"By admiring Jean Monnet so much you depreciate yourself," the general said to André Philipp, Commissioner of the Interior.

Upon returning to the States, Monnet found that, despite his friends and supporters, he was unable to exploit lend-lease for France. The White House refused to accept the existence of a sovereign French committee in Algiers. Only after the death of Roosevelt did Monnet succeed in negotiating a loan that began to put France back on her feet. When General de Gaulle visited President Truman in July, 1945, a loan of $650,000,000 awaited him. But it was not until February, 1946, a bare five months before the end of lend-lease, that Monnet could take advantage of it for France. The Franco-American controversy had lasted a long time.

In refusing to recognize the National Liberation in Algiers, Roosevelt signified that he had other plans. He wanted to set up in liberated France, as well as in Italy and Germany, a military government (AMGOT) with its own currency, "occupation money," and a welfare organization that would distribute flour, milk, gasoline, and cotton free of charge to the people. These supplies, to be unloaded behind columns of armored tanks, would hopefully serve to prevent disorders among the starving masses in the wake of the landings.

In August, 1944, however, the Resistance stationed its Liberation prefects everywhere. The American military government found de Gaulle's prefects in Normandy and Anjou; in Paris there was the general himself, with his provisional government, proudly refusing charity from the foreign occupiers. "If the United States wants to help the French," de Gaulle said, "it must do so through the French government and not by distributing bounty."

Flour, coffee, gasoline, and chocolate, which had not been accepted from the AMGOT, were sold on the black market at prices so high they hastened the devaluation of the franc.

From Washington, Monnet tried to render American generosity both effective and acceptable. He was appointed President of the French Committee for Supplies.

42

IV

The Monnet Plan

SHORTLY after Monnet had worked out the initial financial arrangements with the Truman administration, French purchasing commissions, one for each ministry, swooped down on New York. Monnet met them at the airport and sent them off to Fifth Avenue to shop for decent clothes. Their wooden clogs and threadbare suits made them look like hoboes. Now, freshly attired, they scandalized the American administration. "We were told that the French people are in a sorry state. But look at them. They even have nylon shirts!"

Even Monnet was shocked by the commissions. They arrived with lists of purchases that had been drawn up in Algiers when people believed that liberation would mean devastation—battles at the front and aerial bombardments of the entire country. Their requests included monumental amounts of food, as if famine were about to grip 45,000,000 Frenchmen. All kinds of requests had been included. The Corsicans demanded tobacco rather than cereals, which infuriated Monnet because he failed to grasp the subtleties of the Mediterranean economy. Since there was no state monopoly on tobacco in Corsica, people could use the American cigarettes in trade for items, such as ham, that were especially scarce.

Literally invaded by demands and pleas from every part of the globe, the United States found it difficult to distribute the necessary supplies. The commissions had to justify their requests. Appropriations for lend-lease were limited. The ridiculous waste had to be stopped.

43

Monnet recalled a recent conversation with de Gaulle about the grandeur of France. Monnet had said: "France will be great if she becomes a great, modern, industrialized country. But she is weak in production, her protectionist system is archaic, and her matériel is out-of-date. France must be modernized."

"Write me a memorandum on this," the head of the Provisional French Government had answered.

Monnet decided it was time for him to act, and he hastened back to France. First, he would have to put a stop to the chaotic orders the commissions were placing in the United States. Late in the afternoon he arrived at the Bristol Hotel, which had been requisitioned. Monnet called together a group of young economists who had attracted his notice. They met in his room at one o'clock in the morning. Present were Étienne Hirsch, J. Gascuel, Fourastié, Sauvy, and Delouvrier, all of whom were to play an important role after the war. Perched on the armrests of chairs and seated on the bed, they listened to Monnet explain his ideas, which at that time were unprecedented.

"The officials now buying in the United States know nothing about the real needs of the country," he said. "What good is it to buy mountains of wools and cotton if four thousand bridges have been blown up and nothing can be delivered to factories, if the textile mills are not operating because there's no electricity, no coal? It would be better to order tractors and fertilizers than shipments of cereals. France is rich. Our most urgent task is to restore her productive capacity. What we need most of all from abroad is equipment, tools. But first we must draw up a list of our shortages, determine our priorities, and then draft a plan.

"This plan must aim at the modernization of the French economy. To do a job that will prove lasting, we must improve the general standard of living, break the vicious cycle of rising prices and wages. And we must do it quickly."

At the top of the list Monnet put transport: bridges, highways, railroads, ports. Next came coal and electricity. Then certain basic industries that had to be restored: steel, cement, fertilizers.

Business leaders, whether their industries were nationalized or not, were the only people who could provide essential information. But, in order to make the plan acceptable to the public, experts of every kind would have to participate. This could not be the work of a small group of bureaucrats.

That night the entire economy of the country began to take shape. "I'm going to discuss this with de Gaulle," Monnet said. "And for Pleven, at the Ministry of Finance, we must prepare a statement announcing a reduction of military appropriations. Without such a reduction, there's no way to finance our plan."

On December 13, 1945, Monnet handed de Gaulle a seven-page memorandum explaining the plan.

Rumors of the plan provoked an outcry among businessmen. The only plans they knew about were those of the U.S.S.R. The Soviet plans had become a bureaucratic straitjacket which, as the Russians themselves were later to acknowledge, turned out to be as harmful in some respects as they were beneficial in others. This was pure Communism, people said.

However, responding to the urgent pleas of Léon Blum, de Gaulle accepted Monnet's plan and appointed him High Commissioner. The ordinance decreeing the plan was drafted by Monnet himself, who then took it to Gaston Palewski, head of de Gaulle's staff. The general signed it and had it published in the *Journal Officiel*.

Meanwhile, de Gaulle, provisional president of the Fourth Republic, was trying to organize a new government. He failed to gain the support of the leftist parties, and shortly after the plan had been authorized, he retired and withdrew to Colombey, leaving an enormous void and a gathering tempest in the ranks of the Constituent Assembly. He was certain that he would soon be recalled. But the various political parties accepted the challenge. Félix Gouin was made head of the government.

Monnet called on Paul Delouvrier to serve as his financial adviser. The son of a banker, Delouvrier hails from the Vosges. He is an enterprising realist with the physique of a boxer. Tremendously dynamic, he speaks with authority. As soon as Delouvrier had settled down in an attic office, Monnet sent for him. "Together we are going to draft the government's investiture declaration," he said. "The plan will be the main document. We must obtain a reduction in military expenses."

Delouvrier was dumbfounded. How could Monnet take it upon himself to draw up a ministerial declaration? But behind Félix Gouin was Léon Blum, an influential advocate of Monnet's ideas.

With the rise and fall of so many cabinets during the Fourth Republic, Paul Delouvrier was to draft more ministerial declarations

than financial reports. This was so true that his friend Jean Don-
nedieu de Vabres was to say to him one day: "Good heavens, you
ought to open a shop—The Little Investiture."

"A prodigious epoch," Pierre Uri recalled for Georgette Elgey,
who reported his remarks in an excellent history of the Fourth Republic entitled *La République des Illusions*. "Jean Monnet, Hirsch,
and I did everything: the plan, the financial policy, international
policy. . . ."

To what can we attribute the power of Monnet in the political
corridors of the postwar era? It seemed almost incredible to the few
people who were aware of it.

First of all, it was undoubtedly due to the inexperience of the
politicians who emerged after the Liberation. They were overwhelmed
by gigantic problems: universal shortages because so much had been
siphoned off by the occupiers; the poverty of the devastated areas;
the decline of production to one-fourth of the prewar level; an
anarchical black market and a scandalous food administration; gal-
loping inflation and the rise of prices; the inability of the assemblies
to organize a majority and a stable government; the disconcerting
problems posed by Germany, the U.S.S.R., and the Allies.

In the tumult of the Palais Bourbon where 500 deputies supposedly
governed—the shadow theater as de Gaulle called it—nobody had
the time to think or to make himself heard. In this mad whirl of
cliques, of good intentions gone astray, of questions left unanswered,
Monnet intervened with authoritative, simple ideas and concrete
solutions. His little team constituted a secret cabinet, functioning behind the scenes. The ministers who came and went were seeking
collaborators, appropriations, formulas, solutions to insoluble problems.

General de Gaulle's personality entirely eclipsed Monnet. But
after de Gaulle withdrew to Colombey, Monnet became the *deus ex
machina* of the Fourth Republic. The most significant achievements
of the period—the Monnet Plan, the Coal and Steel Community, the
Common Market—were his creations.

Like the story of the *Man Who Lost His Shadow,* the little man in
gray produces a competent chief of staff from his pocket, or a magic
purse filled with endless dollar bills, a formula for Germany, support
from the outside. Monnet did not buy those shadows, as did the

hero in the story. On the contrary, he himself put them there; they were his own shadows.

"There were twenty of us working with Jean Monnet," recounted Bernard Clappier, the assistant director of the Bank of France, who at the time was a young inspector of finance. "We took care of everything."

"Our greatest strength, when we had to launch the Coal and Steel Community, was that in all the key jobs we had men ready to back us up, men we had put there ourselves," said Pierre Uri.

Monnet attaches little importance to personalities. "Petsche in the Finance Ministry, that's going to be terrible," someone said to him one day.

"Not at all, not at all," Monnet answered. "All we have to do is brief him thoroughly."

Monnet's quasi-magical power doubtless stems from two essential attributes. First of all, his ability and personality; his pragmatic imagination, his capacity to concentrate, and his extreme care in making plans. Second, his political selflessness: He has never sought a ministerial portfolio or the slightest material reward for his work. He is quite willing to let others take credit for his ideas and profit from them in any way they choose. In fact, he is always seeking godparents for his brainchildren. Monnet is immensely persuasive. He has a way of asking questions, of suggesting answers that make his interlocutors feel extremely intelligent. His own faith and optimism serve to counteract skepticism. His constantly repeated truisms somehow turn into dogma, and his convictions inspire his audience with the feeling that they can change the world, that anything is possible as long as everyone cooperates.

When Monnet wants someone's approval, he invites him to dinner, explains his idea while the first course is being served, sends urgent emissaries to him, awakens him in the middle of the night, sends him the letter that he wants returned to him signed. No one has any peace until he gets his way.

Another of his strong points is his influential friends in the United States, his access in Washington to the sources of wealth. America's French favorites are Albert Schweitzer and Jean Monnet.

"Two miracle workers," say their detractors, "two false Messiahs. Schweitzer's philosophy rests on very weak foundations and his hospital was a cesspool. Jean Monnet has been written up in the American magazines only because he is achieving Washington's objectives in Europe." And yet in Algiers we have seen how Monnet, although he was Roosevelt's envoy, opened the way that led to power for de Gaulle—the very reverse of what the White House wanted.

The truth is that Monnet enjoyed the confidence of leaders and administrators in the United States, and without him nothing could have been obtained. Moreover, his ideas harmonized with those of his American contacts. Monnet realized that America was fifty years ahead of Europe industrially, and two centuries ahead in regard to the unification of states. He shared with enthusiasm the far-reaching views of Roosevelt: the abandonment of isolationism, the lowering of frontiers between America and Europe, free trade between the two continents. Their ideas foreshadowed the 1964 Kennedy round of trade talks between the U.S. and the Common Market. He wanted the nations of Europe to end their archaic quarrels and adopt a twentieth-century outlook.

The scope of Monnet's plan for the economic reconstruction of France required innumerable consultations. It was necessary to discuss such things as coalfields, shipyards, agriculture, rural engineering, railroads, bridges and highways, metallurgy, reconstruction, and the establishment of twenty administrative offices. After 1944, 50 company unions worked out their own individual programs. The sole drawback was that they could not all be achieved at once. Essential priorities and a general plan for modernization had to be established.

"When will we be ready to present our plan?" Monnet asked at the close of February, 1946.

"We're just beginning to see daylight. In a few months."

"You mean in two weeks," Monnet cut in. "I have to leave for the States."

For two weeks there was frantic activity. General projections were rushed through, a method was adopted, ways to satisfy and integrate the various needs were worked out. Finally, a small group tackled the major job of writing the introduction: two pages in all. Delouvrier wrote and rewrote the text four times. Then Monnet showed it to the others. The introduction was now crystal clear. Monnet pored over every word.

"We must show this paper to the government," said Emmanuel Monick, director of the Bank of France and one of the major authors of the plan.

"Not on your life!" exclaimed Monnet. "I have to talk it over first with the doorman at the Waldorf-Astoria."

This, of course, was a figure of speech. Monnet never stayed at the Waldorf-Astoria. But in 1946 the financing of the plan depended on American generosity. France was virtually bankrupt, and inflation was proceeding so rapidly that the Bank of France was afraid that a two-pound loaf of bread would soon cost 100,000 francs. It was essential to get the approval of leading Washington circles before Monnet presented the plan to the French government. No plan in the world is worth anything unless there are appropriations to implement it.

The "doorman at the Waldorf-Astoria" was in very bad humor at that time. Georges Bidault had just sent him about his business. After serving as de Gaulle's Foreign Minister, Bidault had remained at the Quai d'Orsay, where he continued to implement the policies of the Colombey exile: dismemberment of Germany, internationalization of the Ruhr, a Franco-Saar union, to be followed by association of the German state with the Western Allies in a European confederation.

On February 6, 1946, Bidault had replied to a request from James Byrnes, the American Secretary of State, that France consent to the unification of Germany, which would be formed into a federal democratic state with a central government. Despite the United States' view that a reunified Germany would block Soviet aggression, Bidault's answer was no.

But the ideas of General de Gaulle and Georges Bidault were not Jean Monnet's or those of the Socialists. Without consulting Bidault, Monnet persuaded Léon Blum, the aging Socialist leader whose international prestige was considerable, to accompany him to Washington to settle the matter with the Americans and obtain the appropriations that would save the plan.

Bidault was apprehensive about Germany's recovery. Blum was concerned about the Soviet threat. An Anglophile, he hoped to establish an Anglo-French alliance with the help of the British Labour Party, which was then in power. His aim was to prevent fresh German or Russian aggression.

Monnet was in total agreement with Blum. He had not abandoned his 1940 plan for Anglo-French union, or at least for an Anglo-

French partnership that would lay the groundwork, with American support, for a United States of Europe.

Blum wanted first to go to London to see his old friend Attlee, the Labour Prime Minister. Together, Blum thought, they might make a joint foray on the American treasury. France was beginning to struggle out of chaos, while England was collapsing amid order. The two countries urgently needed a transfusion of dollars. They might as well act together. The members of His Majesty's government listened attentively to their illustrious French friend. But Lord Halifax was already engaged in the process of negotiating a loan from Washington and was impatient to see Congress vote special aid to Great Britain, on exceptionally favorable terms.

For Léon Blum the discovery of America was an emotional experience. He was struck by the difficulties in obtaining appropriations for the purchase of American goods. American supplies were depleted. One had to wait eighteen months for a Ford. Blum asked for 2 billion dollars. But Monnet had already received $405,000,000, and an additional $550,000,000 had been loaned by the Import-Export Bank.

"Americans are shocked when we show too much reserve in expressing our gratitude. The French have not been effusive enough," Blum noted.

But what shocked the Americans most of all, although they did not say so openly, was the fact that there were Communist ministers in the French government. Americans were also surprised by Bidault's inability to understand their attitude, which was determined by the Soviet Union's 225 battle-ready divisions.

The negotiations were to drag on for six weeks. This mortified Blum, but fortunately Monnet had contacted "the doorman at the Waldorf" upon arriving. For two days he was busy on the phone, talking to the Secretary of State, the Secretary of the Treasury, important senators, and leading bankers. By the third he knew all about the current climate of opinion in America, the ins and outs of American policy. Any request for a loan had to be solidly supported by a blueprint for industrial modernization, by a willingness on the part of the French to give up their protectionism, keep an open mind about free trade, and throw open their frontiers to foreign competition. It would be highly desirable to make an initial gesture: for instance, to permit the export of American technicolor movies which until now had been prohibited in order to save dollars. James Byrnes had friends in Hollywood who were having a hard time. And undoubtedly other considerations played a role.

Monnet slightly modified the emphasis in the two-page introduction to the plan. It made a favorable impression on the White House. He also took the opportunity to explain to his contacts that the Communists had an unstable position within the French government. He obtained another grant of $300,000,000, a new loan of $650,-000,000 from the Import-Export Bank, and a promise that the French debt ($2,774,000,000) would be forgotten. It was less than half of what Blum had hoped for and he hesitated to accept it. But Monnet pressured him to sign. Another trip might would take care of things. Meanwhile, French policy could progress on its own.

It was said here and there that the Americans exacted nothing in return. This was not the opinion of the Communists. Nor was it that of de Gaulle at Colombey. The press alluded to American movies that were to be imposed on French film houses one week out of every four. This, they felt, was not necessary. But the public rushed to see the technicolor films.

Upon his return to Paris, Monnet concentrated on implementing the plan. He moved into a house on the Rue de Martignac, within the shadow of the belfry of Sainte-Clotilde Church. The drawing rooms were turned into conference halls and the few bedrooms into offices. Monnet wanted a very small staff, thirty people in all, including the secretaries. The budget was kept at a minimum to avoid criticism from opponents of the plan as well as temptation for those who craved power. He cautiously refused to accept any already established ministry that was controlled by outsiders. He was dependent upon the head of the government, but at the same time he was the government's moving spirit.

At the offices of the High Commission the only free space was a small dining room, where Monnet lunched with collaborators and visitors. A large trestle table was covered with documents and papers. But he hardly used it. He would give instructions, ask his assistants for the notes, correct them word by word and have them rewritten. Then he would add the finishing touches so that the simplest phrases were effective. Everything else was done through personal contacts, through conversations, luncheons and telephone calls.

Although Monnet was satisfied with modest quarters, he used them

51

to put others to ambitious work. In a capitalist country, the first experience with economic planning should not be the task of an administration, he said, but the result of concerted action.

The word "plan" disturbed the employers' associations and worried the nationalized public services. The High Commissioner reassured the heads of public and private enterprises who stormed his offices, asking for permits and import quotas, subsidies and priorities. These were the people who would draft the plan. Wasn't it logical, he asked them, to classify needs, to list them in order of priority when determining subsidies and supplies? He also appealed to the unions. He knew the plan would never get anywhere if workers and miners were unwilling to work full time. Labor, more than any other group, should be interested in the development of industries, in recovery. He called in experts and ranking bureaucrats, and made sure that the ministers, especially those who were Communists, would cooperate.

But he selected his spokesmen carefully. "I want men who are truly representative, not company or union representatives who come here with categorical demands and faked claims." Nor did he want representatives of ministries. He sought only specialists. He surprised the bureaucrats by refusing them the presidencies of eighteen commissions and their subcommissions. Men who commanded the largest audiences, those who could best direct teamwork, were named: the secretary-general of the buildings branch of the General Confederation of Labor (CGT), an ironmaster, a cattle breeder, a member of the Institute, the chief executive officer of a ministry—these were the men he chose, each for his personal qualifications.

"We're not interested in restoring prewar France," Monnet told them, "but in building a France of tomorrow. Modernization is not a state but a state of mind." He seated side by side Georges Villiers, Léon Jouhaux, Benoît Franchon, and a thousand others who had never met before except in conflict over strikes, wages, and with the government.

Monnet astonished his listeners by his "enormous ignorance." He knew little about production figures. He confused millions of tons with millions of francs. The professionals and technicians, who were overawed at the thought of confronting the man who had armed England, put America on a war footing, and frequently arranged deals with the United States, found themselves suddenly at ease.

Everyone quickly realized that it was impossible to work with the available figures. In the confusion left by the Liberation, no statistics were reliable. All the inventories and appraisals had been faked during the war to fool the Germans. Whatever was left in the way of clandestine supplies or tools was falsely described to avoid forced deliveries or to obtain priorities. The black market kept no books.

In a general way people knew that only a fourth of the merchant marine was left, that industrial equipment—or what was left of it—was twenty years old, that a French factory required eight times more workers than did its American counterpart. The only fairly reliable statistics were those of the nationalized industries. And even here the figures had been deliberately inflated. Bureaucracies have always had enormous needs.

The planners had to feel their way amid the wartime ruins. The plan was inching ahead with an average 30 percent rate of error. But Étienne Hirsch, an engineer who had directed a branch of Kuhlmann before joining Monnet in Algiers, had a gift for distinguishing real needs from exaggerated claims.

Monnet was a remarkable salesman, an idea man, a leader. He did not think of himself as omnipotent; on the contrary, he refused to settle anything solely because he had the power to do so. He bent his efforts toward achieving unanimity, refusing to dictate to others. No expert, Monnet had spent his life wrestling with figures. For him, a given figure was in itself neither good nor bad. What mattered was agreement among people working together. But this did not mean that he sought compromise. Rather, he was intent on finding the most practicable solution.

"Why compromise on anything you know is wise?" he said. "I don't understand what's so good about compromise. I know only poor compromises, whose sole effect is to reduce a problem to the lowest possible denominator. There is no such thing as a satisfactory compromise. There are only good or bad solutions."

Finally, thirty-five industries were identified as warranting priority in regard to financial assistance. They were to pave the way for others. Monnet regrouped them into five basic sectors: coal, electricity, metallurgy, cement, transport. At that point he realized that farm machinery had been omitted. The six basic sectors, which included 75 percent of the nationalized industries, represented only 30 percent of the total economy; but they were essential.

Additional capital was needed. Monnet persuaded François Billoux, the Communist Minister of Reconstruction, to agree that the appropriations earmarked for housing be reassigned to the construction of factories. The unions, led by the CGT, agreed to extend the working week. Parliament voted for a forty-hour week, but the ministers and unions agreed to forty-eight hours with, of course, additional pay for extra time.

Monnet's colleagues wanted to present the first plan with great fanfare. A new era was beginning, an era of economic planning, of capitalism administered by the producers themselves. "You don't know Frenchmen. This is no time to make a big fuss," said Monnet. "If we launch this operation with a lot of fanfare, the public will think it's nothing but bluff. Let the trade unionists and the experts who have collaborated with us present the plan and explain it to the employers. They're the ones who should see to its adoption as a work of their own conception."

This decision proved wise. The plan won unanimous approval. It was, after all, nothing more than a rather elementary assessment of essential needs. But it paved the way for modernization and opened up the prospect of international competition to Frenchmen entrenched in protectionist traditions. It held out hope for continuous expansion.

Now arrangements had to be made for financing the plan. The subsidies obtained by the Blum-Byrnes agreements enabled the planners to place immediate orders for top priority needs—tractors, cement, machine tools, and cranes to clear the ports. "As for the rest," said Delouvrier, "we have faith in the future."

France had become a proletarian country. She could no longer rely on the income from capital invested abroad to cope with the chronic deficit in trade. She could only gamble on the possibility of obtaining foreign loans, on generosity that would not last forever. But she had to get back on her feet or perish.

V

The Failure of the OEEC

JEAN MONNET was the businessman of the Fourth Republic, its intimate adviser, the man in charge of financial relations with the United States and family affairs in Europe.

He lived in an elegantly furnished cottage at Houjarray, near Montfort-l'Amaury, the fashionable part of Seine-et-Oise. He would rise at five in the morning, put on ski pants, sturdy shoes, a sweater, and a windbreaker. He wore an old felt hat and carried a cane. This was his "thinker's costume." Then, rain, snow, or wind, off he would go for a walk in the country.

Monnet is a thinker by trade. And he thinks best as he walks. No statesman can take the time this requires, can indulge in the luxury of reflection as intensively as he does. Churchill used to get undressed at 6:30 P.M., put on his pajamas and go to bed to reflect for an hour. He would think about the approaching dinner, the stories he would tell, what he would say to seduce or convince his visitors. At 7:30 P.M. he would have to get up and don his dinner jacket. His time was monopolized by his duties as Prime Minister.

The gentleman farmer of Houjarray had only one serious competitor in the art of combining walking and thinking: General de Gaulle, who, in his Colombey retreat, walked around his garden forty times each morning. Both men, at the beginning of 1947, were thinking in terms of Europe, each according to his own temperament and inclinations. And both were thinking about going into action.

During the war, in his conversations with the Allies, de Gaulle referred many times to the future of Germany, to the prospects of the Continent. America's plans for Europe varied, depending upon who was doing the planning. Secretary of the Treasury Morgenthau drew up a plan to end the industrial nature of the Reich. Rustic and pastoral Germany, he maintained, would be peaceful. His plan was in striking contrast to Hitler's. The Führer had hoped to deprive France of her factories, to make her the granary of Europe. Roosevelt toyed with the notion of putting a control on raw materials such as iron and coal. This would prevent France and Germany, he thought, from rearming for another war. Monnet, who knew everything that was going on in Washington, was well aware of Roosevelt's attitude.

Winston Churchill alluded to Europe with a certain lyricism tinged with caution. He believed that Europe should become first and foremost an association of nations that would surround Germany in order to domesticate her. These nations would constitute a free-trade area that could prove invaluable to British industry. They would assume control of the Ruhr, regulate its productive capacity, prevent crises, wars, and undue competition with British coal and steel industries.

The Ruhr was in the British zone of occupied Germany. On April 19, 1946, at the University of Zurich, Churchill pronounced the famous slogan: "Europe on its feet!" It was here that he said, "If one day Europe were to unite and share its common legacy, there would be no limit to the happiness, prosperity, and glory its three to four hundred million people would enjoy. . . . The devastation, the hatreds engendered by war can recur. . . . What is the supreme remedy? It consists of reconstituting the European family of nations. . . . Is there any reason why we should not see a European association that would give a broader sense of patriotism and joint citizenship to the bewildered peoples of this powerful continent? Under the guidance and within the framework of the United Nations, we must recreate the European family which perhaps will be called a United States of Europe. . . ."

This appeal was to have no echo save among groups of idealists everywhere who entertained the dream of a continent devoid of frontiers. Seven different movements were working for a unified Europe, but all failed to convince their governments.

De Gaulle alone, toward the close of the war, had very precise ideas about Germany and Europe. They were traditional, in the French sense, and wide-ranging. They were inspired by, or at any rate akin to, the notions of Maurice Barrès who, toward the end of his life, sought reconciliation with the Rhenish people.

The general's plan called for the occupation of West Germany by French, British, Belgian, and Dutch armies; a Rhenish Republic, freed from the Prussian influence that Bismarck had imposed and open to French culture and friendship; internationalization of the Rhine Valley, with France receiving as reparations a share of the coal; a Saar state economically united to France, contributing its coal to Lorraine's iron—all this would resolve the sticky question of reparations. As for the rest, he hoped for a confederation of disarmed Germanic states. Then the period of reconciliation could begin. Germany, plus France, England, the Benelux countries, and Italy would constitute a Western economic and political confederation.

De Gaulle foresaw that the Red Army would occupy the states of Eastern Europe and that for a long time fear of Germany would serve to bind the Slavic bloc together. But one day, when Germany was no longer a threat, the vassals of the U.S.S.R. would not tolerate their subjection. And the Russians themselves would no longer wish to remain outside their own frontiers. "In the end," he wrote in his *Memoirs,* "it will be possible to effect a rapprochement between the East and Western Europe. The latter's unity could be worked out in the form of an organized association of peoples, from Iceland to Istanbul and from Gibraltar to the Urals. . . ."

Many factors combined to defeat the Gaullist plan. One was the partition of Europe which Churchill and Stalin effected with large strokes of blue pencil in Moscow early in November, 1944. Another was the Russians' terror and rage in the face of the American atomic bomb, and their enslavement of East Germany.

The Americans and the English were in agreement with the French about the internationalization of the Ruhr. But they had to give up the idea at Yalta because Stalin demanded that his troops participate in the occupation of Essen or Dortmund. When de Gaulle went to the Kremlin, Stalin told him he would not support his claims. For his part, de Gaulle refused to recognize the Communist Committee of Lublin in Poland, or the Sovietization of Central Europe and the Balkans.

"The absence of natural frontiers," said Stalin wisely, "constitutes an absolute guarantee of security."

The Anglo-Saxons could see perfectly well what was brewing: The

Russians were preparing to draw all of Germany into the Soviet orbit by promising her reunification. The United States and Great Britain refused France the Rhineland for the present in order not to give Stalin any pretext for converting the Soviet zone into a Communist state.

In 1945 Germany had already become a bone of contention between America and the U.S.S.R. This was precisely what de Gaulle had hoped to prevent. Ever since 1944 he had been opposed to the hegemony of the two superpowers.

In Monnet's opinion, all the mistakes of 1919 were being repeated. He was opposed to de Gaulle's plans for postwar Germany. To impose a new *Diktat* on Germany was inevitably to invite a new conflict. He preached the idea of a unified Europe to all his English friends, but without success. In London, only one group, headed by Duncan Sandys, Churchill's son-in-law, campaigned for the concept. But with his usual optimism, Monnet believed that if a united Europe were some day organized on the Continent, Great Britain would surely join it.

For many years Monnet had been an Anglo-Saxon by adoption. He was attracted intellectually by the Americans. He admired their youthful, adventurous spirit, their talent for business. They found it very natural to think of Europe as a group of states like their own country. During one of his innumerable trips, he urged a unified Europe on his many American friends. And he also discussed it with the American generals stationed in Germany.

In 1947 Monnet was accordingly far more concerned with international problems than with the inventory of French national resources that was being drawn up in the Rue de Martignac. Ricard, the president of the ironworks, criticized him for it. In France the situation was tragic that year. There was a terrible shortage of coal, and the harvest had been catastrophic. The U.S.S.R. sent 500,000 tons of wheat to France. But bread rations nevertheless had to be cut by 200 grams per day—worse than during the Occupation. The replenishment of stocks, the system of rationing, economic planning—all had failed. In the black market the price of goods had tripled; in some cases it was ten times the official rate. During the early days of 1946 the Communist ministers who remained in power after de Gaulle's departure managed to avert strikes, but they could do nothing about the general disaffection.

The plan for modernization and equipment was in danger of being wrecked. It could hardly be implemented in view of the terrible conditions in France at that time—the poverty, the inflation. The strictly controlled currency and the import quotas stifled all trade. How would mass production be possible for 45,000,000 inhabitants? A large output, plus the cost of industrial research, requires enormous markets. American prosperity was the offspring of business which had behind it a population of 175,000,000. Wherever they looked, the men who labored over the plan saw nothing but a dead end.

Monnet was constantly preoccupied with the urgent need to unite Europe and to organize free trade. To his assistants, Robert Marjolin and Étienne Hirsch, he left the task of doing what they could to implement the plan, while in London, in Washington, in Germany's American zone, he pondered the future, seeking a solution. Above all, he sought answers within himself.

Peace, he thought, can only be obtained through equality of rights, by consent freely given. Atlantic Europe must be closely allied to the United States, which would contribute to the economic stability and prosperity of Europe, and guarantee it protection. Unification must be accomplished in harmony with the process of civilization itself. Every nation, province, and individual must be willing to submit to common regulations—to political, judicial, and economic institutions that establish equality before the law. In the superstate that would thus be created, every country and citizen would have to submit to supranational institutions that guaranteed equality for all nations and citizens.

According to Monnet, traditionalists like de Gaulle and Bidault, influenced by history, failed to take into account the deterioration of the European nations. To insure Europe's independence, to preserve its uniqueness, a United States of Europe would have to be established. Only then would it be strong enough to defend itself, to elude Soviet enslavement as well as the invasion of the big American industries; only then could it safeguard its freedom, its own culture. In this troubled postwar era, France could not wage a secret war against allies who had rescued her from Nazi hegemony.

Returning from his morning walk for breakfast, Monnet would find his wife, Silvia, seated at her easel. As she worked, she listened to her husband's ideas. For Monnet, she was the sounding board he needed to refine his concepts.

Ravaged and hungry, Western Europe was turning into an encampment of beggars. It was occupied by its benefactors, the Americans. For the first time in history, the victors, far from demanding spoils from the defeated peoples, fed them, and offered them aid. When flour was distributed in the Italian peninsula, a famous Neopolitan singer celebrated the good luck of Italians on having lost the war. "Imagine," he sang, "if we had won the war. All those Americans to feed!"

In 1947, UNRRA, which had enabled Germans, Italians, Greeks, and Turks to survive, was about to fold. The United States was bearing with growing impatience the heavy weight of a disorganized Germany. But Stalin wanted no part of the French plans for a divided and federalized Germany. Nor did he want to see Germany back on her feet, reunified, and controlled by the Western Allies, the masters of the Ruhr. In fact, he did not want to discuss the matter at all. He had a hysterical fear of Germany, whose assault on Russia in 1941 had left him prostrate for a month, while Hitler's tanks approached Moscow. And he was equally fearful of American nuclear capability. Placing no faith in coexistence with the capitalist countries, he attacked Iran, Turkey, and Greece. But he exerted a measure of self-control. Time was on his side. Every passing month brought an increase in the misery of Western Europe—inflation, deprivation, a growing sympathy for the Communist Party. Before long, revolution would establish Stalinism from Vladivostok to Brest.

"There's only one way out," Monnet kept repeating. He was filled with anguish by the growing difficulties of France. Wages were frozen, and black market prices were soaring. All this threatened his plan. The one way out, of course, was to unify Europe with the help of the United States, to rid the Western nations of chaos and unite them into a prosperous, powerful entity. Americans had not fought the war and conquered Hitler only to abandon Europe to Communism.

The German problem was a serious one for Europe. Monnet believed that it could be solved by including West Germany in a European economic and strategic bloc. His views were similar to those of General George Marshall who had succeeded James Byrnes as Secretary of State. Marshall would not wage war in order to free Europe from the East. But he was determined to put West Germany back on her feet, to make her strong and tie her economically and militarily to the free world. He was also determined to persuade Frenchmen to give up their obsolete ideas.

On April 10, 1947, Marshall, British Foreign Minister Bevin, and Georges Bidault met at the Kremlin with Molotov to discuss matters openly. Once again Molotov declared himself unwilling to tamper with Germany. She must remain unified, with Berlin as her capital. She must also pay the U.S.S.R. ten billion dollars in reparations, and this sum did not include the dismantled factories.

"Berlin in the zone occupied by the U.S.S.R. would be a Soviet capital. That is out of the question," General Marshall said. "An indemnity of ten billion would turn Germany into an asylum for the homeless, right in the middle of Europe. That's out of the question, too."

Bidault pressed for the immediate internationalization of the Ruhr. People were dying of the cold in France that year. The factories had no electricity; Paris was desperate for coal from the Rhine.

"The Red Army must participate in the occupation of the Ruhr," Molotov exclaimed.

"The Ruhr is in the British zone. The British army will see to its occupation," Bevin interjected.

This marked the beginning of the split between the U.S.S.R. and the West. Stalin deliberately allowed matters to drag on, hoping Europe would collapse. Bidault was crushed. To cheer him up, Marshall and Bevin signed a note giving him 300,000 tons of Ruhr coal and promised him a Franco-Saar economic union until a final settlement was achieved.

"Bidault has traded French reparations for a bag of coal," the Communist ministers thundered on his return. They immediately voted for a general raise in wages without any increase in prices; they also attempted to stir up unrest.

On May 4, 1947, Premier Ramadier, backed by the President of the Republic, Vincent Auriol, excluded the Communists from the government. As soon as Maurice Thorez and his friends left the government, there were insurrectional strikes against the mines, railroads, and Metro; these were to last until December. The Communists staged riots in Marseilles, Lille, and Paris. Factories were occupied. A loose rail near Arras resulted in an accident on the Paris-Lille train that cost sixteen lives. The prefectures were besieged. In Marseilles, employees of two security companies responsible for guarding the law court against demonstrators joined the insurrection and helped the agitators climb over the railings.

George Marshall sent one of his assistants, Clayton, a big cotton dealer, to study the situation in Europe. Monnet showed him around and explained the situation. The United States would have to come to the aid of Europe as quickly as possible and help put it in a position to contend with poverty and Eastern encroachment; it would also have to assist the cause of European unification.

"France, Germany, and England will all be bankrupt by the end of the year," Clayton concluded. "Italy will fall apart even sooner. Revolution is threatening. The collapse of Europe will be disastrous for world peace and catastrophic for American prosperity which depends on foreign trade."

George Frost Kennan, another of Marshall's assistants, was asked to draw up a blueprint for European recovery. Monnet was one of the few Europeans who was thoroughly well informed. He perceived in General Marshall's generous gesture a chance to set up the first European organization, a possible prelude to the United States of Europe—Monnet's obsession. Earlier mistakes like UNRRA must be avoided. The governments themselves must be the recipients and distributors of American aid. Assistance must be shared by all the nations through a common institution in which the participants, whether former allies or enemies, would learn to become a community. Monnet thus hit upon a mechanism that would start the ball rolling without offending national sensibilities.

On June 5, 1947, addressing an audience at Harvard University, General Marshall delivered his Santa Claus speech. America was ready to spend huge sums to aid the economic recovery of nations victimized by war. To share this aid, the countries of Europe would have to unite.

Marshall came to Paris for the opening of the Peace Conference. Sixteen nations, from both East and West, were gathered here. Monnet conferred with Marshall and outlined his ideas in detail. "Be careful not to humiliate the Europeans," he told the American. That was the day when everything began, Monnet recalled.

Marshall was in total agreement with Monnet, whose ideas he used to reinforce his own. In principle, the American offer was being made to the nations of both Eastern and Western Europe. Either the men at the Kremlin would be disarmed by it or their satellites would break away from them; at least, so it was thought. But from the start the Russians refused the "tainted gifts."

"The United States should state right off what they intend to give," Molotov asserted in the presence of Bevin and Bidault. The latter naturally hoped to keep this manna from America for the Western countries alone.

"First we have to submit a plan for economic recovery," Bidault maintained.

"This is an intolerable infringement on our national independence," Molotov replied. "If you accept the Marshall Plan you will unleash a tempest."

And indeed, the East-West rupture did produce a tempest. The world was divided into two blocs. On September 23, 1947, the Cominform was organized. The Sovietization of East Germany and the satellite countries was accelerated. Czechoslovakia accepted the Marshall Plan, signing Jan Masaryk's death warrant. Eight months later came the coup in Prague. Masaryk leapt from his office window. In France a virtual civil war erupted. Robert Schuman succeeded Ramadier as Premier. The Minister of the Interior, Jules Moch, mobilized the police and the army to combat the agitators.

Having just launched the Rassemblement Populaire Français (RPF), which was expected to restore him to power, de Gaulle made a speech at Rennes on July 27, 1947, in which he denounced the great and perhaps imminent threat of Soviet aggression. "Four hundred million men endanger our freedom. The distance that separates them from the Rhine is equivalent to twice the distance around France." The American general Lemnitzer put it differently, "The Russians need only a good pair of shoes to reach Brest."

De Gaulle demanded a strong Europe: "The defeated must recover their place in the world. The United States must help Europe recover its prosperity." The general was thus outlining a new policy for postwar France. It implied a Franco-German reconciliation and a cohesiveness among European nations, supported by American aid. How far would he push this policy when he resumed power?

Monnet, meanwhile, assisted by his right-hand man, Marjolin, was preparing to found the Organization for European Economic Cooperation (OEEC). It was to be a very novel, charitable organization: The poor would distribute among themselves the mills, generators, bulldozers, refineries, and various machines contributed by the United States. The businessmen and farmers who ordered the machines would pay their own governments for them. The more the Americans gave, the more the European governments would collect. Monnet hastened to see that orders for the subsidies earmarked for commercial equipment were credited to Paris.

Both the OEEC and the Marshall Plan were slow in getting under way. General Marshall had no intention of throwing millions of dollars away. "Europe must organize its own defense," he said. "It is making no effort to arm or to form a military alliance. Here we are, about to make an immense effort, and as soon as we send the money to Europe, Stalin will grab it."

Germany, the number one beneficiary of the Marshall Plan, as well as France, the number two, would be obliged to participate in the European organization. But Germany did not exist. France, through her spokesman, Bidault, opposed the recovery of the Reich.

In effect, the shower of American gold would not begin until France accepted the idea of a West German state. At that moment Paris called for help from the United States. The U.S.S.R. was threatening France, to say nothing of internal subversion. In October, 1947, Jules Moch and General Revers made preparations to apply Plan Y in case of an uprising of the extreme left.

"Europe must organize its own defense," Marshall repeated. "Only then will America come to its aid." What he meant was that France must consent to the restoration of Germany as a nation and organize her defense in association with her allies and the Germans. But Bidault could not reconcile himself to such an about-face. The Marshall Plan was stalled by French obstruction.

In the autumn of 1947 a solution seemed possible; it was inspired by de Gaulle and is relatively unknown. General Billotte dreamed up the Atlantic Pact and the doctrine of deterrence. It was no longer a question of unifying Europe but of creating a free world under French, British, and American supervision.

Pierre Billotte, son of the youngest French general in World War I, was himself the youngest French general of World War II. An army man, a politician, economist, and author, Billotte was above all a man of imagination. Wounded and taken prisoner in 1940, he escaped from Pomerania, Poland, Russia, and Spitzberg. Five companions escaped with him, but before he arrived in London he had gathered

132 Frenchmen and Belgians along the way. In 1941 he was the first representative of the Free French in Moscow; later he became de Gaulle's chief of staff. As the commander of an armored brigade in Leclerc's division, he captured von Choltitz, the German general, who asked the famous question, "Is Paris burning?"

Billotte headed the French delegation to the Committee of Chiefs of Staff at the United Nations. In China he had met Marshall when the latter was attempting to mediate between Mao and Chiang Kai-shek. Marshall confided his deep concerns to Billotte: "The Europeans are unwilling to struggle, unite, and organize to defend themselves against the Stalinist threat. I proposed to help them out of the misery and chaos in which they are bound to flounder amid all the subversion. But they paid no attention. The United States will be forced to abandon Europe."

Billotte had been influenced by the ideas of General de Gaulle, with whom he had often discussed postwar plans. De Gaulle had always envisaged the solution of major problems in the perspective of an Anglo-French-American directorate devising a global strategy for the free world.

The new Premier, Robert Schuman, took office on November 22, 1947. General Billotte urged him to offer the United States a military and political alliance that would bring all the countries of the West —about fifteen—under the aegis of a Big Three Directorate. Such an alliance would assume worldwide responsibilities, whereas Denmark and Sweden would be concerned solely with matters involving their area. The United States, France, and England together would organize a defensive, economic, and financial system of cooperation between Europe and America. At the same time they would determine the status of Germany and include her in their defense plans.

As he talked, Billotte dreamed up his theory of deterrence. If the United States would guarantee to use atomic weapons against the Russians in the event of a Soviet attack on Europe, Stalin would be forced to abandon his plans for aggression. Billotte explained all this to the French military leaders, but they did not seem to understand him. He broached it to General de Gaulle, who listened to him for an hour, then gave his approval. Schuman asked Billotte to open secret negotiations with Marshall.

France was in the midst of Communist subversion. Any moment, it was feared, there might be a Russian offensive. To prevent the

Kremlin from learning of Billotte's plan and consequently hastening the disaster, it was agreed that the greatest secrecy was vital. Diplomatic channels would be shunned. No ambassadors would be informed of the conversations. No secretaries would be employed. Every communication would be written in longhand and transmitted by special messenger.

Billotte told Marshall about the French proposal: an Atlantic alliance with a three-power directorate; rearmament; the organization and reconstruction of Europe; the American atomic umbrella over all countries west of the iron curtain. "If you allow the Russians to conquer Europe," Billotte said to Marshall, "the American military budget will have to be doubled. It would cost you less to arm the Europeans, who are eager to defend themselves, and to come to their rescue with your plans for reconstruction."

General Marshall allowed himself to be convinced. He adopted the idea of an Atlantic alliance with a three-power directorate as if it were his own. Bidault, who was visiting the United Nations, was brought up to date by Billotte, and came to an understanding with Marshall. He did this without informing the French ambassador, Henri Bonnet. Now that the Europeans were willing to form an organization and defend themselves with American help, Marshall declared that he was ready to expedite his plan for economic assistance. The way was thus cleared for the signing of the Marshall Plan on April 3, 1948. A year and a day later, on April 4, 1949, the Atlantic Pact was signed. This was one of the conditions of the Marshall Plan.

Georges Bidault informed the English. The negotiations were conducted in longhand between Paris, Washington, and London. American isolationist laws prohibited the White House from entering into an alliance. Truman and Marshall prepared and took steps to submit to Congress a bill that would permit their country to belong to an already existing pro-American organization. It was therefore up to the French and the British to establish a European alliance with which the United States could be associated.

The negotiations for the Atlantic Pact were transferred to London, to the great annoyance of Bidault. The British had in mind the Brussels Pact. It united Great Britain, France, and the Benelux countries in a defensive alliance which the United States was to join. It also included all the nations that were to sign the Atlantic Pact—fourteen in all. By sabotaging the idea of a three-power directorate,

the British hoped to take the lead in Europe and, as privileged partners of the United States, to establish with the Americans an Anglo-
Saxon directorate for the free world. France was to be excluded from
the formulation of global strategy. The Atlantic Alliance—as envisaged by de Gaulle—was torpedoed.

Bidault bristled. This was not at all what had been agreed upon
in New York. But the Americans and the English ignored him. They
were in a hurry to be done with French demands and objections.
"If the Soviet offensive is unleashed, everything will be swept away,"
they said.

On February 9, 1948, they decided they would wait no longer for
French acquiescence in regard to the future of Germany. The Frankfurt charter substituted a single zone for the British and American
zones of occupation. A government was set up under the presidency
of Konrad Adenauer. Studies made by the chiefs of staff foreshadowed
the absorption of German contingents into the Allied armed forces.
"We cannot dispense with the Germans if we are to defend Western
Europe in Germany," General Ridgeway kept repeating. "They have
the best infantry in the world."

The Prague coup occurred on March 4, 1948. French ambassador
Dejean cabled the Quai d'Orsay: *The Red Army may head for Brest
any day.* Bidault sent another anguished appeal to Washington. The
American government again replied that the Europeans must first get
together and organize. Then the United States would help.

Thrown into a state of panic, the European allies proceeded to
organize. On March 17 the Brussels Pact established a common military force for England, France, and the Benelux countries. The
Germans were to contribute some infantry units. But Paris still could
not bring itself to accept German troops or a German nation until
the fate of the Ruhr and the Saar had been settled.

Meanwhile, twenty countries that had been devastated by war were
growing impatient. The help promised by General Marshall had failed
to arrive. If France was causing the delay, it would be better to go
ahead without her.

"Only Europe can give France her former position," Monnet repeated. He used his influence to get the OEEC under way without
further holdups. As the French High Commissioner of the modernization plan, he was directly involved. On April 16, 1948—although
Bidault continued to fight it until June 3—the first European organ-

ization held its inaugural session in Paris. The American horn of plenty was being emptied for the benefit of the Old World. It was an assembly filled with hope, radiant with the prospect of prosperity, and, for many, imbued with the dream of unity.

The golden trumpets that were sounded at the Château de la Muette brought Bidault, who was in London, to bay. How could one resist the magnificent Marshall, who was about to save the French economy, especially at a time when France and her allies were demanding additional subsidies to arm themselves? Was it possible to tell the world, in case of Soviet invasion, Frenchmen, Englishmen, and Americans will be killed in Germany to protect the Reich, that slope of Western Europe, but Germans will not be mobilized because the Allies cannot agree on the status of Germany?

On June 3, 1948, after interminable discussion, Bidault dropped most of his demands. A centralized federal government would be established in West Germany by a constituent assembly. The Ruhr was to remain German but, in theory, at least, would be controlled by an international authority. The Saar would be autonomous but linked to France by a customs union until a plebiscite could be held.

A definite arrangement with Germany was not the purpose of the conference with German representatives that was to meet as soon as they were elected. But France was no longer demanding the traditional safeguards in regard to the Rhineland. Acquiescence to the unification of West Germany was the price France had to pay for the Marshall Plan, which was to insure her recovery. By consenting to the implicit participation of Germany in European defense, France obtained American participation in the defense of Europe.

"A decisive step has just been taken. France is the gainer in every way—economically, militarily, and in the furthering of European unity. Now she must take the lead in unifying the Continent," Monnet said.

French public opinion was shocked. "A distressing solution, but one we will have to accept," said the President, Vincent Auriol. "We are not responsible for Franco-German reconciliation; we are allowing others to force us to accept the restoration of the Reich. We are merely being dragged along by the Americans," lamented Premier Robert Schuman. On June 10, 1948, de Gaulle stigmatized these defeats as "the final abandonment." General Billotte resigned from the army.

But individual expressions of indignation were overshadowed by a sudden uproar. On June 19, 1948, the Americans introduced the new mark in West Germany. The Germans awakened at seven o'clock that morning, broke. They discovered, when the banks opened at nine o'clock, that the new mark was as solid as the dollar. On June 22, 1948, the Russians closed the highways and canals leading to their zone of occupation. The Berlin blockade had begun. Coming to the rescue of the 2,000,000 Berliners who were condemned to famine, the Americans launched an air lift that was to last 300 days. Within the space of a few hours, the people of Berlin had become the martyrs of liberty. The unity of the West had been achieved amid the anguish of confrontation.

The OEEC, which had just begun to operate in Paris, welcomed victors and vanquished alike with American promises and that spirit of solidarity danger so often engenders. Jean Monnet, the specialist in internationalist techniques, provided the organization that was being installed in the Château de la Muette with its most effective tool. Majority rule had been adopted to settle the question of distributing the American subsidies. But it was important to prevent the dissatisfaction of an individual or a minority from paralyzing the operation of the system. Monnet suggested that the Secretary-General of the Organization take the initiative in making proposals. Four wise men were to supervise the sharing of grants according to needs. The Secretary-General, Marjolin, who for months had been directing the operation and making all the preparations with Monnet, was familiar with Monnet's technique for organizing teamwork. He was to have the invaluable help of Hervé Alphand who, displaying his usual brio, headed the French delegation.

Whereas Monnet has no university degree and owes the success of his extraordinary career in part to his open-mindedness, Marjolin has amassed diplomas. A degree in philosophy and a Yale University scholarship enabled him to discover America, the lovely American girl whom he married, and his vocation: political economy in the new style of Keynes, which explains crises, seeks ways to prevent them, and inspired Roosevelt's New Deal. When he returned to France, Marjolin studied law, obtained a doctorate in economics, and became a professor. Monnet discovered him at the Institut Scientifique de Recherches Économiques and took him to London to work with the Anglo-French Committee for War Supplies. Although a pupil of the well-known liberal economist Charles Rist, Marjolin tends toward Socialism.

At the Château de la Muette he adopted Monnet's methods for the modernization plan and surrounded himself with experts from every country. Their task was to draw up an accurate list of the major needs of each nation and obtain the cooperation of ministers, businessmen, and union leaders. The experience of the Rue de Martignac was to benefit approximately twenty nations.

One of the first things Marjolin did was to gratify a wish of Monnet's. He presented himself to Sir Stafford Cripps in London and asked, "You want to tackle the problem of Europe?" Sir Stafford Cripps agreed immediately to England's participation in the OEEC. His country would enjoy all the advantages of the Marshall Plan since no commitments were required. But he had no intention of going any further.

America, the donor, was finally joined by Canada, the lady bountiful. In spite of the drawbacks of majority rule, and thanks to Monnet's techniques and the impartiality of Marjolin and "the four wise men," the distribution of the bounty from overseas—$5,000,000 for the first year—was accomplished in an efficient and dignified manner.

The OEEC was to render a great service to the nations of Europe by waging war on protectionism. The British, who were impatient to see international trade reestablished, opened a campaign in the other European countries in favor of reducing or abolishing import quotas. This was very helpful, because ever since the crisis of 1929 these quotas had barricaded national frontiers more effectively than tariffs.

Marjolin organized a European Payments Union in which member states could arrange among themselves for subsidies or loans. The strictly controlled currencies were gradually becoming convertible, and existing regulations were relaxed in 1950 and 1951.

But England was drawing away from the OEEC. Her situation had been improved by the Marshall Plan. Stubbornly isolationist, she was to resist all attempts to transform "the charitable organization" into a structured economic organism. Monnet's pleas and American encouragement proved fruitless. "Because of majority rule," Marjolin explained, "when one nation ceases to participate the whole affair can be jeopardized. This experience must not be forgotten."

Meanwhile, at the Château de la Muette, Monnet found the necessary resources for his plan for modernization and equipment. Twenty percent of all the appropriations went to France. Financed in part by American gifts and in part by inflation—a great deal of suffering and injustice was caused by the devalued currency—Monnet's plan was paving the way for the economic recovery of France.

VI

The Opposition of the Labour Party

WINSTON CHURCHILL, the leader of the opposition in England, presided over the Congress of Europe at The Hague from May 7 to 10, 1948. Seven organizations to promote European unity had assembled there under the leadership of Duncan Sandys, the son-in-law of the old lion. Present were 16 former premiers, 800 former ministers, parliamentarians, scholars, churchmen, and industrialists. Churchill read them a "Message to Europeans." "The hour has come," he said, "for the nations of Europe to transfer certain of their sovereign rights in order henceforth to exercise them in common, to coordinate and develop their resources. . . ."

A wave of enthusiasm swept the Western nations.

At that time, Joseph Stalin was unifying the free world. The tremendous fear that gripped the Western countries and the privations they were suffering because the Soviets were preventing a peaceful solution engendered a spirit of solidarity. This had resulted in the Marshall Plan and the OEEC. It was also to bring about the Atlantic Pact, the new Germany, and the Europe of Churchill.

The applause that greeted Sir Winston's peroration was followed by demands for the establishment of a Council of Europe. Idealists, disciples of Briand and Coudenhove-Kalergi, Europeanists of all tendencies, and also many statesmen of goodwill participated in this movement.

72

In France the unanimity was striking. Socialists, Popular Republicans, and Gaullists called with a single voice for the establishment of European unity. The government was favorable to the idea, and Bidault, the Foreign Minister, enthusiastically supported it. Even the great opponent of the regime, General de Gaulle, campaigned in favor of it.

But in reality, the stirring unanimity expressed at The Hague concealed violent conflicts and a multitude of doctrinal quarrels. On the Continent the Socialists favored a Europe very different from that of the businessmen and liberal economists. And in England the Labour Party, on this occasion, proved to be more nationalist than the Conservatives.

"Churchill is preparing for his forthcoming electoral campaign against the Labour government by promoting a united Europe," his opponents in power were saying.

"Having survived the worst ordeal successfully, England can manage by herself. She doesn't have to join the former occupied countries, the losers," Labour's leadership contended. "The British will never allow anyone who is not English to manage their affairs."

Once the echo of bravos had faded, The Hague, to the initiated, seemed to have served merely as the setting for a swan song. At this point the Foreign Ministers of Belgium and France intervened. Paul Henri Spaak, the organizer of the Benelux countries, was a dynamic Europeanist. Although unable to forge the three Netherlands monarchies into a single state, he had succeeded in setting up a customs union. In a unified Europe, he told himself, the irritating, insoluble problems of his small and cruelly divided country would be submerged.

For his part, Bidault believed that European unification would be one way to solve the German problem in a manner advantageous to the French. It could also achieve a complete regeneration of the Continent. Bidault was reacting to the philippics of General de Gaulle. From the platform of the RPF, the party he had founded in 1947, the ghost of Colombey reproached the governments of "the Establishment" for not having sought a European framework that would include a renascent Germany and provide guarantees for France, especially in regard to the Ruhr. Ever since his visit to the French zone of occupation in 1946, de Gaulle had kept repeating that Europe

73

could be unified only if a direct understanding was reached between the Gauls and the Germans.

Events pressed. On June 24, 1948, responding to the creation of the new German mark, Stalin ordered the total blockade of Berlin. That gigantic test of strength, the air lift, began. Panic impelled Europeans to unite. On July 20, 1948, Spaak and Bidault together suggested that a prestigious European Assembly be formed, a Constituent European Assembly of sorts. The free world applauded the proposal.

The least enthusiastic expression of approval did not come from the major opponent of the regime. De Gaulle requested a referendum in order to induce all the nations to join the project and thus insure popular support. But he saw Europe in his own fashion. On September 12, 1948, he declared at Nice, "Europe will be united in the only way possible, around France." He had long favored a united Europe. As early as 1932, he had written in *Fil de l'épée* of the internationalist trend: "Today, individualism is in the wrong. Everywhere the need to unite is becoming clear. . . ." On January 9, 1941, de Gaulle had spoken in London about reconstructing Europe with the Allies, and had mentioned it again in the Albert Hall on November 11, 1942.

The French Resistance regarded a United States of Europe as a means of encircling Germany. In September, 1943, de Gaulle had consulted the members of the Liberation Committee in Algiers, and René Mayer handed him a memorandum on the subject of an economic organization for Western Europe.

On February 24, 1944, the general sent a note to René Massigli, asking him to initiate conversations "with our allies on the Continent" and the three countries of the future Benelux union that Spaak was organizing. "There is good reason to consider joining the Rhineland to a Western bloc," he wrote, "to a strategic and economic federation between France, Belgium, Luxembourg, and the Netherlands—a federation in which Great Britain could participate."

On March 18, 1944, the day before he was to give a speech, de Gaulle received a visit from Jean Monnet who talked to him about establishing close cooperation between France, Holland, Belgium and Luxembourg.

"A four-power Europe? It would be too small," the general insisted. "If a unified Europe is to become a reality, it must include Italy, Spain, and Portugal, provided these countries choose to live under the democratic system of government—Switzerland, if she so desires; Germany, too, but partitioned and deprived of her large arsenal. The Ruhr could be used to pay us back in kind. The Rhineland must be the joint property of such a newborn Europe. And in an organization such as this, France must play the leading role."

In Algiers, de Gaulle, as the head of the Liberation Committee, alluded to the "great design": "We believe that a Western association of sorts, organized by us, as broad as possible in membership and stressing economics, would be very advantageous. Such an association, extending to Africa and maintaining close relations with the East—especially the Arab states, which quite justifiably are seeking to pool their interests—and in which the Channel, the Rhine and the Mediterranean would serve as arteries, might constitute the major center of a global organization concerned with production, trade and security."

At the time of liberation, Europe was not uppermost in de Gaulle's thoughts. But once he had retired to Colombey, he studied the problem carefully. He mentioned it to Gaston Palewski and Georges Pompidou. And most of his correspondence with Michel Debré was devoted to this subject. The RPF program included the formation of a European union around France and a decentralized Germany. Its most prominent exponents were Gaston Palewski, General Billotte, Michel Debré, and Alain Peyrefitte. De Gaulle periodically alluded to Europe before the assembled multitudes. A unified Europe, he declared, must encircle Germany and render her harmless.

In de Gaulle's opinion, Europe would not be a single nation—at least not for a long time—but rather an association of states that were in agreement on economic, military, and cultural matters. "France will be the geographical and moral center of this association." He envisaged a delegation of sovereignty to the common organism. This would be done through "the states, each of which will preserve its body, soul and image."

Now, faced with the Soviet threat, de Gaulle campaigned for a European union which would accept American aid in order to strengthen its defenses but which would nonetheless remain independent. He asked for a referendum in order to draw all the nations into the project and to stimulate the adherence of peoples as well as of states.

Spaak and Bidault convoked a group of prominent Europeans—

eighteen big names from ten countries. Led by Édouard Herriot, the group went to London to see the ministers of the five governments that had signed the Brussels Pact. There Spaak and Bidault opened the door to discussion. Once all these ministers and illustrious citizens were assembled, the result was a European Tower of Babel that might have been conceived by deaf men.

Supported by the Scandinavians, the British cabinet was primarily anxious not to concede to the proposed institutions any power that might infringe on its own government. In particular, it wanted no part of the kind of supranationalism so dear to Winston Churchill. It was feared that the old Tory would take advantage of a trend in favor of supranationalism to defeat his Labour opponents.

Bidault and Spaak wanted to lay the foundations of a European nation governed by an assembly elected by universal suffrage, and a ministerial committee. The Gaullists wanted to see the beginning of a European Europe. Among the eighteen illustrious men there were federalists who wanted to found a government, an Assembly of the United States of Europe. They were confederalists who hoped for a powerful ministerial committee constituted by governments that would begin to cooperate with one another. In addition, they also wanted an assembly with limited power.

In the end a compromise was reached between the supporters of Bidault and Spaak, and the British, who were backed by the Scandinavians. On May 5, 1949, a treaty establishing the Council of Europe was signed in London. This Council was to comprise a Consultative Assembly in Strasbourg and a ministerial committee in Brussels, where the permanent secretariat was to be located. The Consultative Assembly would not be elected by popular vote but would consist of parliamentary delegations "designated according to the procedure adopted by each government." The Labour cabinet, alarmed at the thought of Churchill installed in the Strasbourg Assembly, insisted that the British delegation be directly appointed by His Majesty's government.

De Gaulle welcomed the new body. "On the economic and political level," he said, "the Council of Europe should become an effective and executive organism. To expedite this, peoples everywhere in Europe must express their opinion through a vast referendum which the RPF advocates."

The ministerial committee in Brussels in no way constituted the beginning of a European government. The British viewed it as a sort of Upper Chamber, an Assembly of States holding meetings in Brussels and exerting more influence than the Lower Chamber, or Consultative Assembly in Strasbourg. The committee would bring together the fifteen Foreign Ministers. West Germany, Turkey, Cyprus, Switzerland, and Austria were expected to join. Each member state would have the right of veto.

When the Council of Europe actually materialized, it brought nothing but cruel disappointment to those who had placed their hopes in it. The two chambers were so organized as to be entirely incapable of functioning. The Strasbourg Assembly could only adopt recommendations; it had no authority. It was based neither on universal suffrage nor even on partial suffrage. Tyrannical governments or majorities and political parties would determine its composition. The Communists adopted a negative attitude. The Council of Europe, they claimed, would be merely a tool to be used against the U.S.S.R.

Although its composition was most unsatisfactory and its powers derisory, the Consultative Assembly nevertheless proved livelier than the ministerial committee. During the first session, in 1949, Churchill did his best to stir up revolt against the London saboteurs and their allies. But he managed to secure only a strong minority in favor of establishing a quasi-parliamentary European regime.

De Gaulle was incensed. European union had been sabotaged in London. It had become a mockery. "How can anyone make us believe that this institution, which has no mandate from Europe, no effective power or responsibility, will be able to perform the colossal task of uniting the continent?" he thundered. "I personally believe that the organization of Europe must stem from Europe itself. I believe that only a vast referendum in all the free countries of Europe will be able to launch it.

"A Europe unified in its economy, its culture, its defense, a confederation of people responsible for this unity, an Assembly that has the power to lay the foundations and to submit them for everyone's ratification—that is what the citizens of Europe should be offered. . . .

"Any man with common sense can see that England is drawing away, attracted by people overseas. He can only conclude that the unity of Europe must, if possible and despite all obstacles, include the Germans. There will or will not be such a Europe, depending on

77

whether an agreement without intermediaries will or will not be possible between Germans and Gauls."

"I have always said," de Gaulle later asserted at a press conference held on November 14, 1949, "that Europe must be unified, that this must be done gradually in the economic and cultural domains, later in the military domain and even in the political sphere . . . that it has to be done by Europe alone, without any outside pressure . . . that the foundation of such a Europe must be a direct agreement, without intermediaries, between the French and German peoples—provided, of course, that such an agreement is possible."

He did not believe that such an accord could be reached on a basis of equality. "At the present time, it would be premature—assuming that it will ever be possible—to introduce German military power into the defense of Europe. I have said that a direct arrangement, without intermediaries, between France and Germany must initially be limited to economic and cultural problems and that later we could consider questions relating to defense. In my opinion, this is also true of the Atlantic Pact." In any event, de Gaulle did not believe that the French government was ready to tackle the problem of Europe.

Paul Henri Spaak, the initiator of the Council of Europe, became its president. Bidault, his partner in this difficult undertaking, placed a French diplomat, J.-C. Paris, at the head of the powerfully structured secretariat in Brussels.

Despite his strong personality, Spaak was unable to overcome the lethargy of the ministerial committee. For five years it was impossible to determine a program for the Council of Europe. The secretariat never amounted to anything. Spaak resigned. "We are getting nowhere," he said.

De Gaulle was to become increasingly harsh about "the fanciful schemes encountered at Strasbourg . . . that caricature of European institutions." "Europe will never be unified unless France takes the lead," he said, adding, "I mean a France on her feet and without apron strings."

His former chief of staff, Gaston Palewski, was even more brutal. He spoke of "the parodies and façades of that cardboard setting in Brussels and Strasbourg. . . ."

The Assembly was to become a forum used by brilliant statesmen in search of an audience, by a variety of eloquent speechmakers. But their words were to have only a limited echo. The Robertsau Palace was to remain empty for a long time.

"It is the only meeting place of a divided Europe," the Mayor of Strasbourg, Pierre Pflimlin, objected with moving conviction.

Monnet had never had any illusions about the Council of Europe; it was plagued by talk and lacked a concrete purpose. He had not attended the Congress of Europe at The Hague. He did not believe that European unity would materialize unless it offered the nations practical advantages that would make governments wish to meet "the following week."

The OEEC might have become the framework of a united Europe for businessmen and practical people. But the British had said no. The members of the OEEC, the clients of the Marshall Plan, were, moreover, too numerous. In any case, the atmosphere was not right. Something else would have to be found. Monnet, the initiator of the 1940 Anglo-French union, quite naturally thought of an Anglo-French customs union that could later be opened to other countries.

De Gaulle stressed a Franco-German rapprochement in his speeches about Europe. He was at heart a Continental.

Monnet, during his solitary walks, envisioned a Europe based on an agreement between Great Britain and France. He was a close friend of the Anglo-Saxons. He was encouraged in his leanings by Paul Hoffman, the director of American foreign aid and an enthusiastic champion of a third world force to back up the Atlantic Alliance.

While the battle over the Council of Europe was subsiding, Monnet convinced the Secretary of State for Finance, Maurice Petsche, that his idea was a good one. At that time Petsche was worried about the British cabinet, which was reacting angrily to the devaluation of the franc and the consequent threat to the stability of the pound sterling.

The English, Monnet explained, had won the war. They had safeguarded the pound. They saw no reason why the other countries, whether formerly occupied or hostile, but now their associates, should interfere in British affairs. They had never wanted a genuine OEEC, and they did not want a genuine Council of Europe. They clung to their illusions—the insubstantial pound, the overseas empire, the Commonwealth that was disintegrating, the false sense of security

79

that their relations with the United States gave them. Their only salvation lay in a complete overhauling of their productive system and in an about-face in Europe, where they had 180,000,000 potential customers. They would come to see this. But for the moment they were afraid to commit themselves. An economic union with France, however, might tempt them. It would represent only a limited commitment. If everything worked out well, the customs union could be expanded to include the Benelux countries, Germany, and the other European nations. In this way a concrete reconstruction of Europe could get under way without a lot of fuss.

Petsche approved of the project, and Monnet left for London with his blessings. The Chancellor of the Exchequer, Sir Stafford Cripps, greeted him with marked reserve. Cripps did not, however, reject Monnet's offer. He sent his chief planning officer, Sir Edwin Plowden, together with two assistants, to Montfort-l'Amaury to explore the proposal more thoroughly.

Once again Monnet was to play the role of an official foreign minister. Flanked by Étienne Hirsch and Pierre Uri, Monnet welcomed his English guests at his cottage in April, 1949. But the British officials demurred. They had merely envisaged a plan to increase trade. Now they thought they were being offered a federated Europe, plus a merger of England and France. It was inconceivable. Only Churchill or a state of war could give rise to such folly. No Labour government would embark on an adventure of this kind.

In spite of his incurable optimism, Monnet felt let down by his English friends. They would join a united Europe only when it was an accomplished fact. "I have made a mistake," he told himself. "I forgot Germany; she is about to become once again the most powerful nation on the Continent."

VII

The Holy Year

ON JULY 14, 1949, Jean Monnet stayed up late to listen to the radio. He remembers it as if it were yesterday. Russia's first atomic bomb had been exploded. He feared a storm would break: an American ultimatum, the sound of bombers. But all around his cottage he saw only the fireworks celebrating Bastille Day. Stalin had lifted the Berlin blockade. It had merely served to unite the signatories of the Atlantic Pact and to accelerate the resurgence of Germany despite French reluctance. But now Stalin had the bomb.

"This is our last holiday," Monnet told his friends. "No one in Paris realizes how exasperated the Americans are. And our lack of understanding is holding up a German settlement. The Americans feel they must save Germany from chaos. We oppose this and are trying to obtain a Versailles type of settlement.... Wars are started when impasses such as these occur, when every avenue seems blocked. The Americans might be tempted to forestall the Soviet threat by a preventive action."

On August 24 the first meeting of the NATO Council took place. In the midst of the cold war, the cold alliance pitted France against the Anglo-Saxons on the question of Germany.

A divided but unified Germany was emerging, even as Paris was demanding her dismemberment. On September 8, the Federal Republic was proclaimed in Bonn. On September 15 elections for its first Chancellor were to take place. Between these two dates, on September 10, Robert Schuman, the Foreign Minister who succeeded Bidault, attended a White House meeting. He was flanked by the American Secretary of State, Dean Acheson, who had succeeded General Marshall, and the British Foreign Minister, Ernest Bevin. Schuman was ill at ease. He spoke no English and found himself in an impossible situation.

A conference on the defense of the West was being planned. Scheduled to meet in London in a few months, it was to include the new Federal Republic of West Germany. She was now a power to be reckoned with. The French were demanding that the arsenal of the Ruhr be detached from the Federal Republic and placed under international control to insure French security and the payment of reparations. For the time being, the mines and steelworks of the Ruhr were controlled by the Ruhr International Authority. Although, in theory, this arrangement was designed to prevent a reconstitution of the monopolistic trusts, the International Authority was not at all reassuring to France. The coal and steel tycoons had "regained possession of their property." Among them were men like Thyssen, who had been expelled from Germany by Hitler, and Alfred Krupp, whom the Allies had arrested as a war criminal. The Führer had issued a special decree excusing Krupp from the payment of taxes "in recognition of 150 years of exceptional and uninterrupted services rendered the German army." Acquitted at the Nuremberg trials, Krupp demanded the return of his Essen empire. Aiding German recovery by speeding up her heavy industry, the Americans persuaded the British to allow the barons of the Ruhr to recover their mines and steelworks. French protests went unheeded by the Americans.

Paris demanded the autonomy of the Saar and its economic union with France. In April, 1949, the Allies had agreed that the Saar's coal should be awarded France as a species of reparation pending the outcome of a referendum in the Saar on the customs union. Ever since 1945 the people of the Saar had benefited from this union with France. The elections of November 5, 1949, were to give an overwhelming majority to those favoring autonomy, headed by Johannes Hoffmann. Above all, the French were fiercely opposed to the rearmament of Germany, which was already being contemplated.

Dean Acheson was born a British Canadian, the son of a Presbyterian minister. By nature and birth he was clearly not sympathetic to French concerns or demands. With his English accent, courteous

82

manners, thin mustache, and sober elegance, he gave the impression of having left Oxford one morning when the wind was not blowing in the direction of the Entente Cordiale. "The United States needs a German ally that is strong, highly industrialized, integrated into the Western system and ready to participate in the defense of the West now being organized through NATO," he explained to the French minister. He hoped that France, too, would find some way to become reconciled with her former enemy.

"A dual, insoluble crisis," groaned Schuman, "the Ruhr and the Saar on the one hand, the German army on the other. . . ."

"I believe we can leave it up to France to take the lead in this matter," said Acheson, his thin mustache, which made him look like a sly fox, thrust in the direction of the heavy-set and silent Bevin, whose sole response was a grunt.

Schuman felt that he had been charged with a mission. France must make up her own mind about what she was prepared to renounce, about the future of Europe. To be sure, French public opinion was almost unanimous in opposing German sovereignty in the Ruhr or in the Saar. It also decried German rearmament. But mere opposition was no solution.

For the British, too, no answer was in sight. They were hoping that the Ruhr International Authority would be transformed into a genuine allied guardianship, which could intervene and slow things down should there be a crisis in the production of Rhenish steel and coal which competed with England's. But it would be idle for the French to expect Great Britain to cooperate steadfastly in a genuine internationalization of the Ruhr; the British were too closely tied to the Americans.

The British were embarrassed about the question of a new *Reichswehr*. After all they had suffered, they were not enthusiastic about hearing fifes and drums celebrating German might on the other side of the Rhine. Nonetheless, they had resigned themselves to the idea, and were waiting to determine the form of German rearmament. But they insisted that Germany must be denied a navy, an air force, and atomic weapons. From the opposition benches, Churchill and Eden were to propose that the European army should have a German contingent. But first Europe had to be unified; the Labour Party was against it.

When Schuman returned to France, he consulted with the bureaucrats of the Quai d'Orsay. What could France suggest? The answers were written in the same ink and conceived in the same spirit as the Treaty of Versailles: strict internationalization of the Ruhr, reparations in coal, Franco-Saar union, no rearmament.

Monnet, who learned about this, was disturbed. The neurotic passion for written guarantees, the continuing desire to be punitive toward Germany, to keep her isolated, would once again cause endless trouble. This time, the French attitude would doubtless push the Germans, who wanted reunification above all else, into the welcoming arms of the Russians. The men at the Quai d'Orsay seemed completely unaware of realities—the presence of the Red Army in Europe, Europe's dependence on the Americans for survival. They appeared unmindful of the aid given by the Marshall Plan that had furthered French economic recovery, or of the American subsidies that had enabled her to arm within the Atlantic Alliance. Monnet was desperately seeking a way to forge the kind of European unity that would resolve the impasse.

Meanwhile, Schuman thought that the providential moment had arrived. A pope, Pius XII, who seemed almost transparent so delicate and ascetic was his appearance, experienced supernatural visions and held strong political beliefs. To aid the cause of peace with the help of fellow Catholics, he and the leaders of the Christian Democratic Party had formulated a plan. He proclaimed a Holy Year, to be dedicated to strivings for peace. For the first time, the leaders of Catholic organizations headed the French, Italian, and German governments. The Christian Democratic political parties aroused hopes of a new Christianity. This movement arranged religious gatherings at which political action was planned. Vatican Europe, as it was called, became part of the political scene.

Robert Schuman, Konrad Adenauer, and Alcide de Gasperi were three exemplary Catholics, three men who had lived near foreign borders and were themselves of divided nationality. All three had been hunted down by the Nazis and Fascists; all three were politicians with high ideals—virtually lay saints. If reconciliation were to be achieved between countries that had formerly been enemies—and these men had been brought to power by the desire of people for regeneration—these three were the ones most likely to achieve it.

Schuman, a Lorrainer, was born in Luxembourg in 1886 when Alsace-Lorraine was German. He had a cranium that almost came to a point—to the delight of caricaturists—the face of a clown, and a marked Germanic accent. With close friends he often spoke German. He grew up in Metz, studied in Bonn, Munich, and Berlin, and donned the Prussian uniform for his military service. Then he practiced law in Metz. On the death of his mother he wanted to become a priest but gave up the idea to serve his faith in other ways. His delicate health spared him the ordeal of bearing arms against France during World War I (he was an officer of a military court). After the war he entered politics to defend religious freedom in Alsace-Lorraine and in the rest of the country.

Since 1918 he had been Deputy Mayor of Metz. For him, politics was a priestly duty, but this did not prevent him from being practical or realistic, or from becoming embroiled in political activities that would have shocked a saint. He would do anything to bring about agreement among his associates on important issues.

Schuman had the habits of a studious and economic bachelor. The last to leave the ministry in the evening, he would turn out all the lights. He collected stray bits of string. His hobby was browsing in bookstores during his leisure time. Undersecretary of State for the Refugees in 1939, he voted for Pétain in 1940. But after two months he quit the government and Vichy and returned to Lorraine. There his anti-Nazi remarks provoked his arrest. The Germans, however, offered to make him the gauleiter of Alsace-Lorraine.

"An interesting idea, but difficult for a French deputy," Schuman replied. He was then sent to Neustadt, in the Black Forest, where he was kept under house arrest. In 1942 he escaped, hiding in monasteries as he made his way back to the free zone.

Schuman was Bidault's rival in the Mouvement Républicain Populaire (MRP)—the Catholic Democratic Party. When Bidault became premier in 1949, Schuman succeeded him as Foreign Minister. Bidault favored the dismemberment of Germany and the continuation of the Versailles policy. Schuman was an ardent supporter of European reconciliation, but he was also cautious and very distrustful of the Germans.

In *La République des Illusions,* Georgette Elgey recounted how Bidault had made fun of Schuman's slow Germanic mind: "His motor runs on low-grade gas."

"Not everyone can afford a motor that runs on alcohol," Schuman countered. His wit was quicker than his speech.

To lay the foundations of European unity—first economic, then political—Schuman turned to France's closest neighbors: Holland, Belgium, and Luxembourg. During the war, when their governments had been in exile in London, de Gaulle had approached them with a plan for a four-power entente. In 1945 he had resumed these talks with the object of an economic and strategic federation to organize security against a possible German act of revenge. But the little countries proved reluctant, especially Holland. They were alarmed by the size of the association and feared they might be absorbed by France. And England, their traditional protector, had frowned upon the plan.

Now Schuman proceeded to sound them out again. The three countries were soon to form a customs union under Spaak's leadership, and their response to Schuman was not encouraging. The Dutch rejected the idea of supranational and political institutions established on such a grand scale. Their kingdom would disappear. They also feared the restraints that might be imposed on their ocean and river traffic. This would be harmful to their shipbuilders, their resourceful bargemen, at present so free from regulations and paralyzing union statutes.

The Dutch and the Belgians, who already had their own customs union, were engaged in interminable discussions about problems related to the price of endives and the size of teaspoons. It was to take them seven years to do away with their frontier tariffs. How could they possibly settle such minuscule questions with larger countries? Their problems might seem trivial, but they played an important role in local elections.

Schuman then turned to Italy. No sooner had de Gasperi, the leader of the Christian Democrats, defeated the Communists and the Socialists in the Italian elections than Schuman opened negotiations with him. The two men understood each other well; they had similar life experiences and the same way of looking at things.

Tall, thin, and ascetic, de Gasperi was an Italian Irredentist. Born in Austria, a native of the Trentino, he had fought for the Trentino's liberation. The victory of 1918 gave his province to the House of Savoy. A militant Catholic activist and an anti-Fascist, he was hunted down by Mussolini's police and had to hide in a monastery for many years. Schuman and de Gasperi signed a Franco-Italian customs union treaty—a first step toward the unification of Europe.

There was a great outcry in the French parliament. "A European customs union or nothing," shouted the champions of Western integration.

Actually, France's economy paralleled rather than complemented Italy's. French automobile manufacturers feared the competition of the Italian Fiat; French farmers were leery of competing with the fruit and vegetables from Lombardy. The unions in France were also apprehensive lest an influx of 2,000,000 unemployed Italians flood their market. The treaty was therefore never ratified.

But Schuman was not discouraged. He began planning a customs union that would embrace France, Italy, and the three countries of the new Benelux union. Called the Fritalux, it died a natural death amid a good deal of laughter. "We must give Providence enough time to enlighten us about what we should do," his chief of staff, Bernard Clappier, told him. European unification, apparently so difficult to achieve, would perhaps spring into being all at once.

Schuman had yet to discharge a mission assigned him by the Anglo-Saxons: to come to an understanding with Germany. He turned to Adenauer. The meeting between them should have been a fraternal one. Both were Catholics inspired by the spirit of the Holy Year; both were born close to a frontier and spoke the same language, German. And both desired reconciliation—Schuman, cautiously, Adenauer, ardently.

If, as Adenauer's enemies claimed, it was not his feelings but his intellect that dictated his policy, it was nonetheless true that he wanted to execute an about-face for Germany. He wanted to turn her toward the Rhine, anchor her in the West, and bind her to France. He despised all that Prussianism stood for—domination, militarism, pan-Germanism, the march toward the East, Hitlerism. "Is there anything more idiotic than a Prussian general?" he would ask.

But the meeting was a disappointment to Schuman. Adenauer could not accept the attitude of Bidault, the leader of the French Christian Democrats. Bidault was too imbued with the spirit of Versailles. And Schuman showed himself to be wary of the Germans, especially of Adenauer's imperious manner.

Son of a legal counselor at the court of Cologne, Adenauer was filled with a spirit very different from that of the somber Wagnerian romanticism which had been systematically extended to the Rhine.

Raymond Cartier wrote that Adenauer typified the Germany of wine, in contrast to the Germany of schnapps, a romanticized Germany in contrast to the Germany of the Teuton knights, a Catholic Germany in contrast to a pagan Germany.

Adenauer was born in 1876. Like his father, he was a lawyer. He became president of the Zentrum group (the Catholic Center) in the municipal Assembly of Cologne, and in October, 1917, he was elected mayor—Germany's youngest big-city mayor. He was only forty-one at the time. After World War I he began to play a bigger role. On February 1, 1919, Adenauer called together all the mayors of the big Western cities. Strongly opposed to Prussian domination and centralization of the Reich, he suggested to them the establishment of a Federal Republic of Western Germany that would be large enough to play a decisive role. The republic, hopefully, could prevent Prussia from determining German foreign policy.

"The suggestion was made that I should appeal to the separatist movement," he later explained.

But in 1923 the Rhineland was occupied. Separatism was reawakened under the leadership of Dorten. During a separatist demonstration in Cologne, Adenauer, who happened to be standing close to doors that led to a balcony, was tempted to step out and proclaim a Rhenish Republic. But he held back, shocked by the behavior of Dorten's followers, who were a bunch of young hooligans.

In 1926 Adenauer almost became the Chancellor of the shaky Weimar Republic, at the head of a coalition government with the Socialists. He was horrified by Nazism. Flags emblazoned with the iron cross were flown from the bridges over the Rhine. The day before Hitler entered Cologne in Hindenburg's car, Adenauer had the flags on the main bridge removed. As a result he was expelled from the city hall and hounded. The Nazis persecuted him, not only as an adversary of the regime but also as a former champion of autonomy for Western Germany. Among the misdeeds with which he was reproached, not the least was his opposition to the Prussian centralization of the Reich.

He sought refuge in the Santa Maria Lach monastery, within the shelter of high Roman towers overlooking a volcanic lake. The abbot was a former classmate. In June, 1934, the day after "the night of the long knives," he was arrested, then released, but accused of embezzling public funds. He managed to clear himself of this false accusation and obtained a pension from the city of Cologne. With it he bought a house at Rhöndorf, at the foot of the Petersberg hill, across the river from Bonn. But he was driven from his home and forbidden to remain in Cologne. After the plot against Hitler in July, 1944, he was again arrested by the Gestapo. Actually, he had refused to participate in the plot, telling Goerdeler, the former mayor of Leipzig, "I have no faith in any enterprise led by you." He was hospitalized, escaped, recaptured, and finally released.

While he was watering the rose bush in his Rhöndorf garden one day, a volley of shrapnel knocked him down. The Americans were crossing the Remagen bridge.

"Were they shooting at you?" he was asked.

"Yes, of course."

The Americans proved friendly. They reinstated him as the mayor of Cologne. But the city was included in the British zone, and General Barroclough relieved him of his post on the grounds of incompetence. In reality, the Socialists in the municipal administration had managed to gain the confidence of Britain's new Labour government.

The second phase of Adenauer's career now began. In 1945 he helped found the Christian Democratic Union (CDU). In February, 1946, on the day the Constitutive Assembly met in the British zone, Adenauer mounted the platform, took the president's chair, and declared the meeting open. Claiming the presidency of the party on the basis of seniority, he led the discussion before the meeting's organizers, taken by surprise, could catch their breath. He soon acquired authority. In the midst of the ruins of Nazism, he lent his supporters dignity and restored a measure of good conscience to Germany.

In 1947 Winston Churchill visited Georges Bidault at the Quai d'Orsay. "It would be such a good thing," Churchill told him, "if you were to take the initiative in effecting a Franco-German reconciliation. For a former president of the National Council of the Resistance, everything is possible."

Bidault sought out the "good Germans," the Christian Democrats.

It was soon apparent that Adenauer dominated all the others. He looked like an old Sioux Indian, strikingly stiff in bearing, with straight, coarse hair the color of a balding scalp. He was slated to head the party in the three zones.

"It's too bad you're placing all your bets on Adenauer," Koenig said to Bidault on the telephone. "He's reached the end of his career. He's seventy-one!"

But Adenauer now spoke as the future head of the German government. He detested the British and had never forgiven them for ejecting him from the city hall. Nor did he like the Americans any better. "They don't understand a thing. . . . They fired at me with their artillery." He felt, however, that he could reach some understanding with the French. But he imposed certain conditions. The Ruhr and the Saar must remain German. Germany must be reunified. The Polish border was unacceptable.

"He'll just have to agree to our union with the Saar," was Bidault's response.

In his own way, Adenauer elected himself Chancellor of the new Reich. He had received only 201 votes instead of the 202 that were needed. So he voted for himself. Having installed himself as head of the government, he chose his capital, which was almost directly opposite his villa and his rose garden. Frankfurt was the largest city of West Germany, and it had an excellent communications system. But this city of Goethe had become American: Bonn was in the French zone.

Unfortunately, there still remained the question of the Saar, and Adenauer could not reconcile himself to handing it over to the French. The German press was raging against Paris at the very moment Schuman was trying to arrange a meeting with Adenauer.

The Ruhr International Authority, established in December, 1948, was more or less acceptable to Adenauer. In exchange for his tentative consent, he had obtained an almost total cessation of the dismantling of factories. Seven enormous steel mills were saved, including those belonging to Thyssen, plus eleven chemical firms, including Bayer at Leverkusen and Borsig in Berlin. To achieve this, Adenauer used a telling argument: the 13,000,000 refugees who had fled from East Germany and had to be lodged, fed, and employed. He groaned over the restrictions on Ruhr production imposed by the English. Of what use was the Marshall Plan if the Ruhr—the heart of Germany —was not to beat at its normal rhythm?

Adenauer gave vent to a continuous stream of complaints, threats —the German people would turn to the East—and demands. He haggled. He wanted certain questions discussed, he made concessions one minute only to renege the next. He gave André François-Poncet,

France's High Commissioner to Bonn, a hard time. But his most violent explosion of rage occurred over the question of the Saar. Negotiations were scheduled to open in February, 1950, at the Quai d'Orsay with the government of that small autonomous republic, the Saar, headed by Johannes Hoffmann.

The meeting between Adenauer and Schuman should have been a warm one, as befits two Christian pacifists. When the train came to a halt in the new German capital on January 15, 1950, the station was illuminated but empty. On the platform stood helmeted soldiers and the Chancellor, as stiff as a telegraph pole. Smiling, Schuman began to speak to him in German.

"Let's hurry," Adenauer answered coldly. "I'm afraid of an attempt on our lives. That's why I had the station cleared and all the lights turned on."

What occurred between the two men was not so much a conversation as a near scene.

"You want to annex the Saar," Adenauer accused. "That would be another Alsace-Lorraine." The Chancellor dreaded finding himself seated beside an independent Saar delegation at the forthcoming London conference scheduled for May 10, 1950. A *Diktat* imposed on the Ruhr by the victors was not his only fear. He might be treated as the representative of a defeated country. He demanded that Germany's equality of rights should be acknowledged on the spot. Backed by Washington, he felt sufficiently strong to do so.

The Americans were seeking some formula that would give the new Reich government equal rights in regard to the Ruhr and the Saar, and that would also enable Germany to rearm. They wanted to remove any obstacles that might hinder the industrial development of the Federal Republic, which they were trying to set up as a fortress of the free world. They wanted to tie Germany to the West, include her in the Atlantic Pact, and give her an army that could be used by NATO. The United States hoped to prevent the new government from turning to the Russians in order to achieve reunification. To businessmen on the other side of the Atlantic, a prosperous Germany would open up sizable foreign markets and constitute an economic dominion. The Americans realized, of course, that it would be difficult to fashion Germany into a world power without French help. France was in no position to create a great power, but she could certainly prevent one from being created.

Robert Schuman demurred. France was not demanding annexation, but she too could threaten. Realizing and fearing this, Adenauer became impossible. He was tense and bitter. His government was to begin with a territorial amputation and a *Diktat* on the Ruhr. The task of making Germany peaceful and of reconciling her with France was bound to fail. The German youth would become involved in nationalist or Communist extremism—a catastrophe for Europe and for the cause of peace. Schuman had hoped to soothe him by speaking in German, but the gesture was of no avail. In Paris, Schuman was criticized for not speaking French. Schuman returned to Paris, deeply worried.

Rumors of this testy encounter reached Monnet. His friend General McCloy, the American High Commissioner in Germany, was pessimistic, as were many prominent people on both sides of the Atlantic. The situation was a serious one. If it should prove impossible to establish a Germany as solid as iron, united to the Allies, and opposed to the Soviets, Washington would be forced to concede the failure of its European policy. The Russians would emerge triumphant. A divided, chaotic, and impoverished Europe would fall into their hands like ripe fruit. The atomic stockpile the Soviets were amassing would make them omnipotent. Washington's reaction was easy to foresee; it would be better to forestall a Soviet victory by knocking out the U.S.S.R. before it could increase its atomic arsenal.

Meanwhile, Adenauer began to realize that he had perhaps gone too far. One week after Schuman's visit, he executed a dramatic about-face, suggesting to McCloy that instead of internationalizing the Ruhr and making the Saar French, it would be better to internationalize the steel and coal of the two regions. On March 9, 1950, he went even further. In a statement to Kingsbury Smith, the director of the American I.N.S. agency, he proposed that France and Germany should merge, that they should unite economically and have a single common parliament. Citizens would have a dual nationality. This was a Rhenish replica of the idea espoused by Monnet and Churchill in June, 1940.

A few weeks after the London Conference, Adenauer bombarded world opinion with sensational proposals: a purely economic Franco-German union that would amount to a merger of all coal and steel production. He reminded the public that he had entertained such ideas before. In 1923, seeking ways to avert war, he had suggested a merger of French and German mines and of the steel industries of the Ruhr, the Saar, and the Lorraine. The French steel magnates had rejected the plan.

Adenauer's aim was crystal clear: to resolve the controversy over the Ruhr and the Saar by industrial and national merger. But his ideas met with little enthusiasm in France or elsewhere. He was demanding equal rights, the suppression of Allied control—all of which was deemed unthinkable at the time.

"One should beware of spectacular proposals, as well as of ill-humored gestures," was Schuman's response.

General de Gaulle alone, at a press conference on March 16, 1950, took up the offer: "Looking at the thing coldly," he said, "one is almost dazzled by what the combined valor of Germany and France might bring about, especially if France's African territories were taken into account. . . . In short, it would be like undertaking anew what Charlemagne had attempted, but on a modern basis. . . . For the last thirty years I have followed with interest the actions and words of Konrad Adenauer. I have perceived in what this good German says the echo of an appeal to Europe. The fate of Europe depends on Franco-German relations.

"I am convinced," de Gaulle continued, "that if France, once she is on her feet and properly led, should take the initiative in calling upon Europe to unite, especially with the help of the Germans, the entire atmosphere from the Atlantic to the Urals would be changed."

"Nothing will be possible," he added a little later, "until a balanced Europe has been refashioned, without Russia and her satellites, and without America, about which our country must not be confused."

Shortly after de Gaulle's press conference on March 16, 1950, the French government published a communiqué stating that it was willing to examine any concrete proposal from Bonn. This statement went unnoticed and was not followed by any action.

Adenauer returned to the charge. On April 2, in another interview, he envisaged a merger of England, France, and Germany, with a common government and parliament.

De Gaulle was not the only one to pay attention to Adenauer's proposals. Monnet, too, was mindful of them. He discussed them with his friend McCloy. The Chancellor's proposals were too vague to have any diplomatic effect, he told himself. They came from a defeated country that would always be suspected of using dilatory tactics—especially the day before a conference at which it might be treated haughtily, divided, or partitioned.

On the other hand, an initiative from Paris which, instead of asking Germany to yield to the imperious decisions of her conquerors, offered to reach an understanding on a completely equal footing, would seem a generous departure from the past. It would have every chance of winning general approval and might be the beginning of European unification. But what sort of initiative should it be?

VIII

The Monnet Plan Becomes the Schuman Plan

ON APRIL 14, 1950, Monnet had a visitor at the Rue de Martignac. Paul Reuter, the professor of international law at Aix University and a Quai d'Orsay lawyer, had come in search of certain statistics. It was a chance meeting. He was a personal friend of Fernand Rabier's, Monnet's chief of staff. Through Rabier, Monnet had consulted Reuter earlier about an antitrust law that had seemed indispensable at the time. The big companies were deriving many advantages from Monnet's modernization plan.

"Have you seen this?" Monnet asked Reuter, unfolding some newspapers that had been red-penciled. They were reports of interviews with Adenauer in which the Chancellor alluded to a Franco-German union, the internationalization of production, a joint parliament, and so on. "What do you think about a joint parliament?"

"The Council of Europe has amounted to nothing. I can't see what a Franco-German superparliament could accomplish. It would have to have something to do," said Reuter.

"The Council of Europe is done for," Monnet replied. "There's no use continuing something that got off to such a bad start. What do you think of Lotharingia?" he continued, as if he were tossing out an idea merely to see how Reuter would take it. Yes, he thought to himself. Reconstitute Lotharingia! The Dutch, the Belgians, the Rhinelanders, the people of the Saar, and the Lorrainers all have a common origin; they share the same mine basin. Could they be made into a single state?

"Look here, Monsieur Monnet," Reuter answered, "I am from Metz, like Robert Schuman, and like him I have relatives in Luxembourg. My great-uncle Emile founded the Luxembourg Catholic Movement. . . . But if we are trying to make a deal, political innovations should not be attempted in those border states. They are too sensitized. Talk to the Alsatians about forming a state with the Rhinelanders, they'd be delighted!"

"You see," Monnet resumed, "French policy, Bidault's policy, is idiotic. The Saar, the Ruhr—they are German. You can't tear them away from Germany. Lotharingia would not be a separation but a regrouping of Germans, Frenchmen, Belgians, and Dutch!"

"A political Lotharingia would be impossible," Reuter answered. "But an economic organization might work. The Saar and the Ruhr —that's coal. Lorraine is iron. You can always make a match between minerals. They have no patriotic sentiments."

But the two economists quickly realized that it would be impossible to isolate the Ruhr-Saar-Lorraine complex from the north of France and from Belgium.

"Let's set up a Monnet Plan—an economic Lotharingia," Reuter threw out. "All production pooled. Something very localized. A regional enterprise with a merger of coal mines and nationalized steel works on both sides of the Rhine, with an investment plan for modernizing the equipment and the mines."

"You must come back tomorrow morning," Monnet concluded. "This is very important."

On Saturday morning Reuter and Monnet met again. Monnet was flanked by his collaborators, Hirsch and Uri. The discussion of the day before was resumed—an economic Lotharingia.

"What you're setting up is a combine," Pierre Uri said. "That would call for nationalized mines and steel works in several countries under a single administration. You're going to come up against insurmountable obstacles. The Germans and Americans won't like nationalization. They favor a free economy. You'll have to create a single market for coal and steel in all of Western Europe." (The terms "Coal and Steel Community" and "Common Market" were introduced later by a German, Ophuls.)

"Let's resume the discussion tomorrow morning at my place, in

96

Houjarray," Monnet said. "No, not tomorrow morning. It's my daughter's first communion. I have to cut down some trees to decorate the church. Tomorrow afternoon."

On Sunday, April 16, 1950, the four men met again at Monnet's cottage. Paul Reuter, who, like Monnet, inclined toward Socialism, outlined a plan for a strongly centralized internationalization of the mines and steel works in the Rhineland and Lorraine. It was to be administered by a supranational authority. Included was a project for joint renovation and improvement. Uri favored a free market but one that was powerfully controlled by a sovereign and supranational authority. But they soon realized that a market of this kind could not be limited to certain regions. Lotharingia was abandoned in favor of a market open to all the interested countries.

Should there be a single authority or a free market? The two were finally fused into a system based on a single, planned market. In the famous declaration of May 9 Reuter's plan was adopted, and his provision for joint equipment was included. According to the declaration, half of the project would be based on the principle of a planned economy. But when the treaty of the Coal and Steel Community actually materialized, it was reduced to one-fourth, and in its actual implementation, to only one-eighth.

"I would like to see a small staff and no management," said Monnet. "I only want to handle the producers."

"An economic planner's naïve idea," it would be said later.

They leafed through yearbooks. They counted 360 producers and thousands of distributors of coal, steel, and iron. Monnet believed he could control the market if he held all the producers in the palm of his hand. This would have been true if the operation had been the European Steelworks and Coalfields, a Socialist trust organized by several states. But the community would be based on a free market. The anti-economic planning companies handled most of the steel production in Germany. The international companies were unanimously against economic planning. When the professionals wanted to draft the treaty they had to do it the way it was done by the big companies who had learned all the tricks of the trade.

"Put all this in shape for me—a very clear condensation. Two and a half pages," said Monnet to Reuter as the latter was leaving. "I need it tomorrow."

"Are you asking me for a letter, an article, or a diplomatic note?"

"It's urgent. See you tomorrow morning."

The law professor returned late that night to the home of his former teacher, Achille Maistre, who put him up when he was in Paris.

"He's been drinking," Maistre said to his father.

Reuter was not drunk, but he was in an extraordinary state of exaltation, a dreamlike state, he recalls. At nine o'clock in the morning he brought the text of his plan to the Rue de Martignac, where it was typed.

"Well, that's fine, perfect. We'll polish it up a bit. But the important points are there," Monnet told Reuter, who was taking the train back to Aix.

On April 20, Monnet handed the memorandum to Bidault's aide, Falaize. He then telephoned Reuter at Aix to tell him that he had all the necessary backing for their scheme.

But five days passed and Bidault did not respond. It turned out that he never saw the memorandum; it had remained in Falaize's coat pocket. At that time Bidault was preoccupied with a different plan. In a speech at Lyons on April 16, he had suggested the establishment of an Atlantic High Council for peace and a three-power directorate composed of Great Britain, France, and the United States—the idea so dear to de Gaulle. But Washington was not enthusiastic. The Americans thought that the plan was vague, imprecise and totally unrelated to the realities of the situation. Dean Acheson sent the French Foreign Minister an official note asking him to explain how France planned to integrate Germany into Europe, including NATO, and to indicate what solutions France favored. The London Conference was to meet in three weeks.

To hurry things along, Acheson visited the Rhineland and discussed German rearmament with Adenauer. At first Adenauer very adroitly declined to discuss the matter. Germans had become very antimilitaristic, he claimed. He wanted no part of a large general staff. If Germany were to recover her sovereignty, he would only agree to a German contingent if it were part of a European army and on an equal footing with the other contingents. This was the suggestion that Churchill and Eden had made to the House of Commons.

Schuman, overcome by his failures and isolated from Premier Bidault who was pursuing a different policy, was dismayed by the prospect of German rearmament—of a Reich that would recover its full powers. France would have no guarantees regarding the Ruhr or the Saar. The Quai d'Orsay had only legal arguments to offer Acheson: A German army was an impossibility because an army symbolized sovereignty and a partitioned Germany could not be sovereign.

"In view of Russia's atomic bomb and her 225 divisions, the French answer is a joke," one American remarked.

Reuter returned to Paris to obtain the latest news. "Things are moving ahead. We've made excellent political contacts," Monnet told him. But Monnet had merely lunched on May 4 with a friend, Bernard Clappier, Schuman's chief assistant. He had read him the memorandum, and Clappier had assured him that he would speak to "the boss" about it immediately. "This tallies entirely with Schuman's views."

"Robert Schuman became acquainted with the High Commissioner of the modernization plan when he was Finance Minister," Clappier recounted after he became vice-president of the Bank of France. "I used to go to see Monnet very often. There were about twenty of us officials helping him. We worked behind the scenes in the various ministries. One hour with Monnet was most rewarding, it brought us all up to date. He is a man of remarkable imagination and disarming optimism. His plan had been launched. At that time he was becoming more and more preoccupied with foreign policy. From February to March, 1950, onward, he was seeking a solution to the Franco-German problem.

"Robert Schuman nourished a very long-standing ambition, that of a benevolent man of the Eastern marches who wanted to put an end to the antagonism rampant on both sides of the Rhine. He was also anxious not to sacrifice French guarantees.

"The Anglo-Saxons were putting pressure on him. The London Conference was to take place on May 10. If France failed to come up with some sort of agreement, which Washington had been urging on Schuman, her allies were prepared to put an end to Allied occupation of Germany, especially to control of the Ruhr. Schuman was dismayed by the idea that the formidable German arsenal would again become independent and that no valid guarantees would be given France.

"He left for Metz for the weekend. I accompanied him to the station. 'Do you recommend this memorandum?' he asked after I handed him Monnet's note. 'Can coal and steel be controlled, can their production and sale be organized among states that adhere to different policies? You're a better judge of this than I am. We would have to study this with reliable people. . . .'

"The minister returned on Monday afternoon. 'I am in agreement,' he said as he stepped down from the train. 'But we'll have to act quickly and with the greatest secrecy. If the news leaks out, there'll be such an outcry in the steel industry that we won't be able to accomplish a thing.' "

The next day, May 5, Schuman had lunch on the Rue de Martignac with Monnet and his staff. Paul Delouvrier remembers the occasion vividly and has described it.

"Make yourself comfortable," Monnet said to his visitor. "It's stifling in here. Take off your jacket. And if you don't mind, I'll take mine off, too. It's an American habit. I've lived in the States for such a long time."

"No," Schuman protested gently. "You know, at the Quai d'Orsay we rarely have a chance to lunch in our shirt sleeves. Besides, I have a confession to make: I'm wearing suspenders."

"Monsieur Schuman, I have something very important to tell you, you can't imagine how vital it really is. You look like an honest man . . . you can make any kind of a proposal and you will be believed. Let me explain. Take this plan for a single coal and steel market, which could eradicate war, reconcile France and Germany, and enable the Germans to be treated as equals. If presented by some undistinguished government official, it would come to nothing. It would be just another scrap of paper. The Americans, British, and Germans would see it as a maneuver on the part of the French to appropriate the Ruhr and the Saar. But you would be believed. It would be regarded as an extraordinary proposal made by an honest man."

Schuman was stunned. He was certainly interested in the memorandum Clappier had told him about. But presented in this way, the Monnet Plan was a revelation. For the first time he would have a chance to realize what he had been praying for—a union, on the basis of a reciprocal agreement, of the two banks of the Rhine, the upper and lower branches of the Moselle; the consolidation of Western Europe by an equal and peaceful division of activities and wealth. And he was now being offered the opportunity to bring it about. He was deeply moved. "You can count on me," he said.

100

From then on, the coal and steel pool was called the Schuman Plan.

Schuman stood up. The other guests, who had remained silent, thought that he was about to embrace Monnet. But he merely shook Monnet's hand warmly, saying, "I will discuss it tomorrow with the other members of the cabinet."

Later, Monnet was congratulated by his associates. "To get statesmen to listen to you," he observed, "all you have to do is give them an idea at the right time, when they are floundering, and ask nothing for yourself."

Like Schuman, Monnet was convinced that the element of surprise was important. If the rumor should spread, thousands of questions would be raised. The German, French, Italian, Belgian, and Luxembourg steel industries, the mining companies, the economists, the political parties of ten countries, the chancelleries—all would ask to see the text of the memorandum, demand further explanations, pose prior conditions, and offer counterproposals. The bomb would set off a chain reaction.

Schuman said not a word to the Quai d'Orsay. He consulted no specialists. He merely whispered in René Pleven's ear, because Pleven was a long-standing confidant of Monnet's and René Mayer's. In Algiers in 1943, Pleven himself had conceived of a plan for European federation. Schuman was naturally obliged to talk to Premier Bidault about it.

"Another soap bubble," said Bidault. "One more international body." Later Bidault was to regret that he himself had not initiated the idea. It would have been called the Bidault Plan. A few weeks later, he said to Monnet, "Why didn't you talk to me about it?"

"You were the first to get my memorandum," Monnet answered. A search was made for it. The memorandum was found in Falaize's desk drawer.

For three days Monnet and his colleagues hammered out the text of the statement, which had already been rewritten thirty times. On Monday evening, May 8, every preliminary draft, every carbon copy, every note was burned. No trace remained of the first draft of the Schuman Plan. Then Uri, the principal editor, suddenly realized that they had neglected to include Africa. One page was rewritten. Then the text was read over again. The introduction was redrafted and the entire text reread.

"Gentlemen, let's stand up," Monnet exclaimed. "A text such as this should be read standing."

The definitive document was handed to Clappier on May 9. He took it to Schuman who was attending a meeting of the cabinet. Schuman kept it in his briefcase. At eleven o'clock that morning the cabinet meeting broke up. Monnet was waiting on the telephone. He was crushed: the cabinet had not had time to discuss the project.

Actually, Schuman had requested the cabinet to adjourn. He was awaiting a call from Bonn. The night before he had sent his colleague Mislich to Bonn with a letter for Adenauer. Mislich was received by the Chancellor at the very moment the cabinet was deliberating in Paris. Schuman was pacing up and down on the carpet, awaiting the answer.

"There's nothing I want more," Adenauer answered at 11 A.M. The Chancellor could not believe his eyes. He read and reread Schuman's letter. If it had any meaning at all, it would signify the end of the Ruhr International Authority. Any limitation of German production would henceforward be out of the question. It would also mean the quick end of the Saar nightmare: The question of the Saar problem would be submerged by the Coal and Steel Community. Both the politicians and the public in Bonn would find it hard to believe that Germany's deputies could join the Council of Europe along with the separatist deputies from the Saar. But above all, this meant the acceptance of the Bonn government's offers, association with France, the launching of a unified Europe that would include a rehabilitated Germany.

"It is understood, of course," the Chancellor said to Mislich, "that our approval in no way signifies that we recognize the Saar government." After a call to Paris, this was conceded.

So providential was the advent of the Schuman Plan that Adenauer's biographers have taken it for granted that the whole affair had been his doing and that it was Adenauer who had whispered in Monnet's ear, perhaps through Monnet's friend McCloy. The truth detracts in no way, however, from Adenauer's reputation as the grandfather of Europe.

The cabinet reconvened later that morning, and at one P.M. Schuman left the meeting, radiant. He had merely read a simple note. But René Mayer had immediately risen to the occasion. "Your speech was like a torrent," President Vincent Auriol told him when the meeting was over. There was little debate. In reality, most of the ministers, including Bidault, looked upon the proposal as a pious wish of small importance.

Schuman was obliged, of course, to confide in the Americans. Secretary of State Acheson was in Paris on his way to the London Conference. In order to avoid a last-minute indiscretion, Schuman waited to meet Acheson at a private reception given by David Bruce, the American ambassador. "We will have a constructive proposal to make tomorrow in London," Schuman told him. And in a few short sentences he explained the plan.

"We will have to look into it. Your project implies a good many things. We'll see each other tomorrow in London," Acheson replied.

That very day, Monnet was interviewed by a *Times* correspondent. The interview had been promised some time before, and Monnet did not want to call it off for fear of arousing suspicion. "He forgot to ask me the thousand-dollar question," he thought to himself as he saw the newspaperman off.

Leaving nothing to chance, Monnet had arranged a big press conference to launch the Schuman Plan. Schuman was to address a crowd of journalists in the Salon de l'Horloge at six o'clock that evening. In the presence of the assembled press representatives, in the glare of the spotlights and the golden chandeliers Schuman's tortured expression revealed such emotion that it increased everyone's curiosity. Awkwardly, he put on his glasses, drew a bunch of papers from his pocket, and began to read in his heavy Germanic accent.

"World peace cannot be safeguarded without creative efforts to cope with the dangers that threaten it. . . ."

In 36 pages of the text, written in the grand manner, each word having been carefully weighed by Monnet, Schuman unfolded the idea of a coal and a steel pool that would prevent war between Germany and France. It alluded to a supranational High Authority, independent of governments, and to the European integrated institutions that were to follow in every domain. Schuman was so unfamiliar with the text that he skipped from page 31 to page 33 without noticing it.

The journalists rushed to the telephones. The London Conference was over before it began. Because of the historical importance of the document, the United States Congress voted enthusiastically for its inclusion in the *Congressional Record*.

At Nice, where he was teaching, Professor Reuter opened his newspaper and exclaimed, "It's a success. Monnet is a genius. No one else could have spread the word so easily. It was as simple as mailing a letter."

De Gaulle was disconcerted by the Schuman Plan. Its purpose was not clear to him. "What Europe needs is a new economy," he said on May 19, 1950. "We are offered a potpourri of coal and steel without knowing where it will lead." Later he was to say, "It is not at all surprising that the Coal and Steel Community was accepted so readily by our neighbors. The mines and steelworks of the Ruhr, which the Allies had agreed to assign to an international institution and which were to serve as reparations for France, have been definitively returned to the magnates of Germany's heavy industry.

"The Saar, whose territory and mines should have become part of a customs union with France, has been restored to German sovereignty with the massive consent of the Saar people.

"At the same time, the sponge has been passed over everything that Germany might have owed France. Her sovereignty has been acknowledged. She has been treated as an equal by her victors.

"Since the Italians possess neither steel nor coal, they had no heavy industry before the war. Those who sold Italy her minerals and steel charged excessive prices. This was especially hard on the Italians because of the impoverished state of Piedmontese and Lombard industry. The Coal and Steel Community provides the Italians with minerals and metals at the same prices paid by highly productive countries, plus, of course, the cost of transportation. Thus, Italy enjoys all the advantages of a highly industrialized country without having to sacrifice anything in exchange.

"It is France that will bear the cost of this idea. When Chancellor Adenauer suggested pooling the production of the Rhine, the Saar and Lorraine, he did not expect to gain so much."

"Look here. In 1950 we were wrong," Monnet was to say later to Professor Reuter. "We should have organized Europe politically right from the start. We should have taken advantage of Adenauer's suggestion of a joint Franco-German government, a joint parliament, or a joint Anglo-French-German union. We should have jumped at the chance. The Western states were in such a mess they would have accepted it. We probably could have initiated a United States of Europe as easily as we launched the Coal and Steel Community."

"No, you're wrong," Reuter answered. "People were not ready at that time. They were willing to have a community of minerals and metals but not a community of former enemies. There was no deep-rooted solidarity between peoples. And you can't do it without a sense of solidarity."

In France, Schuman's historic declaration of May 9, 1950, gave rise to anxiety. The French steel magnates were especially angry. They feared that this mad scheme, if it materialized, would make it impossible for them to compete with their Ruhr rivals. "Never again will Robert Schuman be elected a deputy from Metz," some of the natives of the city declared. And it was true that Schuman had great difficulty the following year in getting himself reelected.

It was also true that Schuman's declaration aroused a good deal of irritation among the German steel-mill owners. They foresaw that they would be bullied, perhaps ruined, by the High Authority and that their French competitors would profit. The diplomats, too, were annoyed. In their view, the new status of minerals and metals was unprecedented; it even seemed crazy. Finally, the declaration disconcerted the champions of a unified Europe. They wondered why Schuman had not simply called upon the neighboring countries to join France in forming an imposing assembly that would unanimously proclaim a United States of Europe.

For the most part, however, the document went almost unnoticed in France. It contained nothing precise or of immediate moment. The public was totally unaware of Jean Monnet's activities. It knew nothing of his ambitious plan or of the discreet influence he exerted on the various political parties—of his role as the *deus ex machina* of the Fourth Republic, the architect of French foreign policy.

When Schuman left for London the day after he issued his statement, nobody noticed Monnet's presence at his side. Together, the two would attempt to win the approval of the British government for their supranational organization. Schuman was even more anxious to secure British participation than was his companion. He needed England to act as a balance. Italy carried little weight. Benelux was still a small organization. Without the British, Frenchmen and Germans would confront each other. This was what French diplomats dreaded most, in view of the influence exerted by France's powerful neighbor.

Monnet knew in advance what the British answer would be: His Majesty's government could never subscribe to a federal authority that challenged its sovereignty. But it was ready to take part in any discussion that might strengthen the cause of European unity. In other words, the British were quite willing to participate in negotiations over the French and German coal and steelworks; they were even willing to sign an agreement that would enable them to watch over rival coal and steel production and, if possible, control it. But they would not subject England's mines and steel mills to any High Authority that was not their own.

"Had we accepted British participation under these conditions," Monnet explained later, "we would have been forced to replace the supranational institution proposed by France with something that was bound to make a mockery of our original idea. We made a bold offer to Germany, one that would serve to eliminate war between France and Germany, an offer of equality in a community organization for basic industries. We expected it to bring about reconciliation and European unification. Everything would have been ruined if the English had been allowed to interfere, to challenge the entire proposal. The British are a practical people. They are willing to be part of anything that works. We should have proceeded to unify Europe, knowing that the British would join us as soon as such a union actually began to function."

On June 2, England refused to join the coal and steel pool.

Prior to that, on May 25, Monnet, accompanied by Clappier, had gone to Bonn to see Adenauer. The two initiators of a unified Europe virtually fell into each other's arms. Adenauer expressed great enthusiasm for Monnet's ideas.

"I will entrust you with the most precious of Germany's possessions —the Ruhr," he said.

On June 3, in a speech before the Bundestag, Adenauer emphasized that the construction of a federated Europe would begin with the signing of this pact. "On this," Adenauer said, "I am in total agreement, not only with the French government but with the man who has been the moving spirit of the plan—Jean Monnet." He added, "From the personal conversations that I have had with Monsieur Monnet, I have been confirmed in my own belief that political elements weigh most heavily in the balance. . . . The purpose of the French proposal is to create a European federation. . . ."

Six countries approved the Coal and Steel Community, in principle, but not before the Dutch had expressed their fierce resistance to community supranationality.

106

"We have already been devoured by both France and Germany," said the representatives of the Netherlands. "Now we will disappear completely."

But they were finally calmed down by the Belgians. This was the beginning of a chronic state of irritation and anxiety that was to persist when the Netherlands joined the European organizations. Linked to Belgium by Benelux, the Dutch more or less reluctantly followed her lead in regard to European integration. The Dutch missed England, who was as indispensable to Europe as she was difficult to win over.

IX

The European Defense Community

ON June 25, 1950, a thunderbolt struck that caused everyone to forget the Coal and Steel Community that had just been launched. The North Koreans invaded South Korea. Stalin, blocked in Iran, in Greece, and in Berlin, had opened a new front in Asia. Strategists and diplomats thought it was only a diversion, a prelude to an attack on Europe. There was worldwide panic. From Moscow, Ambassador Harriman sounded the alarm: The Soviets might move beyond the iron curtain at any moment. In Belgium and Switzerland, housewives rushed out to buy rice, sugar, and soap. In France, the South American consulates were besieged with requests for visas. The price of gold and raw materials soared.

Early in September Monnet telephoned Reuter in Aix. "I have to see you," he said. "Please come right away."

Paul Reuter was the lawyer for the Steel and Coal Community. He would know how it had been affected.

"How is our Community progressing?" Monnet asked him.

"The ECSC is dead—killed by the war in Korea. It was conceived during a period of reconstruction for steel, to regularize the production of Lorraine, the Saar, and the Ruhr, and to find buyers for metal in a united Europe. Steel is in demand everywhere. We have to find something else to unify Europe, if there's still time. . . . When an affair of this kind is stymied, there's no use staying with it. You have to move on to something else. Organize a Schuman Plan for a European army," Reuter said.

108

"So you've thought of that, too. I'll take you to see my aide, your friend Rabier. You and he can draw up a plan. We'll do a double job: build the necessary institutions for the Coal and Steel Community and also establish a Defense Community."

Once again Monnet heard the voices beyond the Rhine. For ten months Adenauer had been talking about a European army. On December 3, 1949, in an interview for the Cleveland *Plain Dealer,* he launched his appeal. It was a public reply to the visit Acheson had made to Adenauer on November 13 when the two men talked about placing German soldiers under American command. The Chancellor said, "The Allies disarmed Germany. They must insure her defense. . . . Should they ask us to participate in insuring the security of Europe, I would not favor an independent *Wehrmacht* but rather a German contingent within a European fighting force." He emphasized that he was "absolutely opposed to putting Germans into a non-German contingent. I will not allow them to serve as mercenaries."

"Even if the Allies ask us to recruit a German army, we cannot do anything of the kind," the Chancellor declared to the Bundestag on December 16, 1949. "The most we can concede is a German contingent within a European army."

"The Socialists of East Germany will rob him of his majority. He gives precedence to European over German unity," his enemies said.

Adenauer was sincerely antimilitarist. He was horrified at the thought of a German general staff. He wanted an integrated Europe. It could bring him everything he desired: Germany integrated into the West, protected from the temptation of reunification which the Kremlin kept dangling before his eyes; an army (which the German man in the street no longer wanted) that involved no militarist danger, under Western command; association with the victors, which would give him a considerable voice in joint strategy; then later, through the European army and American support, reunification and recovered sovereignty.

A Germany that is indispensable to Europe should, he believed, be received by it on an equal basis as quickly as possible. The Schuman Plan was conceived in this spirit.

Concern over the war in Korea accelerated events. At Strasbourg on August 12, 1950, Churchill demanded the creation of a European army. On August 17, Adenauer served official notice to the three High Commissioners that Germany must be afforded more protection than could be provided by 2 American divisions, 2 British divisions, and a few French units in the face of 25 front-line Soviet divisions. The White House grew impatient with the way France was beating about the bush. The French did not want Germany to rearm. But since they had to keep troops in Indochina, they begged the Americans, who were involved in Korea, to come to Europe's defense. Paris sent only one battalion to Korea but asked for 20 divisions on the Elbe.

One person, General de Gaulle, opposed Churchill's demand for a European army. On August 17 he answered both Adenauer and Churchill. "Before creating a European army we must first integrate Europe," he maintained. "There must be European economic institutions that emanate directly from a vote of the citizens of Europe. . . . But the practical prerequisite is a Franco-German entente. These are the real strategic and economic possibilities on our old continent.

"Finally, we need a joint defense system whose planning and leadership should normally be the responsibility of France, just as America assumes responsibility in the Pacific and England in the Orient. All these systems should be under a supreme command established by both a council of nations and a general army staff."

Monnet deliberated at his Houjarray farm in the company of his advisers—Hirsch, Uri, and Reuter. Quick action was called for. The situation was distressing.

"It is not possible to defend Germany without the Germans," Monnet said. "And it would be just as unthinkable to reconstitute the old German general staff. Even the Germans don't want that. The French will not accept German rearmament. Even the Belgians and the Dutch are very worried about the possibility. To this insoluble problem there is but one solution: German troops integrated into a European army. Then the former enemies of Germany will be reassured. We are setting up the Coal and Steel Community, thus preventing another war between Germany and France by integrating their metallurgical production. Why not do likewise, using the same supranational bodies—which remain to be defined—for a Defense Community that would integrate Europe's armies?"

Monnet maintained very active political contacts with the Christian Democratic and Socialist parties of the six countries who were to become members of the Coal and Steel Community. By setting up

110

the European Defense Community he hoped to secure their membership in both organizations.

Monnet told Schuman about his new idea. After the fall of the Bidault ministry in 1950, Schuman had remained Foreign Minister under the new Premier, Pleven. Schuman listened, but was hesitant. "A European army? There's something to be said both for and against it." He was worried about allowing Germany to rearm before she had reached an agreement with France about the Saar. And for the time being, he and Bevin were tugging at Dean Acheson's coat-tails, begging him not to abandon Europe.

But the United States could not at one and the same time send an expeditionary corps to Korea and dispatch an army to Europe that would be large enough to protect it from a Soviet tidal wave. It asked its allies to augment General MacArthur's forces. Above all, it urged them to organize their own defense and to accept some German units.

On September 14, 1950, the twelve NATO ministers met in Washington.

"France will never accept even a limited rearmament of Germany," the Defense Minister, Jules Moch, declared.

"That is foolish," the other ministers said. "Should Americans, British, Belgians, and even Frenchmen get themselves killed to defend Germany while the Germans stand by passively?"

"If France does not accept German forces, there will be no inter-allied general staff in Europe," the Americans threatened.

France was judged all the more severely for having sent her finest units to Indochina. "But this is a fight against Communism," the French diplomats replied.

All the other NATO ministers agreed to the creation of a German force. The only question was how it should be constituted, limited, and integrated into the Allied army.

France had six weeks to decide whether to accept the reestablishment of the *Reichswehr*. If she isolated herself, her territory would become a battlefield without the protection of her allies. Pleven could suggest nothing. Monnet approached him with the plan he and his associates had devised. Pleven, long-standing collaborator of Monnet's, welcomed his position paper on the Defense Community as providential. The new Monnet Plan became the Pleven Plan.

Pleven discussed the plan with responsible Americans in New York and Washington. They said very little. The Pentagon believed it would be very easy to recruit a *Bundeswehr,* equipped with American weapons and under American command. But a European Defense Community, with all its complications—treaties, integration, different languages—seemed too confusing, an evasion of existing realities.

President Truman, however, had no intention of abandoning Europe: The fate of the United States depended upon it. He sent reinforcements. He also sent General Eisenhower, who was named commander in chief of SHAPE on December 19, 1950. He was to organize the defense of Western Europe, reassure the Atlantic Pact allies, and set up a German army composed mainly of infantry.

Monnet was a friend of the American ambassador, David Bruce, and a close friend of the United States High Commissioner to Germany, John McCloy, whom he had converted to the idea of an integrated Europe. Accompanied by McCloy, Monnet called on General Eisenhower.

"A Germany army, recruited directly, would weaken the defense of Europe rather than strengthen it," Monnet told Eisenhower. "The French are not alone in their dread of German militarism. The German Socialists are against a restoration of the army. Adenauer is determined not to revive the German general staff. All these dissensions only serve to weaken the Alliance.

"It would be far better for you, and for the unified defense of the Continent, to deal with a European army and one European minister instead of with six national armies, six army staffs, and six ministers. An interallied general staff would have direct contact with the integrated forces of Western Europe."

Eisenhower approved of the Pleven Plan. On October 24, 1950, Pleven presented his plan to the National Assembly. There would be a joint army for the countries that were about to become members of the Coal and Steel Community. This army would be subject to the orders of the Council of Ministers responsible for the Assembly envisaged by the High Authority of the Coal and Steel Community. The integration of the German units into such a joint army would be accomplished at the lowest level, the level of battalions.

"That would not be a merger but a cacophony," the army men observed. They felt that integration would be possible only at the level of divisional combat teams.

After a very bitter struggle, Pleven finally obtained a favorable

112

vote. The Communists and Gaullists were among the largest groups in the Assembly, and they fiercely opposed the plan. The Socialists were divided. "The European Defense Community will assemble European forces in order to put them at the disposition of the United States—that's it in a nutshell," the Gaullists contended. "The French army would be sacrificed."

Convinced by Monnet's arguments, Eisenhower took the proposal to Washington early in 1951. A treaty was negotiated that paralleled that of the ECSC, but it encountered infinitely greater difficulties. England, who had refused to join the coal and steel pool, naturally refused to participate in a European army.

"We were careful at that time," Pierre Uri recounts, "to draft the plan for the Coal and Steel Community ourselves and to discuss it with experts from other countries. The plan for the European Defense Community was to be drafted in the traditional way—by the Quai d'Orsay and the Minister of National Defense. It was negotiated by diplomats and army men, many of whom were hostile to the idea. It was awkwardly patterned after the ECSC, a fact which showed a lack of imagination. The institutions were being worked out in a parallel fashion. I could intervene solely as the shadow of the head of the French delegation, Hervé Alphand.

"The High Authority of the Steel and Coal Community was organized within a highly structured, supranational framework, independent of the states. The European Defense Community (EDC) was being set up in the same way, but it compounded the weaknesses of the other organization. At the very moment that the European army was declared to be a supranational institution, the various governments were demanding that they be allowed to retain control over their own army units and that decisions be made on the basis of majority rule. They claimed the right of veto.

"The EDC was killed by a Belgian, van Zeeland. The project implied a joint military budget to be established by the Commissioner of the Community and voted on by the Assembly of the Six in Strasbourg. Had there been a prior scale of contributions, established according to the resources of each country, difficulties might have been avoided.

"The head of the Brussels government opposed a European army, although Belgium would have only had to pay 3 percent of the cost. Most of the money was being contributed by the United States. The

Belgian leader demanded that the joint budget should not exceed the sum of the military budget of each country, and Belgium beat all records for frugality in military expenditures. The attempt to get each country to contribute its share to the common budget failed."

While the negotiations were dragging on—the treaty was not signed until May 27, 1952—the threat of a Soviet invasion became less and less likely. If there were going to be total warfare it would already have begun: the Korean struggle was a localized conflict. But a political battle ensued over the EDC that was to last four years. According to Raymond Aron, it reached a paroxysm of violence reminiscent of the Dreyfus Affair.

What caused it was not the treaty clauses, although they were poorly drawn—a bad treaty can always be redrafted, Monnet maintained—it was the principle of German rearmament that most Frenchmen could not bring themselves to accept. And the Gaullists and the Communists denounced the Monnet principle of supranationalism.

On November 24, 1951, after the British veto, General de Gaulle indignantly declared, "We alone would be contributing an army. And to whom? To Europe? It does not exist. We would be giving our army to General Eisenhower. Just because the Americans provide us with weapons is no reason to make ourselves their subjects."

He did not criticize the treaty clauses for stipulating that the nations abandon a part of their sovereignty. However, he believed that a federation or a confederation could be established that would not entail a loss of sovereignty for the states. He objected to the formation of supranational communities before a European union had been established. He also objected to the fact that these communities would have sovereign power—they would not be subject to the authority of the states or even of a superstate, since none was set up that had authority superior to theirs. He denounced "these artificial monsters, these robots, these Frankensteins established by bureaucrats, by irresponsible men without a country. . . ." In his view, Monnet's Europe was without a leader. The White House could guide it via television. Washington would become the capital of Europe.

De Gaulle's criticism bore fruit. A clause was inserted in the Treaty of the European Defense Community that called upon the Assembly of the Community to draft a constitution for a United States of Europe. The document was drawn up on the spot. The failure of the EDC was to eliminate the political target at which de Gaulle had been aiming.

114

Monnet, the ardent champion of a United States of Europe, was against establishing a unified Europe at this point because it would have given rise to insuperable differences between the Six. He was trying to set up limited, specialized, intergovernmental organizations that answered real needs of the moment. The very modesty of his purpose facilitated the adoption of his program. Robert Schuman concurred. "A unified Europe must be built step by step," he said.

The treaty signed by the six Western governments on May 27, 1952, was not aimed at counteracting the Soviet threat; it was a manifestation in favor of a unified Europe.

On November 11, 1952, de Gaulle said, "The merger of France and Germany into a kind of economic and military entity, the result of obscure secret meetings controlled by technocrats, is a project worthy of tight-rope dancers—it might even result in a Germanic hegemony."

President Vincent Auriol was appalled. "Germany wants to drag us into a defensive and offensive alliance," he said. "And we are going to be forced to accept it. We can't do otherwise."

Marshal Juin, the Communist Party, the Comte de Paris, and almost all the members of the army's general staff, plus half the Socialist Party led by Jules Moch, announced their opposition to the EDC.

"At no time had anyone thought that the European army might be subject to the orders of a European general," people said. "It is merely a Foreign Legion recruited for the benefit of the United States."

In both houses of the French parliament the lawyers of the EDC stressed the supranationality of the European army—which was quite apparent. This only exasperated its opponents. Michel Debré repeatedly attacked it in the Senate.

General Billotte emphasized one feature of the treaty that shocked all Frenchmen: Germany had demanded that in the joint deliberations voting should be in proportion to the number of units furnished by each country to the European army. Germany had not included in the count the units stationed outside Europe. Since most of the French units were posted overseas, particularly in Indochina, Germany would enjoy military preponderance in Europe six years after her defeat. This was most distressing, especially since the Soviet threat had diminished.

Ratification of the treaty was constantly being delayed. One ministry after another was overthrown by the Gaullists and the other opposition parties just as the accursed treaty was to be submitted to the houses of parliament.

Reaction to the Gaullists was sharp. "A French general at the head of a European army?" one American newspaper commented sardonically. "A commander in chief whose national army is in Indochina, whose arsenals are in America, and who has never seen an atomic bomb?"

De Gaulle impressed Monnet as a man still imbued with the spirit of Versailles, who wanted to organize a united Europe by means of a bilateral treaty with Germany that would impose subservience and *Diktats* incompatible with a community seeking equality among its members. De Gaulle's ambitions for France failed to take into account such realities as the existence of superpowers and a defensive potential no longer controlled by Paris—the atomic bomb. His Europe was not a united Europe but a mere juxtaposition of states. His European army would be but a juxtaposition of national weaknesses. His impotent parliament would be unable to resolve a single problem.

Suddenly, in 1953, General de Gaulle withdrew from the struggle and put an end to the activities of the RPF. On May 6 he released the deputies of the movement, giving them *carte blanche*. The organization no longer followed him. The RPF had received substantial financial support when the Soviets threatened and the Communists were attempting subversion. De Gaulle, the founder of the RPF, had seemed to many the leader of a new Resistance against the enemy both within and without. Gaullist financiers backed him. Indirect American contributions were added to the French, according to the English newspaperwoman Nora Beloff. But Stalin disappeared on March 5, 1953. The cold war was subsiding. The financiers of the RPF were growing weary. The elections failed to give de Gaulle the majority he had hoped for. His offensive against the EDC had led him to assume an anti-American attitude that shocked the French bourgeoisie. His party had a deficit of 80,000,000 francs. After reducing expenses to 2,000,000 francs a month, the general decided to retire.

The battle over the EDC, which had pitted the Europe of Monnet against that of de Gaulle, had assumed the aspect of a personal struggle between the two architects of the Old World's future. Debré accused Monnet of using the Coal and Steel Community's funds to finance an intense propaganda in favor of the EDC. The organ of the RPF even accused him of buying votes.

Neither of the two rival promoters was in power. This handicapped each of them. De Gaulle could only try to combat Monnet's activities; he could not implement his own conception of Europe. And Monnet alone could not negotiate the EDC. It had been misinterpreted by the various governments. Their objections to integration were mere excuses: each country wanted to preserve its own national army. But Monnet had on his side the French government, Chancellor Adenauer, American support, and, above all, the solutions he provided for complicated situations. The general won the battle over the EDC, but the real victor was Monnet. De Gaulle abandoned the political scene.

The Gaullists attributed to Monnet's contacts the loss of resources that paralyzed the RPF. They reproached him most of all for his technocratic innovations in Europe, his Frankensteins that would clutter the field when the general returned to power to promote an association of governments.

On November 12, 1953, General de Gaulle gave his last press conference before he withdrew to Colombey. He attacked the various ministries of the Fourth Republic because they never ventured openly and officially to sponsor a union of states, which he advocated. He favored the establishment of such a union by means of a direct understanding with Germany, but Adenauer had chosen "the trick solution" of approaching Europe through the little door of the Community. He added a philippic against Monnet, "Unfortunately, they used a trick as a solution. The trick was ready and waiting, and the man who inspired it was also ready, with a panacea which he called a merger. He had suggested this panacea once before, in different circumstances. In 1940, as a member of the last government of the Third Republic, I was sent to London by Paul Reynaud. As a last resort, I tried to reactivate an alliance that was about to collapse. At that time, the 'inspirer' brought me a plan for a Franco-British merger which I got Churchill and his government to accept. Churchill and I soon came to see in this project merely an ultimate manifestation of Anglo-French solidarity, merely an argument addressed to the French ministers in order to encourage them to escape the enemy and go to Algiers to continue the fight. But our 'inspirer' believed one could integrate King George V and President Lebrun, the House

117

of Lords and the French Senate, the Horse Guards and the Garde
Républicaine.

"Three years later, when the United States had set up an organization in Algiers that competed with that of France, and when things
were not going very well, the 'inspirer' came to the aid of the Americans by proposing that General Giraud and General de Gaulle unite
to form a new government. Again I accepted the idea of fusion because I knew what would happen. And what did happen, of course,
surprised no one, probably not even the 'inspirer.'

"But . . . the difficulties of reaching some agreement between France
and Germany on the subject of German rearmament—what a mar-
velous chance that was for his panacea. . . ."

In the spirit of a last will and testament, General de Gaulle painted
a picture of the Europe he envisaged: "In order to have a European
army—in other words, an army of Europe—Europe must first exist
as a political, economic, financial, administrative and, above all, spir-
itual entity. And this entity must be sufficiently real and acknowledged
to pursue a policy of its own so that, in case of need, millions of men
would be willing to die for it. . . .

"As for Europe's institutions, I believed and I still believe that the
simplest solution is the best: a reunion, an organic council of heads
of state endowed with the necessary joint tools to implement their
decisions economically, politically, culturally, and militarily; a deliberating assembly; a referendum in all the countries to obtain the
consent of the vast mass of Europeans to the construction of Europe.

"Germany? To my way of thinking, Germany must have a place
in such a confederation. . . . She would be encircled by France, including the French Union, and by England, who would be part of
such a confederation, for there is nothing about this that is incon-
sistent with Great Britain's principles.

"But the United States has never favored a Great European Federation or a Great World Alliance in which it would be possible and
desirable to integrate and encircle Germany. The Americans prefer
to wall off the other countries into many small compartments: continental Europe, northern Europe, the Iberian peninsula, the eastern
Mediterranean, the Far East, South America. They play a special
game in each theater.

"England, too, insists that we ratify the so-called European army,
in which she absolutely refuses to participate. She has no desire to

118

involve herself on the Continent, save for a few divisions and squadrons. Realizing that the United States is likewise unwilling to become involved except in a very limited way, England is afraid of what might happen at the beginning of a conflict on soil that Churchill calls in advance 'the unfortunate Continent.' "

Then de Gaulle disappeared. Nevertheless, the EDC failed. The continuing opposition comprised the Communists, who were hostile to the defense of Europe; the critics of the poorly drafted treaty; the numerous adversaries of German rearmament, some of whom were Socialists; and the defenders of a French national army, the Gaullists, who still represented a rather large group in the Assembly. No government could overcome their combined opposition.

In February, 1953, the EDC treaty, which had already been ratified by several parliaments, encountered a new stumbling block in Paris. Bertrand Goldschmidt, in his informative book *Les Rivalités atomiques* (Fayard, 1967), recounts that a story on the Atomic Energy Commission appeared in the bulletin of a left-wing union. It attracted the attention of the commission's manager, Pierre Guillaumat. The EDC was reported to be reducing the French manufacture of plutonium to 500 grams per year, the very same quota that was allotted to Germany.

"Have you read the treaty?" Guillaumat asked Goldschmidt.

No one connected with the Atomic Energy Commission had read the treaty or helped to draft it. But the French atomic scientists had suggested four years earlier that German production of plutonium should be limited to 500 grams. "No discriminatory measures against Germany," Adenauer had said. So 500 grams was the amount of plutonium to which every country was limited. Ten months after the signature of the Treaty of Paris, the lawyers suddenly woke up. They added further protocols that accorded certain privileges to Germany's partners.

At the Quai d'Orsay, an official spokesman for Goldschmidt summarized the matter thus: "First we tie up Germany; then, in the name of equality of rights, we tie ourselves up. Afterwards, we knock ourselves out trying to get free."

Debré warned: "France is going to find herself in the tragic situation of having to authorize Germany to use nuclear energy for military purposes. She has to do this in order to preserve her own atomic lead."

The cosignatories of the treaty rejected the amendments proposed by Paris. A week later the debate on ratification was opened in parliament. Pierre Mendès-France decided to bring things to a head. One had to vote yes or no. He himself opposed the EDC which, in view of the various units in Europe, would give military preeminence to Germany. This would be true in general of any organization in which England did not participate. She was indispensable to the maintenance of a balance in Europe. Mendès-France left the decision to the discretion of the Assembly.

That very morning, Chancellor Adenauer gave the French ambassador, André François-Poncet, a pathetic message for the Premier: "Tell Monsieur Mendès-France that I will go down in history as the only German chancellor who preferred European unity to the unity of his own country. If France refuses to reach an affirmative decision, she will no longer have me to deal with. I will be defeated and overthrown before long. German unity will be achieved by the Soviets. The question is whether France prefers European unity to that kind of German unity."

Mendès-France was still skeptical. Adenauer was very hale and hearty, politically. And the Germans had not yet reached the point of throwing themselves into the arms of the Russians. On March 10, 1952, Stalin had suggested to Bonn and the Allies that the two Germanies should be reunited; he asked for an immediate peace treaty to be followed within a year by the withdrawal of all occupation troops on both sides. One week later, he even proposed free elections. The offer had been withdrawn after the three Western powers laid down the following condition: A United Nations Commission must ascertain whether free elections were possible in the two Germanies. The Kremlin's proposal would have been more tempting if it had stipulated that the suggested evacuation was to precede the elections.

In August, 1954, ratification of the EDC was rejected by a large majority at the Palais Bourbon. This was a pyrrhic victory for the opponents of German rearmament. Two weeks later, the Americans and the British decided to organize the *Bundeswehr* within the framework of the Western European Union, which included England and the Six. Adenauer viewed this formula as an artificial substitute for his idea of a European army. He was truly the foremost champion of a united Europe. De Gaulle was later to call him the Architect.

In October, 1954, the French Assembly, which in August had rejected the idea of German rearmament within the EDC, ratified the

Paris accords, which included recognition of the sovereignty of the Federal Republic.

Perhaps the most serious criticism one might make of the Pleven Plan is that a European army requires a government to head it. And Europe had no leader, no policy; its army had neither a European commander nor a flag.

A clause in the treaty—an afterthought—gave the Strasbourg Assembly the right to draft the statutes. But the failure of the Assembly doomed the European superstate. Monnet had tried to prevent this by establishing, first, the autonomous communities. Only then would the governments be induced to accept a federation that was already an accomplished fact.

General de Gaulle wanted to follow precisely the opposite course in creating his multinational Europe. First, he planned to establish a common policy through meetings, led by France, with heads of states and governments. This common policy would be based on the Continent's desire for independence. When agreement had been reached on a general defense and economic policy, this unity of thought and will would take the form of a confederation which, like all confederations in the making, would eventually be called a federation.

It is difficult to say which of the two procedures called for the greatest optimism.

X

The Coal and Steel Community

TO trace the beginnings of the first European institution, we must go back in time to the period when the Coal and Steel Community and the European Defense Community were being simultaneously elaborated. At that time the war in Korea was causing great distress.

On October 12, 1950—he will remember that date for a long time —Maurice Lagrange, a specialist in public law, was dining with his wife when the telephone rang. Jean Monnet wanted to see him.

The following morning, Lagrange, a tall, spare man of serious bearing, found himself suddenly a member of the Rue de Martignac brain trust before anyone had taken time to introduce him. A short man with a lordly manner entered. Everyone turned toward him. It was Monnet. "One would have thought this was a royal levée," said Lagrange.

Monnet immediately drew him aside. "I need a court of justice for the High Authority of the Coal and Steel Community. What do you think?"

Lagrange embarked on a discussion of public law which was obviously beyond the ken of his interlocutor. When he was about to leave, Monnet detained him and appealed to him to stay and draft the treaty. "I have to go to Frankfurt," Lagrange replied. "I promised the Americans a plan for the democratization of public offices in Germany."

"Don't worry about that. I'll give McCloy a ring."

Monnet had just launched the EDC. He was in a hurry to set up the OEEC. Some of its institutions—the Council of Ministers, the court of justice, and the Assembly—had to be identical with those of the Defense Community.

Lagrange expected to be overwhelmed with files and projects. But there was almost nothing in the drawers. Pierre Uri, the big brain of the group, went to work and wrote three pages of text and three pages of commentary.

Lagrange was stunned. An idea of revolutionary daring had been launched and was being acclaimed by the Six and the United States— a minerals and metals superstate. Six months later its promoters still were uncertain of exactly how this novelty was to be constructed.

"I hope the structure will stand up," Monnet said dubiously.

The brain trust worked feverishly from ten o'clock in the morning until midnight, without taking Sundays or holidays off, not even Christmas day. Even the secretaries and the office boys were infected by the general excitement, by the feeling that they were part of a fantastic undertaking. This was the psychological atmosphere quite familiar to Monnet. And indeed, as the dynamics of the High Authority began to emerge from the fog, the entire mechanism for the creation of a united Europe was taking shape.

The High Authority for steel and coal was also to serve the EDC. Gradually, it was thought, the supranational authorities, supervised by the European Council of Ministers at Brussels and the Assembly in Strasbourg, would administer all the activities of the Continent. A day would come when governments would be forced to admit that an integrated Europe was an accomplished fact, without their having had a say in the establishment of its underlying principles. All they would have to do was to merge all these autonomous institutions into a single federal administration and then proclaim a United States of Europe.

This creative enthusiasm was not without a measure of naïveté. Actually, the founders of the Coal and Steel Community would have to obtain from the various national governments—justifiably reputed to be incapable of making sacrifices for the sake of a federation—a whole series of concessions in regard to their sovereign rights until, having been finally stripped, they committed hara-kiri by accepting the merger.

Monnet's desire for an integrated Europe led him to exploit the situation. Holland, Belgium, and Luxembourg did not want, nor were

123

they in a position to claim, international policies of their own. The Italians had plenty to do at home. Germany, occupied and divided, directly threatened by the Red Army, could have but one policy, that of seeking American protection. In France, Monnet, who fed ideas to the Fourth Republic, could not address himself to a single head of government who was free to guide the country toward a major European policy. France was unstable and overwhelmed with problems; the war in Indochina deprived it of troops to station in Europe and the cost was a billion francs per day. Each of the Six had agreed to establish autonomous international institutions; they also accepted a Europe that had no overall leader, a Europe for which the United States would be solely responsible. America would have to assume all expenses, including Europe's debts.

Negotiations for the coal and steel treaty lasted a year. They were conducted first by the experts, then by the ministers. Each country feared that its metallurgical industry would fall victim to the common market of minerals, steel, and iron.

The first meeting of the specialists in metallurgy was taken up with bitter complaints. Belgium deplored its shrinking coal lodes, poorly exploited and almost exhausted. A free market for heavy industry would spell ruin for the country. The Netherlands bemoaned its limited resources. It would be submerged by its powerful neighbors. The French representative was deeply distressed. France's dilapidated steel mills and her depleted coal lodes could not compete with the newly equipped Ruhr. The Italian representative pictured himself as Job on his rubbish heap. Italy had no minerals, no heavy industry. She would be the archvictim. Bauden, the German delegate, was the last to speak: "I came here to explain our serious problems. But I have just heard that five of the six countries will be losers in the market you are proposing to organize. Since a market cannot be set up if people lose money, I will hold up what I was going to say."

The Dutch were fiercely opposed to the principle of supranationality. They were afraid of being gobbled up. They were also apprehensive about the absence of their British protectors. "The truth is that the Dutch are afraid of the Germans," one ambassador explained. "And they don't like the French. So when they see the French and the Germans reaching an agreement, they feel they have everything to fear."

Backed by Paul Reuter, an antitrust specialist with Socialist leanings, Monnet was determined to break up the Ruhr cartels. German concerns must not dominate the Common Market. The Americans had promulgated Law 27 in Germany. It called for decentralization but had never been implemented. Monnet was supported by the Americans, especially by their expert, Bowie, in his attitude toward the German monopolies. Behind the scenes, Bowie had had several hard-headed discussions with the German Secretary of State, Walter Hallstein. Naturally, Hallstein defended the cause of the Ruhr industries. With great courage, Chancellor Adenauer sided with Monnet against his chief constituents. He intervened, using his influence to make sure that excessive concentrations were prohibited by Articles 65 and 66 of the treaty.

Robert Schuman had little to say officially. Lagrange, who was to become public prosecutor, noted, "The Foreign Minister not only adopted Monnet's brainchild, he assumed official responsibility for it. He intervened personally behind the scenes to oil the very rigid wheels of the treaty. He studied the project and read it as it was being elaborated, adding notes in the margin as thoughts occurred to him. He insisted on close collaboration between the High Authority and the Council of Ministers and created a coordinating committee. He permitted all those subject to the High Authority—the iron and steel magnates, the unions, and others—to register complaints or make suggestions. It was he who made the treaty pleasant and acceptable. That was very important."

The treaty signaled the death of the Ruhr International Authority. The Conference of Governments was to take it over on April 12, 1951. But before this occurred, Monnet went to Bonn to see Adenauer on a vital mission. The German experts claimed that the influence of each of the Six within the High Authority should be fixed according to the scale of their production. In other words, the Federal Republic would play the preponderant role in the coal and steel pool. "It is my feeling," Monnet said to Adenauer, "that France and Germany should be on an equal footing in any dealings involving coal and steel, as well as in all future moves toward the goal of European unity."

The Chancellor acquiesced without further ado. Practically speaking, the Conference of Governments had nothing more to do except decide where the capital of the first European institution should be. "At that time the prestige of Robert Schuman and Jean Monnet was so great that Frenchmen could easily have obtained Paris as the capital of the new Europe," wrote Lagrange. "But Schuman's modesty and his fear that France might appear to be establishing a hegemony made him refuse the honor."

The Dutch began by demanding that the Community's tribunal should be established at The Hague. The other partners objected; they wanted one capital to house all the Community's institutions. To console the Dutch, they were granted one more judge than the treaty had stipulated.

Since Paris was out of the question, Brussels was the second choice. "Impossible," said the head of the Belgian government, van Zeeland. "Our Flemish population would not allow Brussels to have a monopoly of international institutions. The Walloons and the Flemings have agreed on Liège."

"But Liège has no airport! All Liège can offer is a movie theater."

"I cannot give you Brussels. My cabinet would fall tomorrow."

The negotiations stalled. Schuman, who was presiding over the meetings, seemed thoughtful, but he said nothing.

"I had the feeling that he was hoping for defeat," Lagrange noted. "The treaty settled the question of the Ruhr but not that of the Saar. He seemed to regret this."

And it was true that no one said a word, officially, about the Saar. It was the skeleton in the closet that poisoned all relations between France and Germany. Then Schuman timidly ventured that the European institutions should be set up in the Saar at Saarbrücken. In a way, this would have been the equivalent of America's District of Columbia; independent of the member states, the Saar would have served as their meeting place. Also, France would have had to abandon the idea of annexing the Saar, an idea she had entertained since 1945.

The Germans were unwilling to give up a part of their territory. Amid the euphoria of a Franco-German reconciliation, they hoped to recover it. De Gaulle claimed that underhand deals were being made in regard to the Saar. But Saarbrücken as a capital did not tempt the diplomats any more than did Liège. It offered few resources. The idea was abandoned. A few years later, the Saar question was resolved without tension by a referendum. Meanwhile, it was put under wraps.

A capital had to be found. Lagrange was probably the one who saved the situation. In an elevator at the Quai d'Orsay, he encountered an important member of the Italian delegation. "Nowhere is it stipulated in the treaty that the Coal and Steel Community must have a capital. All we have to do is to announce that a constitutive meeting will take place on such and such a day, in such or such a place." The Italian got the point and suggested that the first meeting take place in Turin.

"It's the only European city that has no convenient communication with the rest of industrial Europe," Uri protested.

Then the natives of Luxembourg suggested their city. Schuman smiled: it was his native town. The smallest state of Western Europe, with its exorbitant rents, became the seat of the first European Community. Moreover, Luxembourg was granted a right of veto which until then it had not enjoyed.

The treaty was filed at the Quai d'Orsay on August 18, 1951. There was only one copy. Written in French, it was printed on Dutch vellum with German ink by the Imprimerie Nationale of Paris; it was bound in Belgian parchment, tied with Italian ribbon, and put together with Luxembourg paste. Monnet has a passion for careful presentations and symbolic details.

It took six months to ready the new institution. This was to have catastrophic consequences for Monnet's second project, which had become the major concern of Europe—the European Defense Community. He was no longer in Paris to arrange the daily diplomatic consultations, parry the objections of France's partners, pull a solution out of his hat, maneuver behind the scenes of the Assembly, put pressure on the ministers, the political party leaders, persuade a Dutchman, rush to Bonn, or telephone Washington. The EDC negotiations were dragging on, but the magician was absent.

In Luxembourg, Monnet had become King Jean. His palace was just an old house, covered with Virginia creepers, the property of the Luxembourg railway. But his team of bureaucrats was organized like an army general staff, and it operated day and night. His work habits terrified the honest people of Luxembourg, the well-ordered, sober Belgians, the Germans who functioned like clockwork, the Dutch who dined and slept at fixed hours. There was a tremendous amount of work to be done.

The problems of the coal, steel, and iron industries were infinitely complex. Prices had been fixed according to the looks of the customer.

127

In each country, intricate, contradictory regulations had resulted in a good deal of cheating in the payment of tariffs. These regulations were the legacy of periods of dumping when steel had to be sold abroad for less than at home; or, conversely, when the state, to protect domestic prices, fixed the cost, leaving it to the exporters to manage as best they could. To the complications of tariff policy were added those of quotas, railway transportation costs manipulated to outwit competitors, and state taxes. And this was nothing compared to the jungle of private agreements, the traps set by the cartels, and the innumerable sales offices. To simplify his task, Monnet wanted to limit his efforts to the 360 steel and coal producers. But the steel and coal industries, especially in Germany, were in the hands of thousands of merchants, all of them ardent free-traders, opposed to any planned control or any regulation of the market.

Monnet would arrive at ten o'clock in the morning, assemble his brain trust and other experts needed for the solution of specific problems, work until two in the afternoon, and then send out for sandwiches. "We're not in good form today," he would observe. "Let's go for a walk."

Sessions would recommence at five and last until eleven at night. "Let's take a break," Monnet would say. "Later on we'll think more clearly." At midnight work would resume and last until three in the morning. At six in the morning he would telephone three or four collaborators to clarify certain points. Then off he would go for a walk in the forest. One night Paul Delouvrier, a giant of a man, simply fell flat on the floor. He had fainted from exhaustion. "What a crazy life!" the Luxembourg, Dutch, and German wives groaned.

Monnet's first difficulties came from an unexpected quarter—the original Europeanists. The treaty provided for a Council of Ministers, an Assembly, and a tribunal. Monnet, the meticulous planner, had taken certain precautions. The relationship of the High Authority to the Council of Ministers was carefully regulated so as to preclude any undue interference on the part of the various governments, although Schuman intervened to enable the various nations to make themselves heard. The tribunal was independent of the High Authority and ruled against it on several occasions. But its jurisdiction was limited in order to circumvent "the power of judges."

The Assembly of the Community, which controlled and could reverse the decisions of the High Authority, was to have been elected

128

by universal suffrage in the six countries. But it seemed to Monnet that the coal and steel pool was too narrow a basis for a European parliament. Besides, the six governments were not overly enthusiastic about such an institution. They feared it might be overpowering. Furthermore, elected parliaments have an unfortunate tendency to harbor opposition groups. The German Social Democrats had declared themselves hostile to the Schuman Plan. Communist opponents could very well be elected in France and in Italy.

It was therefore decided to resort to an Assembly of the Council of Europe. It was without power and had no definite purpose. It assembled at Strasbourg the delegations of the parliaments of 15 countries, including England, the Scandinavian nations, and so forth. Naturally, it was largely composed of uncompromising Europeanists. The flag of the Council of Europe—15 gold stars on a blue background—harbored within its folds the hopes of the idealists of the immediate postwar period. The Assembly was not connected with any organization, neither with the OEEC, which was created later by 17 countries, nor with NATO, subsequently established by 15 states. It was neither legislative nor representative. No government was obliged to read its resolutions. Communists hostile to the "American Europe" were not represented in it. It was merely a forum where Europeanists of every tendency discussed federation, confederation, supranationality, plans, and dreams. Here, people exchanged points of view, gave speeches, and presented reports.

The members of the Council of Europe, particularly Schuman's friends—the MRP leaders like François de Menthon, P. H. Teitgen, and Pierre Pflimlin, Socialists like André Philip—all fervently gathered around the nascent Coal and Steel Community as its sponsors and godparents. As it became the regular institutional Assembly of the High Authority it acquired a function, ceased to be a vague concept, and got off to a fresh start.

The Treaty of Paris stipulated that the Assembly of the ECSC, whose members were to be drawn from the Strasbourg Assembly of the Council of Europe, would consist exclusively of delegations from the parliaments of the Six. The two Assemblies were therefore related, but separate and distinct. But the enthusiasm of the entire Strasbourg forum worried Monnet. The moving welcome given the new Coal and Steel Community by the Secretary-General of the Council of Europe,

129

J.-C. Paris (former director of European affairs at the Quai d'Orsay), seemed especially alarming to Monnet.

According to J.-C. Paris, the Assembly of the Six was merely a small part of the Assembly of Fifteen. The Community's Council of Ministers would become a small part of the phantom Brussels Committee of Ministers of the Council of Europe. The High Authority was not a sovereign, supranational institution but an administrative body subservient to governments.

"This is an extremely dangerous interpretation," Monnet told his colleagues. "The governments would be too inclined to take back with one hand the sovereignty which they had sacrificed with the other, in order to protect those factories the High Authority might shut down, the metallurgical agreements, the tariffs, etc. The Council of Europe will suffocate the ECSC if we allow the ECSC to be absorbed by it."

"The Assembly of the Six is a deliberative and sovereign assembly," Monnet protested in Strasbourg. "It controls and can overthrow the High Authority which is a sovereign executive organ. It has no connection with the Council of Europe. The Community's Council of Ministers will have its seat in Luxembourg. It has nothing in common with the dormant Committee of Ministers in Brussels."

Many members of the Council of Europe, and J.-C. Paris as well, did not seem to understand. The revolutionary ideas of Monnet and Schuman were alien to them.

The meeting hall of the deputies of the Fifteen was offered to the delegates of the Six. These were more or less the same people, even though their membership was reduced by half, but they preserved the same flag with its 15 stars. Monnet decided that his Assembly would not convene until new quarters had been found. He located a room in the stock exchange of Strasbourg and equipped it appropriately. J.-C. Paris capitulated. The ECSC Assembly held its special sessions in the Palais de la Robertsau and was served by a secretariat separate from that of the Council of Europe.

However sovereign the Assembly of the ECSC might be, the recruiting of its personnel was nonetheless somewhat questionable. And however brilliant some of its members might be—Pflimlin, Poher, Pleven, Teitgen, among others—many of the parliamentary appointments were compromise choices. And absenteeism made serious inroads. "You are making a bad mistake if you think of yourselves as Europe's parliament," Maurice Couve de Murville was to say one day, in a contemptuous tone. "You are only a gathering of parliamentarians."

Monnet was uncompromising on the question of sovereignty for the institutions he was creating. To insure adequate funds, the authors of the treaty had authorized the High Authority to levy the first European tax on coal, steel, and iron. The method of collecting this tax was to be determined by the Council of Ministers. The massive Ludwig Erhard, the Economics Minister of Bonn, and a close ally of German employers, came to Luxembourg with his colleagues to settle this problem. The future taxpayers were naturally concerned.

"How much of a tax are you planning?" he asked immediately, chewing on his cigar.

"That is the business of the High Authority," Monnet replied, rather coldly. "There is no reason why I should discuss it with you. We are here solely to regulate the method of collecting the tax, as specified by the Council of Ministers."

Erhard's jovial expression altered abruptly. He scowled like a bulldog. But an hour later, Monnet addressed him amiably enough. "Now that the purpose of the meeting has been accomplished, I am happy to tell you that the tax will be 0.9 percent." The industrialists thought this was rather high.

"For the past two years, our tax payments to the High Authority have been 100 percent greater than the dividends distributed to our stockholders," Ricard, the president of a French steel company, was to say ruefully in 1955.

At the time, the war in Korea had revived heavy industry, and 1952 was a record year for production. The European tax was accepted without much protest. It yielded large revenues that enabled the High Authority to participate in the reconversion of mines that were either depleted or unprofitable. The cost was divided among the states. The Belgian Borinage and certain mines in the center of France and Germany, for example, were subsidized. Housing was constructed for the workers, and tens of thousands of workers were retrained.

Monnet worked hard, and not without difficulties, at abolishing customs barriers, eradicating the impediments to railway transportation, repealing taxation, determining quotas, and so on. The ECSC's first railway shipment of coal was scheduled to cross the Luxembourg

131

border at ten o'clock in the morning on February 9, 1953. Cinema cameramen and journalists were watching for it. The shipment had been freed from all customs formalities, but by ten o'clock that evening technical arrangements had still not been completed. At four o'clock the next morning the frontier was finally crossed, despite the objections of the customs officials, who had not been forewarned.

The metallurgists, who for thirty years had been subjected to restraints, habituated to protectionism, and surrounded by secret agreements, had no conception whatsoever of what a free market would mean. They had had no responsibility for sales. In Germany, 3,000 merchants conducted all transactions. In France, the Comptoir Sidérurgique was in charge of production and did not encourage the steel magnates to create steel industries for unfinished products in Lorraine or elsewhere, although this would have put an end to crises.

The opening of a common market in steel, coal, pig iron, and cast iron restored competition. This enabled the Italians to acquire a metallurgical industry. They reduced by 10 percent the rise in prices caused by the war in Korea. In the United States prices had soared by 35 percent.

Just as a church steeple attracts lightning, the proud title of High Authority drew the ire of governments and the sarcasm of the iron manufacturers. Businessmen, politicians, and diplomats found it difficult to adjust to the idea of an organization with sovereign power over minerals and metallurgical products. To some this creation appeared to be an attack on constitutional rights, to others a Cervantes-like farce, a harebrained scheme.

De Gaulle had alluded to the Coal and Steel Community as a "potpourri." On December 21, 1951, he said, "Europe has an obvious interest in seeing that coal and steel are exploited jointly, but the method employed can only result in the creation of a supranational power."

Gaston Palewski, the general's former chief of staff, said in 1953, "It will have no effect whatsoever." And, in the name of the RPF, he laid before the French Assembly his plan for a European confederation. "When all is said and done, no decision that injures one of the signatory states will be implemented if it has been reached by a committee of experts rather than by a genuine European political authority." Immediate events were to prove him wrong. When the French government wanted to impose a tax for which there was no

132

provision in the treaty, the High Authority forbade it. The matter was taken to the Community's tribunal. Paris lost the case and was forced to acquiesce.

Since the ECSC proposed to abolish trusts, it began to split up the large German concerns in the Ruhr. Monnet convinced Adenauer that these gigantic firms were illegal and should be broken up. This was accomplished by 1951. All cartels would have to be authorized by the High Authority. When Krupp sold an enormous amount of stock all at once, the question of stability arose. Requests for the reconstitution of cartels were made and energetically supported by Erhard. Colossal regroupings were rejected, others were postponed, but some were accepted. This led competitors of the steel magnates to say, whether rightly or wrongly, that the great vassals of the High Authority, who were powerfully backed by their governments, were actually more powerful than the High Authority itself. Monnet denied this.

Those governed by "King Jean" told themselves that the ECSC was there to fix prices and, if necessary, protect them, like a metallurgical sales counter. But in 1953 Monnet warned the industry that the market was flooded with enormous supplies and that a decrease in prices was in the offing. A new price level had to be established.

Prices decreased as soon as the war in Korea ended but before the iron manufacturers had agreed on a lower price scale. The shrewd Dutch staged a few tricks in the ports and canals that enabled them to buy at less than the official rate. German merchants delivered their goods by rail but charged the fee for water transportation. "Make them respect the price scale," the metallurgists demanded of the ECSC.

"The purpose of the treaty is not to maintain arbitrary prices but to reestablish competition," the High Authority answered.

And indeed, the competition proved salutary. A common market was achieved in that most thorny domain, free enterprise. There were many obstacles: decades of protectionism, taxation that varied from one period to another. Firms were organized not to produce and sell as profitably as possible but to satisfy the arbitrary directives of governments. The mines were poorly equipped, the steel mills dilapidated, the administration rigid. The French coal and steel industry had to make enormous efforts to become modernized and adapt itself to competition.

Steel was a jungle. And yet an effective market was established. The industries of not a single member country had been ruined by free confrontation with foreign production. Actually, the opposite was true. In the Europe of the Six, heavy industry made a twenty-year advance within a short space of time. From the prewar output of 30,000,000 tons of steel, 20,000,000 of which were produced by Germany, the figure jumped to more than 73,000,000, compared to 89,000,000 in the United States and 76,000,000 in the U.S.S.R.

The solidity of the High Authority was still to be demonstrated. Was it a mere juridical fiction dressed up in the cast-off clothing of authority wrested from states that had been weakened by the war, or would it prove durable?

The crisis of 1957-59 was the acid test. A dramatic overproduction occurred in the coalfields. The closing of the Suez Canal and the need for fuel had led the United States to subsidize a modernization of its mines while abandoned oil wells were being reopened. Then the canal opened and the transport charges for sea freight fell sharply. American coal arrived at le Havre and was sold for less than coal lying in the pitheads of Europe. At the same time, power plants, factories, and homes began substituting natural gas or oil for coal.

The coal crisis was growing more serious at the very moment de Gaulle came to power. This did not make him any more happily disposed toward Monnet. Determined to establish his European political union, de Gaulle planned to rid himself as quickly as possible of "this carnival of supranationalities," and to merge all the communities.

By January 1, 1959, the stockpile of coal had reached 31,000,000 tons at the pitheads. On March 4, Monnet and the French union leader Paul Finet decided to proclaim "an obvious state of emergency." Article 38 of the treaty gave Monnet, as President of the High Authority, special powers: He could close all unprofitable mines; impose restrictions on production in accordance with the quotas established in Luxembourg; direct the High Authority's negotiations with the coal companies of the various countries in order to stabilize coal production.

On May 14, 1959, the ECSC's Council of Ministers vetoed Monnet's proclamation and proposals. France refused to suspend work in the inefficient coal mines. The miners were calling for help and the federations were besieging the Ministry of Industry. The Germans refused to bow to the directives of the High Authority. Italy, tempted by the low cost of American coal, refused to pay duty on fuel arriving from other foreign sources.

"The governments are preventing the High Authority from settling the crisis," was the cry that went up from Luxembourg.

"The High Authority is making decisions in a vacuum," said the French Minister of Industry, Jeanneney, who had presided over the European Council of Ministers. "It does not have to confront the miners or listen to their troubles and their requests for help. It is the governments that will have to cope with the unrest that is a direct result of decisions they have had no part in."

The Coal and Steel Community was restricted to helping those Belgian miners who had been the most severely affected by the crisis. Subsidies, prohibited by the 1960 Treaty of Rome, were granted to coal miners in distress.

To make matters worse, the steel market was encountering trouble. The Pinay devaluation decreased by 17.5 percent the price of French steel exports. To remedy the situation, the High Authority asked Paris to impose a temporary tax of 4 percent on all exports. But Debré refused. The treaty prohibited two different price scales.

On September 5, 1960, de Gaulle expressed his opinion of the Monnet communities: "As long as nothing serious occurs, the community organizations with supranational pretensions function fairly smoothly. But as soon as a crisis occurs, one realizes that the so-called High Authority has no authority at all in regard to the various national categories, that only the states have such authority."

Deputy Georges Vendroux, the general's brother-in-law, added, "There's nothing more natural than delegation of sovereignty to the European authorities. But abandonment of sovereignty? No! Delegation to whom? Merely to the Council of Ministers of the Six."

During the years that followed, the High Authority virtually lost its authority. The forbidden subsidies were commonly given to coalfields and iron mines as well as to metallurgical concerns. It is quite obvious that the technocratic institutions of Jean Monnet, despite the sovereignty with which they were theoretically invested, had in actuality only as much power as the governments were willing to accord them. They had neither prefects nor policemen, and they were not subject to the verdict of electors—in short, they had merely a fictitious authority. Nonetheless, this fiction enabled them to render important services.

135

The High Authority abolished the regulations that had prevented a wholesome competition from developing in coal and steel, maintained France and Germany in an atmosphere of war, and deprived Italy of heavy industry. This would never have been possible had it not been for the theoretical cession of sovereignty to the Coal and Steel Community.

The ECSC offered a solution to the heretofore insurmountable problems of the Ruhr and the Saar. Could the Coal and Steel Community prevent war between France and Germany, as Schuman's declaration maintained it would? If the two countries should want to fight, the regulations laid down by the High Authority would not stop them. But the existence of a common market has gradually and increasingly united the heavy industries of each country. With the manufacture of vital steel products spreading out over the entire area of the common market, it is becoming more and more difficult for any one country to place itself completely on a wartime footing.

Today, trade is conducted without any concern for frontiers. Goods are purchased on the common market from whichever country sells the needed products at the lowest price. Coke from Germany rather than from northern France, as was formerly the case, feeds the tall furnaces of Lorraine. German furnaces which once used Swedish fuel now consume fuel from Africa. The new route for German iron would be very vulnerable in case of war.

XI

Euratom and the Common Market

THE failure of the European Defense Community in August, 1954, was a serious blow to Jean Monnet. His Europe of autonomous communities was gravely affected by it. France's five partners were furious. The EDC was a French project. The governments of the five other countries had put forth a great effort to make the EDC acceptable to public opinion. Holland had to change her constitution. Then the French said no.

Monnet, too, was deeply disappointed. The chance to accomplish a great work of such magnitude comes only once in a thousand years. The restoration of the German army was not a source of satisfaction to Monnet. Nor did Adenauer like the idea. He saw his plans ruined. He had hoped, with the help of France, to unify Europe, to anchor Germany on the Rhine, and to tie her to France and perhaps to a joint West European army.

Monnet reproached himself for not having worked more closely with those who drafted the treaty. "But a poor treaty can always be redrafted," he kept telling himself. Above all, he reproached himself for having failed to obtain ratification from the French parliament, for not having hit upon some means of persuading the parliamentary groups. He had been convinced that public opinion in the six countries was favorable to European unification.

This defeat, he feared, would discourage the other five, render the European institutions unproductive—the Council of Ministers, the

Strasbourg Assembly, the tribunal—all of which, he had hoped, would lead to the creation of many other communities. The High Authority of the Coal and Steel Community would be adversely affected by the defeat of the EDC.

Monnet believed that Europe could progress only if it enjoyed a permanent recovery. The existing bodies were destined to wither away if they were not constantly reinforced by new institutions. Toying with the idea of a transportation pool and a pool for electricity, he consulted Louis Armand, the general director of the French state railways, a graduate of the École Polytechnique, and a man of many talents. To consult Armand is to open a closet and have your arms filled with an avalanche of startling ideas, of grandiose views about science, industry, and geopolitics.

"Your EDC was a mistake," he told Monnet. "It was an integration of light infantrymen. To merge battalions or combat teams, people who speak four different languages, have six different flags, six national allegiances, rival army staffs and competing suppliers—that was a great gamble.

"What should have been organized was an atomic EDC. There would have been very little opposition. There would be no noncommissioned officers, no generals, marshals, or industrialists in an integrated atomic Europe. Everything would have to be done from scratch.

"An atomic EDC remains to be organized. Europe still has no nuclear defense of its own, yet it is essential. Very soon atomic industry will be the most important element in all the national economies, yet Europe has none.

"We have a unique opportunity to achieve this. The American Congress and Eisenhower have just modified the MacMahon Law, agreed to aid those allies who are sufficiently advanced technically to have the bomb. For the moment, only England is benefiting from this aid. She already has the A-bomb. But Europe can also ask for help. We'll have to form an atomic pool with the British and the Germans. The Germans are the strongest in technology and have the greatest industrial potential; they are also very eager to become Europeans, to join the French, who are the most progressive people on the Continent and who should take the lead. Adenauer has just given up any idea of acquiring nuclear, chemical, or biological weapons. The bomb would not belong to Germany, but to the new Anglo-French-German

Europe. There is no danger that the Germans would be able to use it unilaterally.

"No country of Europe can aspire to become a great nuclear power on its own, on a par with the United States or the U.S.S.R. England has atomic scientists and access to American secrets. But she does not have enough money. France wants to become a nuclear power and has begun to work toward that end. But she does not have the resources in researchers, technicians, and factories, or in the funds necessary for the creation of a great nuclear industry which the ultimate weapon requires. Germany is prohibited from having atomic weapons. Europe could become a third nuclear power if America aided it.

"Atomic science is a great opportunity for Europe," Louis Armand continued. "Europe has become great, thanks to its coal and to the uses Germany has made of coal—dyes, chemical products, nitrogen, oil. But she is bankrupt because she has no gasoline. A nuclear industry would restore her strength. Why? Because she needs atomic power plants far more than do the other developed countries.

"The United States and the U.S.S.R. still have tremendous reserves of conventional energy—coal, waterfalls that can be improved, oil, and gasoline. In America conventional fuel is far less expensive than in our countries. The prosperity of a modern state depends on cheap fuel. Atomic energy is the only kind of energy we could some day produce as cheaply as the Americans do. And that is what will make Europe independent. Since we need more nuclear power plants than the Americans or the Russians, we are sure to be the gainers. We would manufacture more reactors than anyone else; therefore we would make the best and the cheapest ones. Within the next ten years, the atom will become the principal source of energy. We could equip Africa, South America."

The son of a professor from Savoy, Armand was a fanatic about the railways, where he made his career. He was the initiator of the Paris-Lyons-Marseilles run, just as Dautry was given credit for the Paris-Orléans run. A hero of the Resistance, he put all his energy into blowing up the railways and became an expert at it. A Companion of the Order of the Liberation, he proved just as vigorous, as head of the French state railways, in rebuilding and electrifying what he had demolished. He has been criticized for having neglected the canals, the arteries of the great industrial basins, because of his ardor for the railways.

But Armand has other qualities. He is a mustached encyclopedia, a prophet. He knows everything, understands everything, and he explains everything with an animation that makes the driest subjects interesting. He enlightens ministers, big businessmen, and duchesses. He is one of the most sought-after dinner guests in Paris and is also in demand by various boards of directors. No one equals him in the ability to explain, with the help of a salt shaker and a pot of mustard at a dinner table, chain reactions or the mysteries of genetics. He is equally brilliant on the subject of cybernetics and the location of oil wells in the Sahara. He would have been one of France's most brilliant writers had he had the time to devote himself to literary pursuits. He will become a member of the Académie Française for his studies on mineral waters, the maintenance of boilers, and Europe. The Institut de France hopes to obtain his memoirs.

Atomic energy found in him an extremely helpful promoter. In 1952 he was asked to become general director of the French Atomic Energy Commission, which was established in 1945 by de Gaulle on the suggestion of two men: Raoul Dautry, who became its first general director, and Frédéric Joliot-Curie, who headed the Commission. Organized along the lines of the Renault auto works, the Commission had a monopoly of atomic research for civil and military activities.

A scientist of worldwide fame, the pride of the Communist Party, Joliot-Curie could have played an important role in America during the war. He could have made his country an atomic power, thanks to his patents on plutonium and heavy water, which he and Dautry procured in Norway, much to the annoyance of the Germans. These patents were sent in tin cans to England, where they were immediately transferred to America by his collaborators, Halban and Kowarsky. Joliot refused to go to London in 1940; his wife, Irene, was ill. And his political convictions undoubtedly made him reluctant to go to the United States; besides, he probably would have encountered great difficulty in securing admission. Churchill tried in vain to convince Roosevelt that the Frenchman would make a priceless contribution.

As head of the Atomic Energy Commission, Joliot was not expected to produce an atomic bomb. He presided at the meetings of the Peace Congress, led the campaign against the Atlantic Pact, and urged the workers of the Commission to oppose any plans for nuclear armament. But he was dismissed in 1950. A new atomic policy had been adopted. Francis Perrin, Joliot's friend, was asked to take his place. At first Perrin refused, but finally accepted.

When Dautry died in 1951, the young Secretary of State, Félix Gaillard, began to look for a nonpolitical general director for the Commission. "Who is the most brilliant man in France?" he asked everyone. "Louis Armand," was the answer.

Armand was asked to see that the atomic undertaking would emerge from the ivory tower in which Joliot, because of his ideas, had placed it. He was also expected to obtain help from industry, which until now had been looked upon askance, and to obtain the cooperation of other countries. The Americans considered the Commission a Stalinist body, which made it difficult to obtain any help from them. Norway, who possessed heavy water, had proposed an exchange of information, a suggestion that Joliot rejected. Armand's task would be to get some form of European cooperation and to plan the eventual manufacture of an atomic weapon, should the government decide progress in atomic research made this possible.

Armand accepted these tasks in principle, looked around the atomic plant, and recommended the immediate creation of an industrial division. Then he went back to the railways, his passion. He put them in order and electrified them—a task in which the hero of the railways had no political battle to wage.

Pierre Guillaumat was appointed by the government to serve as assistant director. He was an engineer of talent, a graduate of the École Polytechnique, and the director of a motor fuel company. His father was a general who had been Minister of War, and his brother, a professor of ophthalmology, had de Gaulle as a patient. He was eventually to establish a nuclear industry and to make the Commission an increasingly important body. Correctly foreseeing the future decisions of the ministries, he launched the manufacture of the bomb, even before he became de Gaulle's Minister of the Armies on June 1, 1958.

What led Armand, after the rejection of the EDC in August, 1954, to advocate atomic weapons for Europe?

It was the beginning of the nuclear age, a turning point in history. The bomb that imposed peace on Japan in 1945 again played an important role in 1953 by ending hostilities in Korea. General Eisenhower was elected President of the United States on November 4,

141

1952, because he promised to end the war in Korea. Stalin died on March 5, 1953. The new masters of the Kremlin would not accede to Eisenhower's pleas to end the war. He got Nehru to warn the Kremlin through Peking that he would use the bomb. And on July 27, 1953, fighting ceased in Korea. (President Truman, too, together with General MacArthur, had from the very start of the war thought of blocking the North Korean offensive by threatening to use the bomb. But he had consulted his allies, who were horrified; they persuaded him not to use it. The Americans learned a lesson: A deterrent weapon cannot be used by a coalition. Only a state that alone possesses such a weapon can threaten to use it.)

Meanwhile, however, the world was living in fear. The Soviet H-bomb—with power to unleash the equivalent of a thousand Hiroshimas—was exploded in August, 1953. The Americans were readying their superhydrogen bomb to be exploded at Bikini on March 1, 1954. It was 14 megatons, equal in force to ten times the total number of bombs dropped on Germany during the entire war.

No one realized at that time that, paradoxically, this meant peace, at least between the two superpowers. An apocalypse—the two giants could not use this weapon without annihilating each other. This balance of terror made absolute atomic secrecy completely obsolete. The United States had insisted upon it after the war through the Mac-Mahon Law. But the law had disarmed only the Americans. The Soviet explosion had made a mockery of American secrecy. Confidential reports seemed to indicate that the Russians, who were one step ahead of the Americans militarily, were also ahead in the civilian domain. They were working on an electric power station that would provide energy and light for a city of 100,000 inhabitants.

Ironically, the MacMahon Law prevented a spurt in American industry. The atom was reserved for defense, whereas it could have become a huge industry concerned with the peaceful, scientific applications of the transmutation of matter—the most important industry of the next fifty years.

Eisenhower, "the good chap," as Churchill called him, was seeking a détente with the U.S.S.R. He also wanted to make arrangements with America's allies, especially the British, who were impatient to get off to a better start in the modern world, with the help of the atom. They hoped to remove the strings of secrecy that were tying their hands as well as those of the Americans. When Churchill returned to power, he made use of the Hyde Park protocol which he and Roosevelt had signed in 1945. It guaranteed Great Britain a privileged association with the United States in all atomic developments.

Early in December, 1953, Eisenhower met with Churchill and Joseph Laniel, the French Premier, in Bermuda. When Laniel learned that the two Anglo-Saxon leaders were accompanied by atomic experts, he decided to take Francis Perrin with him.

"No point in that," the British told him, "we won't be discussing nuclear affairs."

Actually, Francis Perrin, friend and successor of Joliot-Curie, would alarm the Anglo-Saxons.

"That Laniel doesn't realize what he's doing," the officials in London and Washington commented. "The idea of bringing a Communist to a Western summit meeting!"

"This was merely an excuse," Guillaumat said later. "I was the one who should have accompanied the Premier. But they didn't want to grant Laniel what they later conceded to Churchill."

A faulty air conditioner in Laniel's bedroom resolved the question of French participation at the Bermuda Conference. Laniel had bronchitis, ran a high fever, and was given penicillin.

Surrounded by their experts, Eisenhower and Churchill agreed to do away with atomic secrecy and to alter the MacMahon Law in three major ways: (1) To permit the creation of a private nuclear industry in the United States; to establish an Authority for Atomic Energy in England that would produce and sell reactors, electric power plants, equipment, and fissionable matter. (2) To authorize the transmission—to those allied powers that already had a headstart in atomic science—of the means with which to establish a military force. (This meant England, at that time, but it could apply eventually to other countries.) (3) To permit the sale abroad of reactors, patents, and fissionable matter that might serve peaceful ends. Supervision by the producing country would insure the peaceful utilization of these supplies.

The "progressive" allied powers that were building both atomic arms and power plants (at that time Great Britain alone was so engaged) were to be supervised with some indulgence. They could be the recipients of assistance without having to submit to inspection of their military activities. This tailor-made arrangement was for Churchill's benefit. Essentially, from the American point of view, this was a decision for big business to commercialize the atom.

Returning from Bermuda, the President of the United States proclaimed a balance of terror in a speech before the United Nations on December 8, 1953. "Even were it devastated by a surprise attack," he said, "the United States would still be capable of dealing a death blow to the aggressor." He proposed the partial demobilization of the atom, a world pool for atomic energy, an international agency that would receive from producing countries a monopoly of fissionable matter which it would then distribute equitably.

The Soviets kept putting off any formal acceptance of the offer. President Eisenhower was therefore impelled to enlarge upon his idea. His high-flown plan was called Atoms for Peace. The United States would make a direct transfer of reactors, techniques, and fuels, with instructions for their use. Their peaceful utilization by the buyers was to be controlled by the American government, pending Russian participation in an international agency to oversee sales and verifications, the future Vienna Agency.

When the MacMahon Law was changed in August, 1954, the French parliament was rejecting the EDC and the rearmament of Germany. Until then, atomic energy had been looked upon as a scourge. The Bikini bomb on March 1, 1954, had surprised and "atomized" the Japanese fishermen from a great distance. But now Eisenhower was discovering unknown aspects of the atom, its magical promise of energy and fuel for all the world. There would be no further need of coal, dams, or oil. Nuclear power would provide power and light everywhere. The underdeveloped countries could become industrialized. The popularizers waxed enthusiastic over the miracles of atomic mutation which would girdle the globe. The press and radio spoke of nothing but the benevolent atom. The balance of terror was beginning to make the cold war a thing of the past. The United States was secretly negotiating with the U.S.S.R. The two superpowers were destined to discover together some *modus vivendi,* the road to peaceful coexistence.

The rush of events gave rise to a variety of reactions in Paris. "If, since the explosion of the Soviet H-bomb, the Americans are afraid of seeing their cities razed," said many deputies, especially the Gaullists, "they may soon hesitate to use the supreme weapon to defend Europe. Hence, France must have her own nuclear force."

Voices in the National Assembly demanded that a French deterrent weapon be manufactured immediately. Public opinion resented the way Laniel had been shoved aside at the Bermuda Conference. Some felt that no country had international power until it had atomic power.

The removal of atomic secrecy aroused great hope among French atomic scientists. Perhaps a belated compensation could be obtained for the contribution Joliot-Curie had made through the patent he sent to England during the war. It had been transmitted to the United States through the good offices of Churchill.

Others said, "Let's take advantage of the American offer, in any case, to help us build reactors and a bomb. If they refuse us their direct aid, let's try to make some arrangement with England. We must hurry. Some day or other the United States might come to some understanding with the Soviets to preserve a monopoly of nuclear weapons for the two great powers."

General Crépin, at the Secretariat of National Defense, Colonel Ailleret, and General Buchalet urged the establishment on the Rue Saint-Dominique of atomic laboratories and military factories for the bomb. But the military men had no confidence in the Atomic Energy Commission. They charged that 67 percent of the researchers, technicians, and employees recruited by Joliot-Curie were Communist sympathizers or were influenced by Communism.

At the Commission, military projects aroused a clamor. Six hundred and sixty collaborators rebelled against the intention of the National Defense to start working on the bomb. Guillaumat, however, was determined to undertake the manufacture of this decisive weapon. He hurried over to the Minister of the Armies, Pleven, to defend the civil and military monopoly of the Commission, which entitled it to manufacture the bomb. He got his way. Committees to establish liaison with the army and navy were created. Their mission was to study one atomic missile and two atomic submarines which the government had not yet officially sanctioned.

The Communist members of the Commission did not renew their protests. The only conclusion to be drawn from this is that the Soviets saw no reason to object to French possession of atomic weapons. It foreshadowed insubordination within the Atlantic Alliance.

Bertrand Goldschmidt recounts in his book *Les Rivalités atomiques* that on December 26, 1954, Premier Mendès-France called a meeting at the Quai d'Orsay of the ministers and experts who either favored or opposed the idea that France should have atomic bombs. He was well aware, he said, of the gap between the atomic powers and the others, of the advantages France would derive from Adenauer's announcement in October that Germany would not attempt to acquire nuclear weapons. He had decided to launch a secret program for the manufacture of atomic bombs and submarines. But Mendès-France fell before he had a chance to implement his decision.

It was in this euphoric and expectant atmosphere that Armand began his crusade to persuade Monnet, after the failure of the EDC, that Europe needed atomic weapons. "We must see that Europe benefits from American offers of aid, from the promise of the United States to provide us with whatever we need for military and civilian purposes," he said. "No individual country, not even England, will benefit as much and as quickly as will a combination of several countries: France, England, Germany, and their neighbors. Vexed by the failure of the EDC, the Americans will welcome a European nuclear enterprise. They will be happy to see Europe unite to negotiate with them for deliveries of equipment and matériel." (Indeed, Washington quickly let it be known that Euratom would receive more American aid than the United States would have given to any one of the six countries.)

"Within ten years, Europe can develop a nuclear industry that will be two-thirds as powerful as that of the United States," Armand continued. "The Americans think they can sell reactors and fissionable material to the rest of the world [approximately forty countries were almost ready to become customers]. But the only serious buyers will be the industrialized countriès. The underdeveloped countries, having no industry, no scientific elite, might try to buy nuclear power plants, but they will not know what to do with them. Europe needs American aid in order to get started, in order to become the greatest producer of nuclear arms, of experimental reactors for its universities and scientific centers; it needs atomic power plants to compensate for the growing insufficiency of fuel."

Armand had another idea to sell Monnet. He was trying to convince French leaders that there was oil in the Sahara. As the president of a group of African industrial firms and as a promoter of oil prospecting in the Sahara, he was the first to claim that there was oil in South Algeria. He passed around to bureaucrats an obscure geology official's reports on prospecting. The geologist had been searching the Sahara ever since 1931, but his predictions had gone unheeded. Oil wells were drilled, but to no avail.

One reason no one paid much attention to this was the reluctance of the big French import companies to see oil gush from wells over which the Tricolor flew. A leading banker explained, "If there is any oil in Africa, you have to look for it in the bowels of the earth; but in Arabia all you have to do is to stick your cane in the sand and the oil gushes forth."

Armand wanted to internationalize the desert. It had no citizens, but he wanted all the adjacent countries to benefit from the oil concessions—Algeria, Morocco, Tunisia, Libya, Nigeria, and Mauretania. He suggested to Monnet that the oil wells in the Sahara might be operated in association with the Coal and Steel Community.

A little later, Armand enlarged on his remarks to the ECSC Council of Ministers. His plan implied great faith in an as yet uncertain wealth. Many new frontiers would have to be explored and many private interests interfered with. As a consequence, everyone preferred to find the oil first and then face the resulting complications.

Monnet believed that atomic energy as well as oil could be placed under the aegis of the High Authority of the ECSC. He was not enthusiastic about an EDC for atomic energy because the United States had already promised to insure the defense of Europe. Since Germany had renounced the possession of nuclear weapons, Monnet—the apostle of equality among the members of a united Europe—saw nothing but complications in a community in which all the states would have equal rights. He assembled his close advisers, Uri and Hirsch, at his farm in Houjarray. They seemed less than enthusiastic.

"The Six are poorly equipped for an atomic pool," Uri told him. "The only European nuclear power at present is England, and no one knows whether she will join Europe. Norway has a monopoly of heavy water. The precision tool industries are all in Switzerland and they will play an important role in nuclear installations. You have few resources of your own."

Monnet also spoke of a transportation pool. "We will have trouble with the maritime countries," Uri objected.

"Let's hear what the Germans think about all this," Monnet suggested. "We'll send for Ophuls."

Ophuls was an old friend. He was Germany's legal representative

147

in the preliminary negotiations of the ECSC. At first, he was a disappointment. "A transportation pool or an atomic energy pool," said Ophuls, "means we have to talk about railways and electricity. Unlike coal and steel, which are tangible industries, these are services. And so the first problem you'll encounter is that of developing a single tariff. Governments and industrialists, however, are very jealous of their prerogatives in such matters because questions of commercial policy play an important role in elections." He concluded by stressing that Germany, "especially Erhard, is interested neither in your transportation pool nor in your atomic science pool."

Disappointed at first, Monnet began to think out loud. "Transportation and atomic science, to my way of thinking, may be the beginning of economic integration."

"Oh, if you are thinking about economic integration, that changes everything," Ophuls answered without hesitation. "Then it's very likely that Germany will be quite interested."

Monnet immediately began to draft a text. European recovery, which would compensate for the failure of the EDC, received his close attention. As a matter of fact, the subject fascinated him. To get official action under way, Monnet decided to stir the public with a spectacular gesture. On September 9, 1954, he called a special meeting of the High Authority in Luxembourg. He tendered his resignation, justifying his action by a wish to "participate with total freedom of action and speech in the achievement of real and concrete European unity."

The text of his speech actually had less effect than he had expected. To begin with, it created no new situation, and it indicated that Monnet would not resume his freedom until February 10, the date when his mandate expired. His resignation was therefore not a resignation at all. Since the High Authority had five months' leeway, there was no need to hurry. Everything still hung fire.

Meanwhile, Monnet continued to sound people about his new plan, which would give infinitely broader powers to the High Authority than did the coal and steel pool and would create supranational mechanisms that could be decisive for the unity of the six countries of Western Europe: a transportation community, an atomic pool, a fuel pool, an economic community. He went to Bonn to talk to Adenauer about it, to Rome to talk to Saragat, and to Brussels to consult Spaak; he also talked to those politicians and union leaders who might share his hopes.

Monnet found the Germans very eager to join a European economic community but very wary of fuel and atomic pools. The coal magnates were worried. There was so much talk about the new era of uranium that they feared their mines would close and be replaced by nuclear power plants. The barons of big business were also hostile to the idea. An Atomic Authority seemed to them a monopolistic gimmick like the Communist-infested Atomic Energy Commission. It would prevent them from constructing German atomic power plants in association with the Americans. The large firms already foresaw the possibility of accords with the big American nuclear companies which were presently springing up as a consequence of the lifting of atomic secrecy.

Forbidden possession of atomic weapons, Germany had been raided by the Russians and the Americans for researchers. Leading businessmen felt that Germany had no interest in joining the costly atomic venture. The American nuclear kitchen would one day serve Germany its precooked dishes at far less cost.

Armand, nevertheless, clung to his idea of a European civilian and military atomic organization that would exploit all the possibilities of the modified MacMahon Law. He believed that France's military program, which had been started secretly, would require crushing expenditures and many long years if it were to be accomplished alone. With American help and British and German collaboration, it could be achieved very quickly and at far less cost. It could be developed into a joint atomic industry and become a European force. The fall of Mendès-France on February 6, 1955, offered an opportunity to organize a unified Europe. Mendès-France had been responsible for the failure of the EDC. He would not agree to a Western European union without England, and the British could not make up their minds to join the Continent.

Armand explained his ideas to the new Premier, Edgar Fauré. What the United States denied the French it would readily give to a United States of Europe. Fauré listened attentively.

"You might contact the OEEC," he advised. "England is a member. It is very important to gain her help. Within the framework of the OEEC, you could investigate Europe's requirements in regard to energy. This will interest the British."

But Fauré's cabinet pressed him to follow up the military program begun by his predecessor. The Gaullist ministers—Palewski, de Gaulle's former chief of staff, who was now in charge of atomic affairs, and General Koenig, head of the National Defense—were both determined to equip France with nuclear weapons. They backed Guillaumat, who had opened negotiations with the British Atomic Authority with an eye to getting British technicians to construct a factory in France for the separation of isotopes. France would then be able to produce uranium 235. Small amounts were needed by atomic power plants, and larger amounts for the bomb. Guillaumat had been well received by Professor John Cockroft and Lord Plowden, with whom the French atomic scientists had worked in Canada during the war. When the Mendès-France ministry fell, Guillaumat was in London with Bertrand Goldschmidt, awaiting an answer from Plowden and Cockroft. They handed him a comprehensive list of factories engaged in the work of separating isotopes. But they had to have the list back, they said. The American government had vetoed the delivery to France of any equipment earmarked for military use.

Guillaumat and the ministers who supported him hoped to begin preliminary research for the construction of an isotope plant. It would be an enormous undertaking, like America's Oak Ridge which had been built during the war in eighteen months, at the cost of hundreds of millions of dollars. Fauré counseled patience. "Let's wait a little," he said. "Something is under way in Europe."

In May, 1955, because of the bomb, Guillaumat's budget was increased from 40 to 100 billion francs. Work on the first Marcoule pile began. It was said that each of France's partners would have all kinds of good reasons for refusing to contribute to the joint effort. The Americans promised Belgium a share in the future exploitation of atomic energy in exchange for her uranium from the Congo. Italy, who had very little fuel of any kind, was impatient to buy fully assembled American reactors. The Dutch were buying Norwegian products, but on a very small scale. The German industrialists were hostile to the notion of "Europeanizing" the atom. England agreed with the United States in opposing the establishment of a separate French striking force. In any event, it was extremely difficult to create a pool for countries whose level of development varied so widely.

The French Atomic Energy Commission reacted guardedly to the idea of a European atomic organization. A nuclear EDC would mean the scrapping of the French atomic bomb. In the eyes of many French scientists, Euratom had all the earmarks of a rival shop. France's progress in nuclear research, all the efforts she had made to move ahead, would have been wasted. France was the only country in the Community that had made a considerable effort as early as 1945. Her budget for atomic research was several times greater than the total spent for this purpose by the other five countries combined. The government, everyone said, would not have enough money to finance both the work of the Atomic Commission and a European atomic program. The Commission, its bomb and submarines, would be sacrificed for a European bomb—if one were ever manufactured—or perhaps merely for a European nuclear industry run by the large private corporations.

Despite Armand's contention that a French military program would be best served by a powerful European nuclear industry, an Oak Ridge of Europe, opinion was divided. His plan depended on American assistance. The Gaullists and the extreme left claimed that this would entail the loss of French autonomy.

Actually, the Commission's first request for assistance met with little enthusiasm in Washington. In 1955, the Commission asked for 500 kilos of uranium 235 to power its submarines. The request was turned down although Switzerland and the Netherlands, who had made a similar request, each received 500 kilos. A little later, France was granted a few dozen kilos, but that was all. Moreover, Switzerland and the Netherlands were promised certain secret nuclear data— which they never received—that had been denied France. The French physicists therefore decided to block not only an atomic EDC but also any European Community devoted to the peaceful use of atomic energy, because such a body would be dependent on the United States.

"They had no idea of the invisible forces that were united to establish Euratom," Goldschmidt commented much later.

"I will organize an atomic Europe '*à la sauce Muette,*' or '*à la sauce Luxembourg,*' " Armand said at the time, meaning either with or without England. The OEEC, with headquarters at the Château de la Muette, housed the beneficiaries of the Marshall Plan; Luxembourg was the seat of the Coal and Steel Community of the Six.

Monnet's supranational ideas were not entirely to Armand's liking. The sovereignty of the communities, so dear to Monnet, had little appeal for the people—scientists and business tycoons—whom

151

Armand hoped to assemble in a sort of private club for the creation of a European atomic industry. "What a strange idea—for countries to be represented by their ambassadors at atomic councils," Armand said. "The ambassadors won't understand a thing."

England would never agree to relinquish her sovereignty. She had refused to join the ECSC and the EDC. Armand's contacts with the British at the Château de la Muette proved disappointing. Great Britain imagined herself to be on the threshold of a new industrial era, a second period of Elizabethan greatness. She would become, some Englishmen thought, the world's great supplier of reactors, patents, information, and fissionable material. New uranium deposits had just been discovered in Canada. A new method for extracting both gold and uranium from the sands of South Africa had also just been invented. The United Kingdom was ten years ahead of France and fifteen years ahead of the other European states. The British, therefore, saw nothing to be gained by forming a partnership with countries that lagged behind them but that might become rivals later. They rebuffed Armand's overtures.

This failure brought Armand back to Monnet, whose persistence held promise. Armand also turned toward Germany, whose participation he needed more than ever. He went to see Adenauer. The old man, already convinced by Monnet's arguments, was enthusiastic about a European recovery program and impatient to see it launched. A common market seemed an excellent idea for Germany. But an atomic pool? Very well, he would agree if it pleased the French, but he really saw no advantage in it. He had just relinquished, as Germany's spokesman, the right to possess nuclear weapons. Adenauer was extremely well informed about atomic research by one of his advisers who, although not himself a scientist, had kept in close contact with a number of scientists.

Armand tried to tempt Adenauer by painting a glowing picture of the benefits which nuclear science would confer on Europe. Possession of a European deterrent force, he said, was like having a gun in your own house instead of having to call your neighbor across the sea for help. Another argument, and one to which Adenauer was most responsive, stressed the need to become independent of the United States. It seemed to the Chancellor that it would mean the end of discrimination against Germany. His country would play a considerable part in the powerful European nuclear industry which, hopefully, would meet the challenge posed by the paucity of fuel throughout the world, particularly in Europe. This problem would become increasingly serious with the passage of time; because of Germany's technology and her manufacturing potential, she would certainly play an essential role. An isotope separation plant would bring in an enormous number of orders. With American assistance and with French cooperation in producing reactors for export and for European power plants, Germany would do better than England and as well as the United States in the world market. And the United States would not object to a European atomic force.

Adenauer allowed himself to be persuaded and was confident that he could overcome the opposition of the industrialists.

Shortly after his trip to Bonn, Armand received a visitor in Paris, a German minister who asked that his name be withheld. He came, he said, as a friend and wanted answers to the questions usually asked by the man in the street.

"Is there a great difference between military and civilian atomic energy? Are the differences comparable to the one between different kinds of airplanes? For instance, you can put bombs and guns in a large plane. It's a flying fortress. If you put seats in them instead, you call it a Constellation."

"Nonetheless, it's quite easy to distinguish between military and civilian atomic power," Armand answered. "If the uranium you add amounts to two point five percent, you get enough explosive power for an atomic reactor. But if the uranium added amounts to ninety percent, you have the explosive power of a bomb. But to get that much power is not so easy. In any case, it is very simple to control."

"Is it very difficult to manufacture a bomb?" the visitor asked.

"Atomic industry is very commonplace," Armand answered. "It's fifteen percent scientific skill and eighty-five percent technology. Give me the technology and I'll make a bomb for you whenever you wish."

"When do we begin?" the German asked.

Meanwhile, Monnet had been working strenuously to prepare the launching of his plan for the new communities. Uri had gone over the arguments with him ten times. Monnet planned to present the plan over his signature as the outgoing President of the High Authority of the Coal and Steel Community. At the last moment, he changed his mind. The plan would have far greater impact if it were sponsored by a government.

"International courtesy demands that governments pay attention to the proposals of a member state," he explained.

He therefore handed his project over to Spaak and asked him to become its official sponsor. A good politician, the Belgian Foreign Minister enlisted the cooperation of his Benelux colleagues Beyen and Bech. They agreed to join him in sponsoring Monnet's plan.

Spaak sent the Benelux memorandum to the other governments. Then he went to Paris to sound out Premier Fauré and Antoine Pinay, the Foreign Minister. Spaak was disappointed. "They're not very enthusiastic," he told Monnet.

At that time France's currency and finances were in a chronic state of crisis. Abolishing frontiers seemed like walking on clouds. Moreover, the Gaullist ministers in Fauré's cabinet were very cautious about any plan initiated by Monnet, the champion of the EDC.

When he learned about the reception given Spaak in Paris, Monnet told himself that he had been idiotic to resign the presidency of the Coal and Steel Community. He could have waged from within an effective campaign to broaden its scope. Although it takes governments a long time to make a move, he could have exerted a decisive influence on public opinion and on the various political parties. He had won a great victory of this kind before. In 1945 the German Social Democrats had voted against the coal and steel pool (against a hegemony, they believed, of the Ruhr magnates). In 1955 they had voted against the Defense Community (against a renascent militarism). Above all, they had been eager to oppose Adenauer, who was known to be hard on his opponents. But in Luxembourg Monnet had welcomed the Social Democrats and the union leaders and had completely converted them to the idea of an integrated Europe. He could have done likewise among the Six, he could have used persuasion to secure the appointment of a committee to establish a United States of Europe, thus putting pressure on the governments to follow the path of integration.

By virtue of his official position, at the very center of negotiations, he might have played a determining role. And as head of the High Authority in an enlarged Community, he could have become the architect of a genuinely unified Europe, whose stubborn initiator he was. So, after much hesitation, he withdrew his resignation in order to dramatize the urgency of European recovery.

But his gesture was poorly received in Paris. Fauré was neither a fanatic who favored the immediate creation of a United States of Europe nor a close friend of Monnet's. He had taken Monnet's resignation seriously. His Gaullist ministers insisted that he catch the ball before it bounced. They were determined to prevent Monnet from becoming the Emperor of Europe.

Fauré had taken great pains to persuade René Mayer to become a candidate for Monnet's post. The cabinet decided that France would support only a single candidate, René Mayer. And Monnet had put himself out of circulation by adding a new undertaking to the brainchild he had created: He had announced that he was devoting all his time to setting up an action committee for the establishment of a United States of Europe.

The project presented by the Benelux countries was made public on May 20, 1955. It was just in time. A Council of Foreign Ministers was called to meet at Messina on June 1. There was only one item on the agenda—finding a replacement for Monnet.

In spite of the lack of enthusiasm in Paris for an atomic pool, circumstances were exceptionally favorable for Spaak's proposal. After rejecting the EDC, France owed her neighbors some kind of compensation. Therefore Fauré gave his consent, in principle. Pinay, the Foreign Minister, discussed the matter at the Quai d'Orsay.

"First we should push the atomic pool," said the Mayor of Saint-Chamond. "But a customs union for the Six? French industries might be gobbled up by the Germans, if my tannery is any example."

Wormser commented, "France has just said no to the Defense Community; she can't say no to everything."

"I agree. But we must be careful."

At Messina on June 1, 1955, Professor Martino, the Italian Foreign Minister, proved a hearty host. Rector of the University of Messina, he was busily engaged in an electoral campaign. A successful conference would greatly enhance his prestige.

At four o'clock in the morning, the Council of Foreign Ministers voted to set up a commission of experts to explore the possibilities of establishing a United Europe. England was invited to join it in whatever capacity she chose.

René Mayer was appointed President of the Steel and Coal Community. He proved to be an excellent administrator. But Luxembourg ceased to be the political center of Europe. Only the affairs of the coal and steel industry would be discussed here. When Mayer left the presidency, the pool lost its effectiveness. The administrators did no more than seek a balance among the various political parties.

Monnet's friends were downhearted. He would no longer be the leader of the new venture that he had launched. But the plan that he had originated was to make him the unofficial, backstage orchestra leader of public opinion and of the major political parties of the Six. During his walks in the Luxembourg forest just before handing over the presidency to Mayer, Monnet conceived of a whole series of devices to further the cause of European unity.

He asked the presidents, the secretaries-general, and the leaders of political parties who were sympathetic to his ideas—the heads of free and autonomous parties (with the exception of the Communists) —to come to Paris and try to reach an agreement on the principles of the future of Europe. He asked them in the name of the organization rather than in his own.

Six months of travel, of encounters and negotiations were necessary to establish this wide-open conference. From the political and labor leaders Monnet won 34 followers, all of them strong personalities, people who could manipulate parliamentary majorities. The following were among the more important for France—Guy Mollet, Pflimlin, Maurice Fauré, Pinay, Pleven; for Germany—Willy Brandt, von Brentano, Kiesinger, and Barzel; for Italy—Fanfani, Moro, and Saragat; for Belgium—Biesheuvel. Labor supporters included Freitag, Cool, Bothereau, Bouladoux, Theo Braun, Pastore, and others. These names represented the Christian Democratic parties, the Socialists, liberals (some of the French radicals) and ten million workers.

"Your debate will not be publicized," Monnet promised them. "You will have complete and total freedom, including the privilege of contradicting yourselves. There will be no public announcement of your sessions, no press conferences. Only the text of the final motions in which you have all reached agreement will be published. But you must make sure that the motions you do pass are voted on in the parliaments."

This understanding gave Monnet a considerable, if unofficial, power in the six capitals. Through his supporters he continued to influence the various governments and affect their respective parliaments.

"I am leaving for Challes-les-Eaux tomorrow," Monnet said toward the end of 1955. "I've lost my voice because of all this talking."

156

XII

Nasser: Europe's Federator

THE Messina Council of Ministers charged Spaak with the task of drawing up plans for additional European organizations. He lost no time. On July 9, 1955, he called a meeting of experts of the Six at the Château de Val Duchesse, on the outskirts of Brussels.

There was no doubt about Spaak's fitness for the presidency of a United States of Europe. For a long time he had made his presence felt in idealistic European movements as a realistic idealist. As the founder of Benelux, he was the most outstanding of the federalists. His cordial handclasp was disarming. His shrewdness, belied by a jovial plumpness, was quite capable of unraveling the knottiest problems. In short, he was a man of goodwill. Of Swedish origin, he was born a Walloon but had a Flemish-sounding name.

Born at the beginning of the century, Spaak from his earliest youth was a militant Socialist but one who favored cooperation. Deputy mayor of Brussels at the age of twenty-two, Minister of Transportation at thirty-two, he became Foreign Minister at thirty-nine when the avalanche of panzer divisions sent the Belgian government scurrying to London. He was an extraordinary political figure. He was made Premier, but his large, plump figure in no way symbolized the country he represented. Belgium did not triple in importance after she joined Benelux.

It took him seven years to achieve a customs union of Holland, Belgium, and Luxembourg, but this accomplishment failed to foreshadow the coveted political union. Like the early history and stormy, communal life of the splintered Netherlands, the history of the Benelux countries was marked by the difficulties encountered in their attempts to achieve a federation. But this made Spaak all the more persistent in his efforts to achieve a unified Europe. Within a huge political and economic entity, the problems posed by Flemish particularism and the division over languages might very well disappear, or at least become attenuated; in any case, they would be submerged. The countries that were seeking association would export, among other things, their internal difficulties. This was certainly true for France and her agricultural problems.

Spaak became President of the Council of Europe, that "empty carcass," as de Gaulle put it. The Council was stripped of all authority by the compatriots of Churchill, who had sponsored it. Spaak resigned in protest against the failure of European reconstruction. He accepted appointment as Secretary-General of NATO, believing that it would provide the West with a ready-made military and foreign policy. The disconcerting reverberations of this illusion were dramatized in June, 1966, when he was forced to leave both his party and the government. His Socialist friends, opposed to the establishment of SHAPE in Brussels, marshaled an overwhelming majority against him.

But let us go back. For the moment, Spaak is the Foreign Minister, and a good one. His awareness of realities, his plump figure, his elegance and verbal agility—all these were assets. He often would say, "I ought to write a book, although I never will, on 'The Inevitability of the Politician's Incompetence.' A politician has his own ready-made personal remedies. He is incapable of listening to others and selecting the best solutions offered. He is incapable, too, of taking full advantage of the experts' inexhaustible imagination, of getting them to clear away the obstacles. A politician's first requirement is to have an open mind."

The Château de Val Duchesse was a medieval manor that had been restored. Recent improvements, however, had not exorcised one ghost. The presence of Jean Monnet, though invisible, was felt in every room, partly because his friends and associates were there. Monnet was eager to make sure that the future communities would not be stillborn or weak, like the EDC. So he pressured the delegations, showered them with proposals, and left no one in peace. He

158

had not been invited to join the group. Edgar Fauré's government, with all its Gaullist ministers, would not have dreamed of including him in the French delegation. Besides, his proper place would have been the one occupied by Spaak. But one of his incarnations was there for him—Pierre Uri, his familiar genius. Although he, too, had not been invited, he came in via the backstairs, as the director of the Coal and Steel Community. Luxembourg had not appointed him to represent the High Authority at the Val Duchesse. The German vice-president of the ECSC, Franz Etzel, and the Dutch delegate to Luxembourg, Spierenbourg, threatened to resign when they learned that Uri, who was self-appointed, had nonetheless joined the conference. The higher-ranking officials were also displeased by his presence.

A volcano of ideas, a brilliant writer, Uri had all the defects of his virtues. A graduate in philosophy, doctor of jurisprudence, Princeton scholar, Monnet's right-hand man on the Rue de Martignac as well as in Luxembourg, Uri had no patience with people whose minds worked slowly. He spoke so rapidly that it was difficult to follow his elliptical arguments, his iconoclastic and deliberately paradoxical train of thought. It was not easy to forgive him his tendency to poke fun. He got involved in everything, was the fly in the ointment. Some people accused him of being an intriguer. But each day he hit upon ten different solutions for one tricky problem and tossed them nonchalantly on the conference table; he was as indispensable as he was exasperating. No progress was made when he was absent. So he became a sort of permanent troubleshooter. Delouvrier admitted this to the Atomic Energy Commission. But Uri could not sit on two important commissions, the atomic pool and the economic union, nor could he attend a general assembly. Spaak, who valued this generator of fireworks, hid Uri under his chair, had Uri take notes for him, and allowed him to participate in the discussions—an anonymous voice emanating from behind his chair.

On September 6, 1955, President Spaak informed his foreign ministers and colleagues of the results of the first exploratory talks. The transportation pool was vetoed by the Dutch. The Dutch merchant marine and the river barges on the Rhine enjoyed a good deal of freedom. The Netherlands was cautious about the possibility of regulations like those that had hampered the French armaments industry. Rotterdam, the second-largest port in the world and about to become the largest, refused to accept any controls.

England also registered her opposition. The members of the British delegation had not said whether they were present as future participants or merely as observers. But their flag flew over all the waters. A pool with whom? And to do what? Nothing doing!

The other delegations considered the apparently unachievable integration of the railways. Each government wanted to manipulate its own rail tariffs. This would enable it to grant favors to certain regions or customers and to maintain tollgates.

The pool for conventional fuel—electricity, gas and oil—which Monnet had planned to add to his High Authority, also clashed with powerful interests. Private electrical companies did not want to be subjected to supervision by technocrats. Oil was an international matter.

All that seemed feasible was an economic market stripped of frontiers, and an atomic pool. The Common Market—a term coined by the Germans who were particularly interested in its creation—seemed a risky possibility to the other delegates.

One expert from the Benelux countries said there were enough problems for twenty-one years of debate. "It took us seven years to agree on three 'mini-economic organizations,'" he said. "To harmonize the economies of Germany, France, Italy, the Benelux, and perhaps England, we'll have to face the fact that it will take three times longer."

Euratom, on the other hand, was the star performer. It was the "pin-up" of the Val Duchesse, as its initiator, Armand, said. Its report to the OEEC caused a stir: A dramatic lack of fuel was threatening Europe. Only something as powerful as uranium could resolve the Old World's need for energy without exhausting appropriations by ruinous imports.

The plan excited everyone. The universe was witnessing an atomic fairyland. To celebrate America's willingness to dispense with nuclear secrecy, and to derive the maximum benefit for the universe from Eisenhower's gesture and the discussions on disarmament that he had opened with the Soviets, the Secretary of the United Nations, Hammarskjöld, organized the largest scientific congress in history. It was held at Geneva in August, 1955. (One month earlier, in the same palace of the defunct League of Nations, Bulganin and Khrushchev had outlined with their allies a plan for peaceful coexistence.) It was attended by 1,500 scientists; 1,000 papers revealing the secrets of fissionable material were distributed. It was a spectacular event. The Soviets were extremely proud of their first nuclear power plant in Obninsk, 100 kilometers from Moscow, and the Americans boasted of their first atomic submarine, the *Nautilus*.

In the spring of 1955 the British had published a White Book about their monumental projects. They announced that by 1975 they would double their fuel production, thanks to the nuclear plants now under way. They were preparing, with the aid of data from America, to manufacture an H-bomb. The French described their procedures for exploiting plutonium, and this stimulated the other atomic experts to tell about their work.

Thus, a mirage unfolded before world opinion: Atomic energy for everyday use, everywhere. The Soviets announced that they were about to alter geography, to change the course of rivers, and to move mountains. Ships would sail around the world, powered by matter that took up the space of a sardine can.

Ben-Gurion sent for Goldschmidt to come to Israel. He was to install nuclear power plants to pump water into the Negev, to improve vegetation, and to bring light and industry to the desert. Ben-Gurion wanted more reactors along the coast to desalt the sea water and change the course of the rivers.

The prophets of modern alchemy announced the transmutation of species, the production of enormous spikes and buds, of giant farmyard animals with accelerated growth potential. The atom would vastly increase harvests, preserve food supplies, distribute all this abundance, and enable medicine to make giant strides. The science-fiction magazines amused grown-ups and fascinated children.

Louis Armand, the moving spirit of the Euratom Commission at the Val Duchesse, employed all his charm to win over the French physicists to the cause of a nuclear Europe. But at that time the French Atomic Energy Commission was working at full speed. Guillaumat, its director, Palewski, the Gaullist minister instructed by Premier Fauré to look into atomic problems, General Koenig, Minister of the Armies—all had decided more or less secretly that France must manufacture the bomb. Pflimlin, the Finance Minister, authorized a large appropriation for this purpose. General Buchalet directed a Committee of General Studies. The cradle of the French bomb was set up on land purchased at Bruyères-le-Chatel in Seine-et-Oise without the official permission of the cabinet and before parliament had had a chance to debate the matter.

Toward the close of 1955, Armand, anxious to bring about a reconciliation between the Euratom Commission and the French scientific community, made a very tempting proposal to Goldschmidt, the director of foreign relations on the Rue de Varenne: the establishment of a European isotope separation plant, which would produce the enriched uranium so invaluable for perfecting the bomb as well as for future nuclear power plants. This was precisely what Guillaumat had vainly suggested to the British earlier that year. Armand suggested that Goldschmidt should become the director of this European undertaking by assuming the presidency of a union of the Six, a post to be created for this purpose. The undertaking would require 500 billion francs and the cost would be shared equally by the Six. Armand was sure that he could obtain assistance from Washington by pointing out that Euratom was about to be established. The project, like America's Oak Ridge, was colossal; it would be known as Pierrelatte.

"France must take advantage of her headstart to assume the leadership of Europe's great atomic industry," Armand said. "It will give the old country fuel at low cost and put it on the same footing as the United States. It will make Europe a great economic and military power. The Germans are reluctant because their power plants are in private hands and because they have been denied access to atomic power. But they can contribute what we need most: technology and a first-rate industrial potential. To win them over, we will have to make sure that they get big contracts."

But the French Atomic Commission remained unenthusiastic. Goldschmidt seemed in no hurry to assume the presidency of a European syndicate. The French physicists, who were trying to obtain from Washington small amounts of fissionable material and a few tips on how to exploit atomic energy for peaceful purposes, were convinced that the Americans would never accept a French nuclear force, not even an Anglo-French or European one. They knew that the Dutch were opposed and that the Germans were even more hostile to the idea of a factory for enriched uranium that would enable France to make the bomb. The Dutch and the Germans preferred to buy uranium 235 in the United States at a reasonable price.

"If there is not complete agreement about what to manufacture, how to manufacture it, and for what purpose, cooperation will merely result in waste and loss of time," Guillaumat warned.

Francis Perrin, of the French Commission, advanced a technico-political argument. "Euratom is about to be organized with the approval of the United States. American techniques will be important in Europe. It has been suggested that we set up an isotope separation plant in order to produce uranium 235, which we are unable to do at the moment. But the plant would have to rely on patents and supplies purchased in the United States or in England, and it would have to have American authorization and American licenses. We'd never be able to rid ourselves later of these patents and controls. It would be far better for France to go her own way in taming the atom, however slow and costly the process might be. Then she would achieve permanent independence."

This was the beginning of an intramural conflict. The French physicists preferred to pursue their own work on uranium and plutonium —they had mastered the technique—rather than to proceed, with foreign aid, to manufacture and utilize enriched uranium, which was an Anglo-Saxon and Soviet monopoly.

In answer to these arguments, Armand said, "It would be absurd for France to employ outmoded methods. Alone, we could never set up a great nuclear industry. But if other European countries would cooperate, it would certainly be possible, and this would rid us as rapidly as possible of the American monopoly. Otherwise, when our researchers finally arrive at the point already reached by the Americans and the British, they will be ten years behind them. Our power plants will be obsolete, unsalable, and surpassed by the most recent American models. The result will be a bomb that's fifteen years behind the times. But if we get American assistance plus, I hope, British cooperation and the technological and industrial potential of the Germans, we could, with our own know-how, catch up with the United States in ten years. And in the process, as we turn out better work, we'll discover new techniques which will insure our independence."

Val Duchesse received a shock in January, 1956. Unable to control an anarchical parliament, Edgar Fauré dissolved the French Assembly. Guy Mollet and Mendès-France made a pact: Whoever became Premier would name the other Foreign Minister. In either case, the atomic work currently under way would be threatened.

Mollet was an ardent Europeanist, the President of the Strasbourg

Assembly and, like Léon Blum, a friend of Monnet's. Mendès-France had condemned the ECSC and torpedoed the EDC. Champion of a free-trade area, he insisted that England must be part of any community undertaking. Yet the British balked once again at any supranational institution inspired by Monnet. It was plain that they stayed on at the Val Duchesse only out of curiosity, and that they would soon withdraw. Neither the Prime Minister nor the Foreign Minister would accept the idea of a Common Market dominated by Germany, or an atomic pool in which the German potential could achieve preponderance.

Monnet's efforts to launch a European recovery program, and all of Spaak's endeavors, were left hanging fire.

On January 18, 1956, Monnet called the first meeting of the action committee for a United States of Europe. About thirty parliamentary and union leaders were present. They had been carefully chosen because of their influence on large groups of voters. Among the French were Mollet, Pflimlin, Maurice Faure, and Pleven, who dominated the majority in the new French Assembly that was soon to convene at the Palais Bourbon.

The gathering Monnet had assembled in Paris was an attractive one. Monnet spoke in muffled tones. There were frequent interruptions. He fascinated the most blasé of politicians. His faith and optimism were disarming, and he lent force to the most basic ideas by incorporating them into the mechanisms of his plan. He gave his listeners—men with few illusions, inveterate skeptics—the feeling that they were the giants of a holy crusade, the new Knights of the Round Table. They would leave their mark in this world and change the face of the earth.

Monnet was a remarkably well-organized man. His apartment in Paris, 83 Avenue Foch, was a temple of discretion. His offices, furnished in English style with comfortable armchairs and brightened by his wife's luminous paintings, protected his guests from the outside world of newspapermen, rumor-mongers, enemy ears and, more dangerous and important, the ears of friends. Here, party leaders could meet their parliamentary adversaries without being accused of collusion. The Italian Christian Democrats, who knew their Socialist colleagues only through dissension in the Italian Assembly, discovered they were in basic agreement about European reconstruction. The

German Social Democrats had been opposed to both the ECSC and the EDC. Monnet rallied them to the cause of the new communities under discussion. They found themselves in accord with the partisans of Adenauer and Erhard. In regard to the rebirth of Europe, important union leaders found that they were on the same wavelength as the conservatives. Cooperation was a Monnet technique.

It would be necessary to create a parliamentary majority in each of the six capitals that would do its best to champion the cause of Euratom and the Common Market. In Paris the majority would have to fight strong opposition when the Assembly met at the Palais Bourbon. It would have to exorcise the evil spells cast by de Gaulle and Mendès-France and overcome disappointment over the EDC.

To accomplish this, the leaders of the six majority groups would have to be in agreement. They would present the plan to be voted on in their respective parliaments. No general report had as yet been drawn up at Val Duchesse. The Common Market had hardly been discussed; it was so complicated that it seemed an unrealizable dream. Monnet, Spaak, and Mollet were at one in thinking that it would not be possible for several years.

On the other hand, Euratom was discussed a good deal on the Avenue Foch. There it was the number one item on the agenda. The union leaders, the German Social Democrats, like the labor delegates at Brussels, were very hostile to a nuclear EDC and to the economic community of Louis Armand. The German Christian Democrats, despite the ambitions of the Rhineland industrialists, were in agreement with Monnet's formula: a supranational and exclusively pacific Euratom, with a monopoly of fissionable material.

The action committee's initial statement affirmed the need to carry out the plans made at Messina, and designated a Euratom for peaceful purposes as the highest priority.

It was Mollet who became Premier on February 1, 1956. He was one of the founders of the action committee. Instead of appointing Mendès-France as Foreign Minister, he named a Socialist who favored European reconstruction, Christian Pineau.

"Should we create a European industry to manufacture atomic bombs, something that cannot be done on a national level? My answer is no. Whoever possesses the explosive material is in a position to make the bomb. The government will demand that Euratom be given

165

exclusive possession of all explosives," Mollet said just before the opening debate in the new French Assembly. The French Atomic Energy Commission's efforts were not, however, interrupted because of this statement, nor was it deprived of appropriations.

To the general responsible for the manufacture of military weapons, Guillaumat said, "One day, my dear Buchalet, we'll have to get a wheelbarrow, put the bomb in it and trundle it to the Hôtel Matignon. We'll never get the authorization to manufacture it beforehand."

After the opening debate in the Assembly, General de Gaulle, impressed by the concern voiced in the Atomic Commission, went to visit the laboratories at Saclay. He warned those in charge against relinquishing their independence, reminded them of their duties to national defense, and cautioned them against allowing their efforts to become subordinate to Washington's desire for an American-Soviet monopoly in nuclear science.

Armand was indignant. "De Gaulle has been fooled. It's the treachery of the intellectuals! The men on the Atomic Commission are experts on whom the government relies. They and de Gaulle are sabotaging the game. They ought to bring it up at Brussels. They are completely disregarding the benefit our country will derive from a great European industry. They're thinking only of their own military plans."

But the last card had not yet been played, in the opinion of Armand. Monnet, too, was pushing things, leaving nothing to chance, for fear that there would be a repetition of the EDC fiasco. His friends were in key positions in Paris and in Brussels.

The head of the French delegation to the Val Duchesse, Félix Gaillard, was his young companion from Charente, a former general of the Monnet Plan, the youngest Premier of the Fourth Republic. The most active experts included Delouvrier, a former colleague of Monnet's. His former right-hand man, Marjolin, was at the Quai d'Orsay as "community adviser" in Pineau's cabinet. Maurice Faure, the Secretary of State in the Foreign Ministry who supervised the blueprinting of the new communities, was a rising young radical, but already a familiar voice in the Strasbourg Assembly. Monnet had personally indoctrinated Faure. He had also acquainted him with the diplomatic circles that favored a unified Europe. The Premier's chief of staff and the future Secretary-General of the Economic Community, Emile Noel, was an ardent champion of European integration.

While the experts were fumbling their way through the fog of the innumerable problems connected with the Common Market and Euratom, Monnet tested his "machine to prefabricate parliamentary majorities." The action committee's motion was put before the parliaments of the Six. Five of the parliaments voted in favor of it by overwhelming majorities.

The text was presented to the French chamber on June 5, 1956. But in Paris there was no chance of massive support. A battle had begun over Euratom. Communists opposed to an integrated Europe, Gaullists, Independents who favored nuclear arms—all rose up as one against the atomic pool. They demanded a unilateral renunciation of the bomb, leaving a monopoly of deterrence to the superpowers.

The battle began amid great confusion. Champions and opponents of the project juggled in the corridors with kilotons and megatons, fission and fusion, plutonium and uranium 235, with an ease that dismayed the atomic physicists who had come to listen to the debates.

Premier Mollet's trump card was objectivity. Resorting to tactics not commonly followed in the Assembly, he invited both Perrin, the physicist representing the Atomic Energy Commission, and Armand, the promoter of Euratom, to speak. Although this intellectual duel seemed to proceed in a calm and reasonable manner, an expert could detect the contradictions, the thrusts and parries.

Perrin delivered a remarkable speech on the procedures involved in atomic science, pleading that the movement for international collaboration should not be allowed to destroy the efforts which France had made for so many years to acquire knowledge of atomic energy. Only once did he allude to Euratom. "France would suffer a partial setback if she acquired low-cost atomic energy in fifteen years and if all the atomic equipment were made by Dutch, Swiss, or German factories. . . ."

"He talks as if that's not exactly what will happen if we refuse to set up Euratom," one opponent snorted.

Armand's speech dealt with the advantages of cooperation. The sum total of American investments was equivalent to one hundred years of the sum which the French budget set aside annually for this purpose. Armand concluded, "If we do not have Euratom, every European country will have to buy its material from the two superpowers. That would be the end of our independence."

167

"In that case, we might as well sell our entire future to the Americans right away," a Communist deputy grumbled.

Armand's oratorical ardor won the day; it proved more effective than Perrin's technical remarks. It looked as if there would be a majority in favor of an atomic Europe.

The stumbling block, however, was the surrender of nuclear weapons. Mollet shelved this question by changing his position and opposing the Monnet committee's recommendations. He revealed that the scientists were already working on a bomb. He would veto, he said, any treaty restrictions on France's freedom in the nuclear domain. No government had declared that France alone should abandon plans to acquire nuclear arms. The United States and the U.S.S.R. were not renouncing the possession of atomic weapons, and England had just acquired a few. As long as other countries had the right to manufacture bombs, France would not give up her right to have them. However, Mollet did promise that no bombs would be tested until 1961.

"An affirmative vote will obligate the Assembly to ratify the two treaties," Mollet said.

Adherence to Euratom was voted by a large majority. This did not in any way affect the rights of the French Atomic Energy Commission. The Common Market, which aroused less interest, received a much smaller majority.

"There are several reasons for this," said one of the leading experts. "First of all, Euratom is a French invention which Paris regards as sound and highly important."

"Let's not fool ourselves," Mollet insisted, as he gave his instructions. "Euratom is a huge undertaking."

For the members of the French delegation to Val Duchesse, the Common Market was the price that had to be paid to obtain the membership of France's partners, especially Germany, in the Atomic Community. In discussing the Common Market, many factors were passed over very rapidly because no one really believed that it was feasible. The financial and economic situation in France was so bad that the abolition of frontiers seemed unthinkable for many years to come.

For the Germans, the very opposite was true. The Common Market was welcomed by them whereas Euratom was a bitter pill that had to be swallowed.

Moreover, in this procedural exchange, there was a certain tactical Machiavellianism. Because of public opinion in France, the less said about the abolition of customs the better. This foreshadowed the end of the good old protectionist days, the old, easy, nationally independent way of life. It would bring problems, occupational dislocation, and national confusion. Mastery of the atom, on the other hand, augured a golden age. For Europeans, especially the French, it meant a return to power.

A report from the Coal and Steel Community—René Mayer had always supported Jean Monnet in his plans for European reconstruction—laid the question of Euratom squarely before the Six. The report stressed that a fourth of the world consumed seven-eighths of the energy produced on the planet. The beginning of industrialization in the underdeveloped countries would bid up the cost of oil. In fifteen years the oil supply might be depleted.

"The oil reserves would last only fifteen years," Armand explained. "This was an error due to the excessive cautiousness of the big oil companies. When they discovered a new deposit, they did not exploit it immediately, thinking they still had fifteen years before the oil reserves would be depleted. These fifteen years were constantly being extended."

The report made a strong impression on the Six, especially on countries that were experiencing monetary difficulties. For example, France, Italy, and Holland had to pay for their oil imports in strong currency, of which they had little. Euratom seemed to them an increasingly urgent necessity.

On September 20, 1956, the Monnet committee made a proposal that called for ratification of the treaty before the close of the year. Three Wise Men were designated by the Six to work out how much power was needed in the atomic power plants of Western Europe: Louis Armand, Franz Etzel, the German member of the Coal and Steel Commission, and Francesco Giordani, a professor of theoretical physics who had done an extraordinary job as organizer of state industries in Italy. Their report assessed the enormous needs for energy by 1970: 570 billion kilowatts plus twice the present consumption.

Armand took his two colleagues to the United States to see what they could obtain from the Americans. They were given a rather cold reception by the atomic industries. They were customers, but it was plain that they would soon be competitors. On the other hand, President Eisenhower's highest officials received them with open arms. A European atomic pool would spare Washington France's demands that she be given royalties for her scientific contributions; Belgium's reminders of the promises made to her in exchange for the Congolese uranium she had contributed during the war; Germany's embarrassing claims; Italy's plaints of poverty; Holland's needs, and so on. Since Euratom would have a monopoly of fissionable material in Europe, there was every reason to believe that controls would be instituted to insure that atomic energy was being used exclusively for peaceful purposes.

"I must be frank with you," said Armand. "I cannot guarantee that we will not manufacture the bomb."

"A European bomb? We would have no objection to that," was the answer from the White House.

This ready acceptance left the French physicist skeptical. Nevertheless, the Three Wise Men returned to Brussels with the feeling of having won a great victory.

"We obtained American aid for the creation of a powerful nuclear industry," Armand recounts. "An isotope separation plant, to begin with. This represents a further concession, despite the MacMahon Law. And instructions have been given to the American industrialists to furnish us with fissionable matter, equipment, and technological data. Euratom will control the use that is made of American supplies to make sure that they are employed for peaceful purposes. We will even have the right to do away with controls should a nuclear Defense Community be established in Europe. And finally, we secured 60 billions francs' worth of uranium at a very low cost."

But Armand, back from America with these royal gifts, got a cool reception from the French Atomic Energy Commission. Many of the French atomic scientists claimed that the bitter gifts from America would only deprive France of her bomb and her nascent atomic industry. "Euratom was set up for the benefit of Germany," de Gaulle commented.

"Germany has the lion's share of Europe's nuclear industry and this will compensate her for having been denied nuclear weapons," the Gaullists explained.

"France has to get this organization under way," Armand repeated in Paris. "She will head it. We must show the Germans that we are broad-minded by laying the foundations for a vast European industrial undertaking in which the Germans will receive a considerable share of the orders."

It was very important to obtain Germany's cooperation in European industry because the British were raising all kinds of objections at Val Duchesse. They wanted a cloistered Common Market, refusing to allow the Germans any of the advantages they themselves would derive from free trade. The atomic pool did not tempt them at all. They had no desire to tie themselves to people who were so far behind them but who could become competitors. But above all, Great Britain could not accept the idea that part of her sovereignty would be sacrificed to joint supranational authorities. Yet the negotiators at Val Duchesse, influenced by Monnet, held that supranationality was essential.

"What you need is not a community but a free-trade area," Uri told the British. "It could come to some understanding with a continental Common Market."

Subsequently, a British diplomat told Uri: "You gave us the idea of the Free-Trade Area of the Seven."

So ambiguous and perplexing was the British attitude that one day Uri came out from behind Spaak's armchair. He asked, "Have you come to the conference table merely to advise us or do you intend to participate in the bodies we are planning to set up?"

No definite answer to this question was given until November, 1956. Then Maudling, the head of the British delegation, said he was pulling out. "I am not in the habit of wasting His Majesty's money. And that's what the United Kingdom is doing by its presence at this table. You have become entangled in something so complex that you'll never extricate yourselves from it. And even if you should, the mass of regulations and institutions do not interest England. I no longer belong here. I'm going back to the Board of Trade."

An historic event was to change the entire nature of things. Suddenly, to Europeans, atomic energy seemed the only road to salvation. On July 26, 1956, Nasser, who was quarreling with the United States, nationalized the Suez Canal. Henceforth, for Europe, the transport of oil would depend on the goodwill of the dictator, and he was arming the Algerian rebels. Guy Mollet and Anthony Eden had secretly planned an expedition to Egypt. The Anglo-French landing in Port Said was blocked thirty-six hours later by Bulganin and Khrushchev, who threatened that the Soviets might drop bombs on London and Paris.

That very night Chancellor Adenauer was at the Hôtel Matignon with Mollet and other leading statesmen. "Tell me," Mollet asked Guillaumat, "is your bomb nearer to completion than people think?"

"Unfortunately, no."

"Ask your ambassador in Washington if you can still count on the American umbrella," Adenauer advised.

The landing at Port Said took Eisenhower by surprise. It occurred on the eve of his reelection. Secretary of State Dulles replied that the American umbrella would be closed if the offensive against Cairo did not cease immediately. This was the first crack in the fabric of the Atlantic Alliance.

Paris bitterly resented this demonstration of French military impotence. The government felt that the only possible retort to such humiliation was the acquisition of atomic autonomy. On November 30, an interministerial protocol, signed by Bourgès-Maunoury, the Minister of National Defense, and Secretary Guille, instructed the Atomic Energy Commission to manufacture and explode the first French bomb and to build a factory for the separation of isotopes in order to produce the necessary explosives—unless, of course, a European factory was to be built.

Louis Armand was indignant. The Americans had promised him a European factory. He interpreted the protocol as proof that the French Atomic Energy Commission wanted to torpedo Euratom.

Meanwhile, the Suez Canal was blocked by the ships that had been sunk in it. Gasoline stations in Europe had no motor fuel to sell and the factories had no oil. Nasser had succeeded in convincing Europeans of their terrible paucity in vital resources.

. The Six decided to hasten negotiations, which had been dragging on. Mollet's cabinet was tottering, and the shadow of Mendès-France was once again emerging from the corridors of the Palais Bourbon, a fact that brought consternation to the negotiators.

Two committees of experts were charged with the drafting of the Common Market and the Euratom treaties. Guillaumat presided over the Euratom Committee. He was better disposed toward the Atomic Community than had been anticipated, but he still favored a European institution headed by France that would give her permission to manufacture her own weapons. There seemed to be no solution to the contradiction between an exclusively pacific Euratom (with reservations, depending upon future developments, which Armand was counting on) and French military plans. The Quai d'Orsay attorney, Vedel, managed to resolve the impasse magnificently by a text that gave Euratom a monopoly on fissionable matter but gave each country a free hand in managing its own affairs.

The French favored a joint organization to prospect for uranium. Go ahead, they were told. But when the question of financing it arose, they found that there were no subscribers.

"The extraction of uranium is something that is of interest to France," the others maintained. "Trapped by their obsolete natural uranium reactors, the French researchers are using only 1 percent of uranium. They're making a frightful mess of nuclear materials. They want European supplies in order to escape American control; the United States insists that whatever it provides must be used solely for peaceful purposes. Well then, let them pay for their own follies."

The French Atomic Energy Commission had been told to build its own Oak Ridge—Pierrelatte—if there were not to be a European Oak Ridge, although it still remained a possibility. The isotope separation plant was to be, according to Armand, the crowning achievement of Euratom. It would open up enormous resources of energy to be used for peaceful purposes. It also would be a means of acquiring, at far less expense, a European army—should circumstances be propitious—or at any rate, modern French weapons.

But the French persisted in their desire to build their own Oak Ridge according to their scientific data, so that they would never again be subject to an American interdiction. They felt that the freedom to use enriched uranium produced in Europe was of major importance.

The Germans opposed an expenditure of 500 billion francs. The Americans were willing to sell their uranium much cheaper, provided it was used solely for peaceful purposes. Since the Germans had no right to possess nuclear weapons anyway, they preferred to buy their merchandise at the lowest possible price.

The French experts were scandalized. Paris had agreed to the Common Market in exchange for Euratom. But when the time came to draft the treaties, the Germans refused to share the cost of Euratom.

"At least, let's not build an Oak Ridge. It's already outmoded and has been abandoned," the Germans said. "Its method of gaseous diffusion is frightfully expensive. Our atomic scientists are very advanced in the gas centrifuge process. This is much cheaper and the operation is more economical."

"In ten years you'll no longer be using centrifuge gas," the French replied. (They were right.)

"But if France works alone it will take her ten years to build her old-fashioned factory for enriched uranium," Armand demurred. "If we get help from the Americans, we can build a modern factory in two years."

"But we'll be paying for the patents forever," the experts on the Atomic Energy Commission objected. "And we'll still be subject to American control."

The discussion dragged on until 1959 when the idea of a European factory was finally dropped.

"It was Louis Armand, influenced by Monnet, who gave up trying to persuade our partners to set up a truly European isotope separation plant," the Parisians said. "Euratom would have been nothing but an empty carcass without that plant."

"Since no one wants Euratom, let's do something else," Armand said. "Let's begin European unification with something that's new. Let's not include uranium, fissionable material, or reactors in the list of dutiable items because we haven't got them yet. Every month a new scientific institute is founded in Europe, or some chair is established for a brand-new subject. Let's decide that these institutes, these chairs, will be part of a new Europe. They are not yet part of any special administration, and they have no national budget. Why don't we say that every new type of plant and every new product, liberated from national regulations and tariffs, will become part of reconstructed Europe and will be governed solely by European legislation. In twenty years everything of any importance will be European, yet not a single law or administrative service will have to be changed.

"A scientific, technological, and industrial community will have been created without any effort. And European education, free from national bias, will emerge. The new generation will be a European generation."

The Germans were seduced by the idea. A European education that taught European history and European geography seemed to them a good thing. The faculty would be European.

174

But the French were shocked, especially the Gaullists. French culture would be stifled. "Dante, Goethe, and Chateaubriand belong to Europe only insofar as they are respectively and eminently Italian, German, and French," de Gaulle commented. "They would not have served Europe very well had they been men without a country, or had they written some kind of Esperanto or Volapuk."

The finance ministers shook their heads. All that was left of this mirage in the Euratom treaty was the European University of Florence. The Mayor of Florence, La Pira, who was quick to seize upon brilliant or spectacular ideas, had slipped it into the treaty.

Guillaumat wrote into the treaty two five-year plans, with a budget of $225,000,000 and $425,000,000 respectively. The allotment of appropriations caused a furor among the scientists, academicians, and diplomats. They quarreled like fishwives. Each administrative service wanted subsidies for its laboratory. Every country wanted its slice of the cake. There had to be an end to this.

Spaak had already charged Uri with the task of sorting out the pile of notes accumulated by the experts. Uri was aided by a German, von der Groeben, a Belgian, Hupperts, and an Italian, Grazzuli. Spaak gave Uri two weeks to draft both treaties.

"It's impossible to work in Brussels," Uri said. "There's nothing but a series of interruptions. The telephone calls slow up everything. We're leaving. And no one is to follow us."

The four man escaped to the Grand Hotel in Saint-Jean-Cap-Ferrat. The final report, which was a preliminary draft of the treaty establishing the European Economic Community (the Common Market), was drawn up in twelve days. The text for Euratom was entirely dictated by Uri between seven o'clock in the evening and three o'clock in the morning.

Exhausted, the four men separated. Uri went skiing at Mürren to recover from the strain. But a phone call from Brussels informed him that the Germans were demanding a change in the text. Uri's colleagues arranged to meet in Zurich, the most central place for all four men. The final touches were put to the treaties at a place that was outside the Europe of the Six. Uri returned to Mürren. Exhausted, he had an accident and broke a leg.

"Finally, he'll have to rest," people in Brussels said with a sigh of relief.

The government heads and the foreign ministers of the Six met at the Hôtel Matignon on February 16, 1957. The impatiently awaited draft treaties were read to them. Spaak beamed.

"I have come here with high hopes," he told Adenauer.

But there were further difficulties. The French insisted that the proposed Common Market must include agricultural products. Her partners frowned. The fruits and vegetables of Les Halles were going to create complications. Finally, France's partners accepted two additional pages of text in the hope that they would be forgotten.

The French also demanded a preferential tariff for the tropical products shipped in from their former colonies. Again there were frowns. The British, alerted to what was going on, sent two officials to the Hôtel Matignon on February 18. They declared that Great Britain was opposed to the entry of overseas territories into the continental market. Mollet bristled. The colonial products were included.

The French made still another demand: The signatories of the treaty must contribute to a fund for the development of former European colonies.

"They want us to pay for their neocolonial venture while they are continuing to fight in Algeria," the others grumbled.

But Adenauer insisted that this provision be accepted. Spaak did likewise: He had the Congo to worry about. France's partners agreed to this final concession.

On March 25, 1957, the Euratom and Common Market treaties were signed in Rome, on the Capitoline hill.

Monnet was not present at the birth of these twins. He had played no official role in this new Europe which owed so much to him. But his penchant for secrecy was satisfied. He had no need for notoriety. Behind the scenes he could pull the strings all the more effectively.

"We ought to erect a statue to Nasser," Armand said at the ceremony. "To the federator of Europe."

XIII

Euratom

"DURING the discussions on Euratom an extraordinary opportunity was suddenly offered Europe," Armand recounts.

Professor John Cockroft, the Nobel Prize winner (in 1932 he had achieved the first nuclear fusion, the first artificial transmutation) and the scientific director of the British Atomic Authority, published a communiqué. In his experiments, he had detected one neutron whose action was different from that of all the others. This was the beginning, he claimed, of the taming of the hydrogen atom.

"It was more than an ordinary discovery," Armand contends. "Uranium had been controlled. A bomb had been made from it. Knowledge had been acquired on how to use it in motors and in power plants. But hydrogen was different. The fusion of the heavy hydrogen atom was achieved by using a uranium bomb as a match. This was the H-bomb, a thousand times more powerful than the A-bomb. But the power of the hydrogen atom—like that of the sun, fire, and stars—had not been mastered.

"Uranium is to be found in deposits unevenly distributed throughout the universe: These deposits might perhaps become depleted half a century from now. Besides, they are almost entirely controlled in the free world by the United States.

"Heavy hydrogen—deuterium—is in the sea, in ponds; it runs in your water taps. One molecule of water out of 8,000 is a molecule of heavy hydrogen.

"If Cockroft is telling the truth, people thought at that time, the entire atomic technique would have to start from scratch. The Americans and the Russians would no longer be ahead of the Europeans.

"Moscow and Washington reached an agreement: Together they would domesticate the power of hydrogen. The stakes were fantastically high, but the difficulties seemed insurmountable.

"The problem was to imprison a sun within walls that would not melt. The ball of fire lasts only a few thousandths of a second. But it must be kept at a safe distance from the walls. One solution was to use electromagnets, but their power was woefully inadequate.

"Then a second miracle occurred. A researcher who, by chance, had mixed tin with niobium discovered a new property of electromagnets. One kilo of this amalgam possessed the power of two tons of conventional alloys. If the electromagnets were maintained at absolute zero (−273 degrees), it would be possible to manipulate the fusion of hydrogen.

"Suddenly the Russo-American accord disappeared. The harnessing of hydrogen could be mastered by any of the big powers. And Euratom was one of the big powers.

"In 1958, however, honest John Cockroft issued another communiqué. His 'wandering neutron' was an illusion. The control of the solar energy that runs out of a water tap was postponed. Rand Corporation estimated that methods to control hydrogen would be discovered around the year 2000, just in time to take the place of uranium."

This dazzling mirage that illuminated the beginning of Euratom was in a way the symbol of Euratom itself. It had been launched by the Suez crisis and the dramatic shortage of energy. Now there was abundance. Washington subsidized the reequipment of American coal mines. Large-tonnage ore ships were launched to prepare for the transportation of equipment to deposits in Africa. Freight charges on the Atlantic fell to $4 per ton. American coal arriving at Le Havre and in the Ruhr cost less than the coal in the local pitheads. The Suez Canal had been reopened. Giant oil tankers emerged from the shipyards. Mollet opened up the Sahara to prospectors and instituted the REP (*Sociétés de Recherches et d'Exploitation Pétrolières*). Everywhere there was drilling. Gas poured over the Dutch river banks. The price of oil, gas, and especially coal, indeed of all fuel, fell.

Nuclear power, which, amid the euphoria of 1955, was thought

178

to rival water power, fuel oil, and coal, was no longer profitable. The grandiose British plan, achieved over a ten-year period, proved a waste.

Westinghouse and General Electric, America's pioneers in industrial atomic energy, scattered experimental reactors and power plants of various kinds all over the country without finding any buyers.

Louis Armand had been right ten or fifteen years too early. On January 1, 1959, when Armand assumed the presidency of Euratom, General de Gaulle, who had been in power for six months, was settling down in the Elysée Palace.

"He found himself in the midst of two communities that were about to blossom," Armand said. "Euratom entailed association with America, while the Common Market was to provide protection against American industry. De Gaulle's attitude toward both organizations was entirely predictable. Scientific, technological, and industrial cooperation with the United States would have enabled Europe to make up for much of the time lost. Anti-Americanism has lost us years.

"The mistake made by the French physicists who opposed Euratom was to believe that the Americans would prevent the development of a large-scale European nuclear industry in order to slow down the rearming of France. It is true that Euratom was breathing down their necks. But Eisenhower and his associates proved very generous toward the delegation of the Three Wise Men."

"It is true that for six months Washington had opened up a new era of generosity toward Europe," said Guillaumat. "The White House felt the need to offset, with the help of the Old World, the lightning progress made by the Soviets in the domain of nuclear and spatial research. (Oppenheimer publicly maintained that there could be no balance or peace in the world as long as the United States refused to share its secrets and arms with its allies.)"

President Eisenhower was remarkably broad-minded. He promised France an atomic submarine, all kinds of help, and nuclear material. But the United States Senate very quickly opposed Eisenhower's generosity. Only Great Britain was treated as a privileged ally, but not for long. The United States soon did everything it could to deprive the British of any nuclear advantages. France never received what she had been promised. The principle of a Soviet-American monopoly and of the nondissemination of arms had been laid down.

In December, 1957, Guillaumat met a very important Washington official at the Hôtel George V (perhaps Secretary of State Dulles). He mentioned the explosion of the British H-bomb, which apparently had not entirely pleased the White House. "But their bomb surely did not bother you as much as the Soviet bomb?" Guillaumat asked.

"Neither more nor less," he was told.

Gauillaumat asked him for the enriched uranium that was needed to power the French atomic submarine. "We have been promised it. I have to calm down the navy."

Enriched uranium might also be used to manufacture the bomb. The American refused.

"We'll make our own someday, anyway," Guillaumat said.

"Try it," the American said with a smile. "I'll be there to shout *'Vive la France!'* "

Louis Armand and Max Kohnstamm, a Dutchman, negotiated the Euratom accord with the United States. It was to be signed on August 25, 1958. There was no longer any question of American assistance for the isotope separation plant that was to have been the prize possession of the atomic pool.

The five partners of France no longer asked for American aid because they had been counting on American supplies at low cost. And the French physicists did not want it because the only way they could be sure of getting enriched uranium which they could use as they pleased was to build their own national plant. Besides, de Gaulle had just opened wide the taps for appropriations. Washington had no desire to help Europe create a nuclear industry to be used for both civilian and military purposes. The American firms that were selling uranium power plants quite naturally preferred to preserve for themselves as much explosive material as possible.

In the domain of peaceful uses of atomic energy, the treaty offered an abundance to the Europeans: electric power plants at reasonable prices to the Italians, who were hungry for energy; large quantities of fissionable matter at low cost for the Germans, who were in a hurry to go to work with the Americans, and for the Belgians and French, who would share the plant at Chooz on the Franco-Belgian frontier.

Through Euratom, France obtained twice the amount of atomic explosives she had received from the United States through accords that had been previously granted the European states and that were not going to be renewed.

Armand secured privileges of major importance for the Six. Henceforward, control of the use of fissionable material would not be exercised by the United States or by the Vienna Agency, acting on behalf of the United Nations, but by Euratom itself.

In Brussels, Euratom President Armand tried to broaden the first Euratom plan. But the atomic pool was different from the one he had planned: a scientific, technological, and industrial understanding between the French, the Germans and, if possible, the English, to build together a great nuclear industry. Armand had hoped that with the help of the Americans, they would join to construct power plants, atomic ships, adding machines, and large planes. But the enthusiastic cooperation that he had expected to elicit from scholars, researchers, engineers, and industrialists, cutting across national frontiers, had not materialized. He had hoped that by the year 2000 Europe would be able to catch up with America.

Perhaps Armand's great mistake was to have believed that the atom, because it was not as yet controlled by generals or industrialists, was an ideal instrument for European cooperation. But the atom, with its Ali Baba cave, its reserves of political and military energy and power which had scarcely been tapped, raised ambitions to a high peak. It created among governments, industrialists, and researchers a feeling of envy and a desire to monopolize the new power. The atom was the number one industry of the future. It was an instrument of terror, domination, and material well-being. No prize was more coveted and fought over than this.

Armand vainly attempted to relaunch the joint plant for enriched uranium, in which scientists, technicians, and heads of industry were to have worked side by side. But the military plant, Pierrelatte, was taking shape. Sufficient progress had been made on the French bomb to warrant the prediction that by 1960 it would be exploded. The EDF was asked to construct French nuclear power plants in cooperation with the Atomic Energy Commission. French physicists turned their backs on the atomic pool in Brussels.

"France isn't playing the game," Armand complained. "She should have been the one to get everything under way. Instead, she used every imaginable argument against Euratom. And it was easy. Although Euratom was the most exciting of all the European institutions, it was also the most fragile. Because of their lack of technical knowledge, the politicians could not possibly have been responsible for the objections voiced against it."

Frenchmen maintained that Euratom would have meant American control over the future of Europe. They said that afterward it would be impossible to get rid of the United States. All the European establishments would be stymied by American licenses. In order to exploit American or Americo-European patents, the companies that built reactors would have to accept American participation. Like oil, the atom would become an American monopoly.

Francis Perrin argued that France should cooperate with others on anything that she could not accomplish alone. "Let the others do what we don't want to do ourselves," was the interpretation France's partners put on his remarks. "The Atomic Commission only offers us work that leads to nothing. It keeps its best researchers for the bomb. In its eyes, Euratom is a scrap heap."

Armand, at grips with insuperable difficulties, was losing his appetite and sleep. Far from the realm of railways, he was out of his element. He became ill from overwork and aggravation. He could no longer serve as a full-time president of Euratom and resigned late in 1958.

On February 1, 1959, Étienne Hirsch took Armand's place in Brussels. Hirsch was an engineer who became an economist while serving as a member of Monnet's team. He had been Monnet's assistant in Algiers in 1943 when the two men helped to equip France's armored divisions. Later Hirsch helped Monnet with the modernization plan, then succeeded him as its director.

It was Hirsch who implemented the United States-Euratom accords that gave rise to so much mumbling and grumbling in Paris. He granted subsidies of $7,000,000 and $8,000,000 to European firms that ordered atomic power plants from Westinghouse and General Electric. The American firms had been impatiently awaiting customers. The German company Gundremingen, which was set up in collaboration with General Electric, likewise received a subsidy; Garigliano and Trino Vercelese, near Turin, and Chooz, at the Franco-Belgian frontier, were also given financial assistance.

Parisians said, "Euratom was conceived in order to create a European atomic industry. But it served mainly to get American industry off the ground by becoming the latter's first customer and enabling it to introduce American techniques and licenses in Europe. The United States thus succeeded in getting a slice of German, Dutch, and Italian profits, and in obtaining long-term contracts to supply Europe with fissionable material.

"These subsidies paralyzed European industry from the start. They prevented the creation of a European consortium. Both Westinghouse and General Electric used the enriched uranium that Oak Ridge and the other discontinued war plants sold at reduced prices. Westinghouse employed pressurized water reactors; General Electric used boiling water reactors for the same purpose. They competed with each other. Their German associates not only competed with one another but also with the French, who were using natural uranium.

"Europeans were divided by Euratom, yet their scientific and industrial association was a unique opportunity to construct an autonomous industry on the Continent and to produce their own power at low cost."

The Germans and Italians began to demand a "fair return," insisting that as much money be spent on them as they contributed to Euratom. Each country had its university laboratories, its research centers. Instead of setting up a joint program, each country wanted a slice of the cake as well as subsidies for all kinds of research. All Hirsch could do was to Europeanize the existing facilities of each country. He made Ispra in Italy the most important of the joint centers for the construction of a prototypic industrial reactor, Orgel. Seven years later, however, Orgel was still only a laboratory because of the absence of a unified policy.

To keep her hands free, France refused to allow her center at Grenoble to become Europeanized, although French atomic scientists joined the Germans in doing research on a high flow reactor.

Alongside the German national center at Karlsruhe, Hirsch created a European establishment that caused a lot of talk. The Parisians said that if the German atomic scientists had not been protected by Euratom they would never have dared to undertake a project that bordered on the military.

At Karlsruhe researchers studied transuranium, a metal consisting mainly of plutonium from which the bomb and engines for submarines are made. They found a plutonium metal, cast it, and molded it. Concurrently, at Hamburg, they blueprinted the engine for the submarine the French had built at Cadarache, and designed the plutonium engine for the first atomic European commercial cargo ship, the *Otto Hahn,* named after the German scientist who, in 1938, discovered how to bombard nuclei. The cargo ship was launched at Kiel in 1966. But prior to these developments, Hirsch was credited with having greatly encouraged the construction of a prototype for fast reactors called breeders. Unlike the first atomic pile, the neutrons were not slowed down artificially. The Russians, with the British close on their heels, took the lead in this new and revolutionary venture. The Soviets were hoping to build their first breeder reactors by 1972. They were two years ahead of the Americans and the Western Europeans whose breeders would probably not become operative until 1975 or 1980.

These breeders, which require natural uranium enriched with plutonium, produce plutonium and electricity simultaneously. The EDF power plants extract 0.3 percent of the energy contained in natural uranium. (The objection to them is that they waste rare raw material, whereas the breeders recover 50 percent.)

France was the first country to seek and obtain from Euratom a $225,000,000 contract to build a prototypic breeder. Constructed at Cadarache with the help of foreign atomic scientists, the breeder (Rapid-Sodium) was called Rhapsodie, and it was a huge success. Immediately, the Germans sought a contract of $230,000,000 for their plutonium models. Long before these new experimental reactors were launched on both sides of the Rhine, Hirsch had left Brussels and resigned from the presidency of Euratom.

The prevailing opinion in Paris was that Hirsch, the engineer-economist, had one grave shortcoming that hampered his usefulness to Euratom: He was an ardent supranational "Monnetist" and anti-Gaullist. In the name of the sovereign Euratom Community he would come to the Quai d'Orsay to chide Couve de Murville. The Gaullist politician did not take the European University of Florence seriously enough, Hirsch would complain, although it had not implemented Armand's plan for a European higher education. Hirsch got a cold reception. He quarreled with Debré over appropriations. When his term as president of Euratom expired in January, 1963, he was not reappointed by the Gaullist government.

His successor, Pierre Chatenet, a former minister in Debré's cabinet, launched the second Euratom plan. Chatenet discreetly played down the supranational character of Euratom, but this did not reconcile Paris to the Community. Squabbles over plans and subsidies continued unabated.

184

Meanwhile, in 1964, atomic kilowatts became a profitable reality, and the consumption of power doubled. Foreseeing a shortage in gas and oil, the big petroleum companies turned to uranium and built nuclear power plants. Between 1964 and 1968, 16 uranium plants were in operation, 17 others were under construction, and 41 had been ordered. The Tennessee Valley Authority added 2 giant atomic plants. By 1980 a third of the current American demand for power— 150 million kilowatts—would be provided by atomic energy, mainly through breeders.

The breeders that were being built in French and German laboratories offered a fresh opportunity for cooperation. The French fast reactor, Rhapsodie, successfully tested at Cadarache, was a Euratom project in the sense that Germans, Belgians, and Dutch had collaborated with the French to perfect it. Two German models were also built at Euratom centers and with European funds.

In this domain, the Europeans ceased to lag behind the Americans, nor were American techniques and licenses any longer a problem. Industrial and political rivalry, however, persisted. Siemens, which was associated with Westinghouse, was building a private breeder and declined to form a partnership with the French monopolies. Chancellor Erhard was at odds with Paris. In 1964 the French planned to test the peaceful uses of enriched uranium. They suggested to the Germans that a second plant be built at Pierrelatte. It would be a joint undertaking to enrich uranium to 3 percent for electric power plants. The offer was rejected.

Euratom seemed to be nearing its end. At the time of the great Common Market crisis in 1965-66, there was talk of doing away with it. When Kiesinger took office, he suggested to the French that the two governments should revive it. The political situation was propitious and there seemed to be a renewed interest in Euratom.

Eastern Europe expressed alarm at the progress being made in German atomic science and at "the demands of the *revanchists* at Bonn." Actually, the Federal Republic was about to become a great European nuclear power. American institutes connected with Germany predicted that in twenty years the Germans would be the principal producers of industrial reactors in Europe.

The first power plant that emerged from the Euratom-United States treaty was Gundremingen, built in cooperation with General Electric. It began to turn out 237 megawatts. The same company built a second plant at Lingen that turned out 160 megawatts. Siemens bought two electric power plants at Obrigheim and Neideraibach (300 and 100 megawatts) and had received orders for two new power plants of 660 megawatts each. Six more plants were being planned. The big chemical firms, for whom electricity constituted at least half of the manufacturing cost, were studying plans for private power plants. Badische Anilian was one of them.

Enriched uranium, patents, foolproof American techniques, and Germany's enormous industrial capacity facilitated the construction of power plants whose kilowatt output was becoming increasingly competitive with gas and oil in terms of price. However, German production of nuclear energy, which was already under way or about to begin, represented less than two-thirds of the French output.

The three EDF's at Chinon (750 megawatts), the two power plants at Saint-Laurent-des-Eaux—one about to be inaugurated, the other under construction and each geared to produce 480 megawatts—the Bugey plant at Ain (545 megawatts), the two plants at Fessenheim that were built in 1967 (1,400 megawatts), to say nothing of Chooz, which was shared with the Belgians, its twin, Tihange, also Franco-Belgian, and the Vandellos plant in Catalonia—all these together represented a total of some 3,000 megawatts.

Although an industry that had a great potential was being organized in Germany, no similar atomic undertaking was being promoted in France because both the Atomic Energy Commission and the nationalized electrical company, Électricité de France, held monopolies. Certain groups met temporarily in offices, banks, or at big corporations whenever there was a concrete plan to implement. Some factories received large but limited orders for very resistant equipment to be used in atomic plants. But these plants were not adapted to this kind of production. There were technical difficulties that could not be solved. Pipes burst, boilers and turbines broke down, and the power plants were paralyzed.

Électricité de France attributed its difficulties to the complexity of the techniques used in handling natural uranium—uranium plants were expensive to install—and to the high cost of the kilowatt yield. In order to reduce the cost of production and obtain the maximum from the bids offered, it revised its plans. In 1966 Électricité de France demanded that the two power plants being built on the Rhine at Fessenheim be earmarked to produce enriched uranium according to reliable American methods, in order to reduce the cost of power. The French contractors claimed that the procedures for building natural uranium plants would make it impossible to create a French industry capable of rivaling Germany's.

The Vendellos power plant was sold to Spain under exceptional conditions (80 percent credit and 50 percent repurchase of its yield). A group called Socia, which had undertaken the task of constructing this plant, complained of the risks involved in using natural uranium. Socia decried it as a thankless job, and demanded the right to resort to American techniques and know-how. Many companies were formed in France to exploit the Westinghouse and General Electric patents. Eventually they supplied power to the big corporations, thus meeting the latter's needs.

A tempest of controversy—the conflicting opinions of the experts —swept through the ministerial bureaus. The Atomic Energy Commission took up the cudgels on behalf of natural uranium as if it were an only child. Natural uranium, the Commission claimed, not only produced electricity but plutonium as well. This was important in furthering the armaments program. In addition, it would save France from having to pay huge sums in royalties to American corporations. The Commission maintained that the troubles of the EDF had stemmed from its attempt to supervise the construction of the plants, a task which should have been left to an industrial architect.

French industry was weak, in spite of the enormous orders it had received, because it had not been structured. But if, to remedy the situation, it resorted to foreign methods, it would never adapt itself to purely French procedures; in addition, it would become embroiled in a tangle of patents and royalties from which it might be unable to extricate itself.

At the close of 1967 the government decided, at least temporarily, to continue the plans currently under way for natural uranium. In any case, during the next ten years the advent of breeding would herald a new nuclear era. The atomic physicists predicted that fast reactors would burn granite by 1980. They would yield a million kilowatts per year and three tons of plutonium, the equivalent of 600,000 tons of coal. Uranium would be used to fuel the engines of submarines, as well as those of ocean liners, giant oil tankers, and mobile nuclear power plants that could be installed anywhere.

The Americans announced that in 1969 they would build a nuclear desalting plant at Huntington Beach, in southern California. It would turn out 1,800,000 kilowatts and 600,000,000 liters of distilled water, enough to meet the needs of a city of 700,000 inhabitants. The Germans were working on three experimental fast reactors, one of which was being built by Siemens in its own center. This plant would produce 1,000 megawatts at a cost of 1.4 pfennigs per kilowatt, instead of 2.4 pfennigs.

The Israelis wanted the future "magic" reactors, hoping to use them to fertilize the Negev and solve the problems of Palestine and of the entire Middle East. Multipurpose breeders along the barren coast of Sinai and the Gulf of Aqaba would furnish the power and light so necessary to vast oases and agricultural-industrial centers. They would draw from the sea millions of cubic meters of distilled water, saline residues for tons of ammonia, hundreds of tons of phosphorus—all of which would enable them to irrigate and fertilize about 250,000 acres around the uranium plant, to harvest a half-million tons of grain, and feed two million people.

Proud of the performance of their Rhapsodie, the French were preparing to build an industrial prototype, Phoenix, at Marcoule in 1969.

Meanwhile, the expiring Euratom, without a budget for 1968, without a program, suddenly resumed the role of star performer. Germany's success in domains that bordered on atomic warfare aroused apprehension among the members of the Eastern bloc. In addition, the latter were irritated by the speeches of various ministers of the Federal Republic demanding for the *Bundeswehr* the right to possess guns and arms like those of Germany's allies and potential enemies. The Russians at Geneva renewed their negotiations with the Americans for a nuclear nonproliferation treaty. This was directed primarily against Germany. Thereupon Euratom assumed enormous importance in the eyes of the Bonn government.

Chancellor Kiesinger's proposal for a two-power Euratom embarrassed Paris. De Gaulle's policy was well known: no atomic arms for Germany in order not to hinder the détente with the U.S.S.R. and the Eastern bloc; the reunification of Germany; a great new Europe that would attract the countries of the East.

But the nuclear nonproliferation treaty drafted in 1967—the disarmament of countries that had no arms, according to de Gaulle—

188

raised Euratom to a position of stardom. The Six were invited to sign the treaty. This would mean surrender of the Community's autonomy and submission to the control of the Vienna Agency and its inspectors "who came in from the cold."

Backed by the Italians, Chancellor Kiesinger rebelled. Since the Soviets did not sell nuclear explosives or allow any on-the-spot control, they had no moral right to examine the German laboratories and plants. The Eastern supervisors might take advantage of the situation to spy for Russian industry.

Since France was a nuclear power, she was immune from Soviet curiosity. In any case, she refused to sign a treaty that contained no provision for the disarming of countries that were armed. Bonn immediately demanded that control by Euratom be maintained. This, of course, did not please the Russians. It likewise displeased the Americans, who were as monopolistic as the Soviets in regard to atomic weapons. The United States was no more willing than was the U.S.S.R. to allow Germany to elude United Nations control.

Suddenly the Germans realized that the American monopoly of enriched uranium could become a powerful means of exerting pressure. Ten years earlier the Americans had rejected a European isotope separation plant. In 1964 they had rejected a French proposal to share the cost of a second generator plant at Pierrelatte which would have insured the independence of the Six. The Russians might serve formal notice on the White House that it must refuse to supply fissionable material to any state that refused to sign the treaty.

This dangerous possibility caused an about-face in German policy. In March, 1968, Chancellor Kiesinger declared that the future of Germany did not depend upon a North Atlantic empire. At Bonn's suggestion, the president of the Commission at Brussels, Jean Rey, relaunched Euratom by proposing a European plant for enriched uranium. The French Pierrelatte was a costly but remarkable success. It was therefore suggested that a generating plant to produce slightly enriched uranium for peaceful purposes could be split into two parts, the second plant to be used for a united Europe.

The European plant could be free from the control of the Vienna Agency because it was situated in France, on the territory of an atomic power that was at liberty to pursue its own activities as it pleased and to supply whomever it chose. France had refused to sign the Geneva Treaty; any control exercised in regard to Euratom was purely on a voluntary basis. The situation was an interesting one because France had at her disposal uranium deposits in Africa, including some newly discovered deposits in the valley of the Niger. This assured her independence.

The extension of Pierrelatte to supply fissionable material to France's neighbors was warmly supported by the EDF and the French contractors. It was now possible to build enriched uranium power plants without being reproached for having to buy American supplies.

But Paris was uncomfortable. The government had to help the Germans elude eventual control of their activities; France was assuming responsibility for Germany and protecting her from sanctions if she failed to use the plant exclusively for peaceful purposes. Franco-German cooperation was altogether justified within the framework of Euratom. But the Germans refused to cooperate with the French in the joint utilization of fissionable material produced in common, or in sharing the construction of future nuclear plants.

On October 31, 1967, Maurice Schumann, the French Minister of Research, suggested to his colleagues at Luxembourg the idea of setting up a Scientific and Technological Europe, outside the confines of Euratom. There would be joint programs for the Maréchal group at Brussels to study such things as adding machines, telecommunication by satellite, air transport, and oceanography.

The plan was well received. It also envisaged joint efforts to set up breeders and power plants in the near future. There was no need to seek American patents for the experimental reactors built in France or in Germany under the auspices of Euratom. With atomic power maintained at absolute zero by fast neutrons, the Euratom breeding industry could flourish in utmost freedom. Maurice Schumann offered the Italians, who had made less progress than the French and the Germans, a chance to participate in this great undertaking.

"Don't rely on the Americans for your breeders," he advised them. "Our atomic centers will be open to you if yours will be open to us."

But the German minister, Gerhard Stoltenberg, became mute whenever breeders were mentioned. Maurice Schumann paid him a visit in Bonn, but this did not loosen his tongue. Siemens had announced as early as 1966 that it would utilize its private breeder for commercial purposes, in conjunction with a Dutch firm and a Belgian firm, and that it considered France a direct competitor and therefore would not establish relations with French scientists. The German minister repeated these statements.

Euratom did not constitute a joint industrial consortium. The German liberal economy did not allow the Bonn government to sign accords of which it disapproved. Previous offers of cooperation made by Alain Peyrefitte, especially in regard to color television, had encountered the same objections. The Germans cited their agreements with American companies and affirmed their complete freedom of action.

Schumann persisted: Franco-German atomic cooperation could become one of the great achievements of the century. How, he asked, could France open up Pierrelatte to the Germans if French atomic scientists were denied access to Karlsruhe? But the Bonn government did not, or could not, give up the advantages of a purely national German industrial triumph in the manufacture of future reactors. On December 8, 1967, the various ministers of science convened when the Council of Euratom met. Gerhard Stoltenberg submitted a fully drafted blueprint for a European enriched uranium plant. This time Maurice Schumann officially repeated his proposal for a program of European breeders. The German minister maintained an icy silence. (A few days later, Siemens announced the signing of agreements with its Belgian and Dutch associates for the construction of a private breeder.)

The French minister suggested that the plan for an enriched uranium plant be sent to an advisory commission for approval. The suggestion was accepted. Now Euratom no longer had a program. Would this spell its demise? No. International political developments were to restore the usefulness of this empty carcass. It became increasingly plain that Kiesinger would become Erhard's successor. He and Schumann were agreed that the Euratom Community should be granted a survival budget. They would give themselves a year to find a suitable purpose for it.

"Let's organize Euratom with England," Foreign Minister Willy Brandt urged in January, 1968. Italy and the Benelux countries applauded him for this. Ever since the British Prime Minister, Harold Wilson, had been converted to the idea of the Common Market, he had kept suggesting that England could make a considerable technological contribution. The offer was of limited interest if it meant the usual negotiations for licenses and royalties. But the proposal would deserve attention if Wilson intended to work for a viable scientific and industrial community, for the creation of European consortiums that would be equal in importance to the big American firms.

The ten years of misfortune experienced by Euratom was something to think about. It remained, nonetheless, the great European venture. One wonders whether Euratom might not have become the modern instrument of peace.

The Soviets, Americans, British, French, even the Germans themselves, aided by Adenauer, had taken extreme precautions to deprive Germany of the supreme weapon, to shield her against the possible resurgence of the old Germanic demons that Adenauer had dreaded. German atomic power, which is now becoming apparent, disturbs the East and embarrasses America. It raises many questions.

Was not a total civilian and military nuclear community, which Louis Armand had proposed and which was declared impossible by everyone, the best long-term insurance against fear? If atomic power had been developed and shared by the Six, would it not have been better protected, more effectively controlled, less dangerous?

Are the Americans and the French wise in allowing a single country, the strongest one industrially, to enjoy the advantages of American assistance?

Is it true that Germany is secretly about to acquire the bomb or perhaps some other weapon even more dangerous, as some capitals in Eastern Europe seem to believe?

"With their knowledge and technology, with the information they get from the United States, which only the Israelis or the Soviets also have, the Germans would need only eighteen months to make a plutonium bomb. They might even be able to dispense with tests. A few experiments would suffice," say the French experts.

To be sure, the German government has no desire to expose its people to the danger of suicide. Official control, parallel supervision, the attitude of the Russians and the Americans, are guarantees that even if the idea occurred to a small group, it could not be carried out.

The real Soviet concerns relate not to the present but to the future. German talents, German inventiveness, might some day surpass Russian power. The most fantastic hypotheses could become a reality within a few years.

Change has been so rapid that a small number of men might find themselves suddenly, through some fortuitous development in a laboratory, in possession of terrible power over the rest of humanity. These are the risks of the period we live in. Would it not have been wiser to pool the research of the nations? Would not that have been preferable to all the controls imposed and so difficult to implement? Monopolies of powers difficult to defend may be numbered among the most dangerous causes of tensions and conflicts.

XIV

De Gaulle's Europe

ON May 20, 1958, Jean Monnet telephoned Robert Marjolin, his former right-hand man of the modernization plan. Marjolin was about to leave for Brussels to take up his position as vice-president of the Common Market Commission of which Walter Hallstein was president.

"Listen, it's very important. Have you got a *Petit Larousse?* Look up what it says under the word 'confederation,' " said Monnet.

"I think I can tell you," Marjolin began.

"No, believe me, the definition in the *Petit Larousse* is more important than the best legal advice."

The dictionary said: "A temporary union of sovereign states that either dissolves or becomes transformed into a federal state. Although Switzerland has preserved the official name of Helvetian confederation, since 1874 it has been for all practical purposes a federal state."

De Gaulle was returning to power. Monnet had just reread the press conferences and speeches of the former head of the Provisional Government, the former RPF leader. He was attempting to penetrate the general's mind. De Gaulle had always wanted a new Europe, his own, one that moved in the direction of a confederation, not the Europe of the Europeanists.

His statements were explicit enough: "In giving up the safeguards presently operative in Germany, we must replace them with a Europe organized into an effective confederation." (Speech delivered at the Vélodrome d'Hiver on February 23, 1952) "A confederation that should be brought into being by a plebiscite. Each country would participate without sacrificing its image or personality. Thanks to the French Union, France would be on an equal footing with Germany. This would reopen for Europe all the avenues to hope." (Speech delivered at the Vélodrome d'Hiver on November 11, 1952)

"As for institutions, I believe the simplest ones are the best: periodic and constitutional consultation among heads of state who have at their disposal the joint means of reaching political, economic, cultural, and military decisions; a deliberative assembly." (Press conference at the Continental on November 12, 1953)

In Bonn, Rome, and at The Hague, and even more passionately in Brussels, Monnet's analysis of de Gaulle's ideas found an echo. It was quite obvious that the general had in mind a closed alliance and a confederation that would be loose enough to leave him free to work out a policy, yet sufficiently cohesive to enable him to fashion his European Europe. The basis of such a Europe was a political alliance between France and Germany.

In a continent that still lacked stability, de Gaulle's Europe was incompatible with the mechanisms of a unified, supranational Europe that was Monnet's goal. But the general would certainly not accept Monnet's ideas. Besides, the Common Market Commission had the right to take the initiative and present proposals to the Council of Ministers of the Six. De Gaulle would therefore try to obstruct the Common Market. Only the dictionary definition, which offered hope that a federal state would some day emerge from a confederation, offered consolation to the Brussels Europeanists.

The diplomats of the Five met to consult. Since 1950, the six governments, leaning heavily on their Christian Democrat and Christian Socialist majorities, had subscribed to the same views. They had adhered to two dogmas: a European federation, even though no government had proposed one; an Atlantic Alliance, which conferred the political and military leadership of the West on the United States.

Belgium, Holland, and Luxembourg were too small to develop foreign policies of their own. They needed to be shored up by a superpower. Germany, defeated and not yet armed, could rely only on the American atomic shield for protection against the U.S.S.R. and, later on, for reunification if Washington were willing. Italy, also defeated and divided, needed the constant support of the White House. The Fourth Republic, beset by colonial wars, government instability, and recurrent inflation, solicited both financial aid and American weapons from Washington.

Europe was nothing more than a coalition of frailties. The customary reinforcement afforded by leagues or a confederation was lacking. Despite the terror that Stalin inspired, Europe had not become integrated. Khrushchev, to be sure, was a more reassuring figure. Nonetheless, Europe remained a group of commensals dependent on American generosity, a conglomeration of men of goodwill who were hampered by the absence of England. Europe's cohesiveness depended primarily on the hope of betterment within a trading community. It also depended on the ingenuity of Monnet and his friends, and on Europe's competitors, all eager to harden this lump of butter through supranational institutions.

General de Gaulle's tall figure, his stiffness, so different from the prevailing flexibilities, aroused more than passing concern among France's partners as well as among the champions of integration. According to de Gaulle, Europe must show itself to be independent of its American benefactors and protectors.

When the war broke out in Korea, de Gaulle reminded the Americans of their promise to maintain troops and bases in France. "War has begun," he said. "The United States intervened tardily, as usual. It must retain its connections with Europe.... The vanguard of the Cossacks is camping 150 kilometers from the Rhine, if you can imagine that."

He had approved the Atlantic Pact. People around him were talking about an Atlantic civilization. But when the question of EDC arose, he was of a different mind. The United States had set itself up as the suzerain of Europe, he claimed, with Germany serving as its vassal. France was excluded from the higher councils of the Alliance. The Alliance was an Anglo-Saxon affair. America was consolidating its hold over Europe in order to have a market for its surplus goods. A Europe that had recovered and was back on its feet would have every right to be treated as an equal, not a slave. The defense of Europe was the responsibility of Europeans.

A small "summit meeting" brought Monnet, Spaak, and Armand together to ponder the situation created by de Gaulle's advent to power. Monnet was optimistic. If de Gaulle would accept a Europe in the making, he could become the incomparable, unhoped-for moving spirit that would unify the Continent. The supranational mechanisms which were beginning to function would, of course, not please him. But he might make his peace with them if he were offered the leadership of the new international regime—or, at least, so thought Monnet. De Gaulle should be asked to assume the presidency of the Union. He was a man big enough to cope with Franco-German reconciliation, and he could bring it off. Such a reconciliation had been the ardent hope of Adenauer for thirty-five years; and the Schuman Plan had just begun to come to grips with it.

Spaak, who had spearheaded the movement that culminated in the Treaty of Rome, had for long regarded himself as the natural choice for the presidency of the first United States of Europe. He was more than willing, however, to withdraw in favor of de Gaulle, if the general were willing to head a unified Continent.

Armand, the father of Euratom, was skeptical. "De Gaulle has no talent for Europeanism," he said. "He might be willing to head some vague union, but he could never be the man we're looking for, someone to promote a real fusion. At heart, he is a national, if not a nationalist. You'll never convert him. If you want to know how a man thinks, you have to know what books he read when he was twenty. De Gaulle has never read anything but French books. He just doesn't understand the modern world, the atomic era. He thinks French!"

On May 30, 1958, de Gaulle resumed power. Within six months, President Coty yielded him his place at the Elysée Palace. The general was in the throes of forming a cabinet. The recluse from Colombey had brought with him the dream of Charlemagne.

He had the French ambassador to Bonn, Couve de Murville, recalled to Paris to join him at the Hôtel Matignon. Murville had been his former Finance Commissioner in Algiers. An Inspector of Finance, Murville had become at an early age a ranking member of the Finance Ministry's bureaucracy. He went to North Africa at the time of the Allied landings. The Liberation and the general's respect for him made him a diplomat. Before taking the post in Bonn he had served as French ambassador to Washington. He was the star of the Quai d'Orsay.

The ambassador was playing golf when he got the call from Paris. He finished the game, then took the train. Tall, thin, with gray, elegantly wavy hair, Couve is remarkable for his self-control, his measured way of speaking. He has been reproached for making boring speeches. He expresses himself judiciously in even, unaccentuated terms. A Protestant, the son of a magistrate in Montpellier, he has the rigidity of the people of Cévenole, the austerity reminiscent of the mountains that dominate the Languedoc plain. In reality, he is a descendant of an old planter's family from the Île de France in the Indian Ocean, which was ceded to England and became Mauritius. French traditions and the French language are still current there. In private, he is full of humor. His extreme reserve should perhaps be imputed more to the secret tactics that are part of the Gaullist strategy rather than to anything in his personality. His Europeanism is devoid of warmth or enthusiasm.

In diplomatic discussions, Couve is a very effective debater; his manners are perfect but glacial, his arguments are extremely clear. At times it was said in Brussels that he was "diabolically clever." In Washington, his talents were greatly appreciated by the State Department. In the advice he gave with brutal frankness to the foreign ministers at the Quai d'Orsay, he proved to be a loyal supporter of the general's foreign policy, bristling like de Gaulle at the "give-aways" on the Rhine.

Yes, of course, he was for Europe, but not for the "leaderless Europe of Mr. Monnet, who wears the Washington hat"—not for communitarian, supranational institutions without a superstate. He was for the Gaullist Europe, which would take shape gradually on the basis of an independent, concerted policy of a Union of States that would eventually embrace the countries of Eastern Europe, thus settling the German question.

De Gaulle told Couve that he wanted to achieve as quickly as possible an Economic Europe which the Treaty of Rome had inaugurated. An Economic Community would be a sort of business venture from which a political Europe would take shape. In the modern world, major economic problems were political as well. A common currency had to be created to harmonize production as well as major imports such as oil. A solidarity of interests would inevitably lead to a political entente if the United States or Eastern Europe refrained from placing obstacles in the way of unification. The Brussels Commission had received highly questionable powers, particularly the exclusive right to initiate. This was entirely understandable, since heretofore there had been no desire among the Six to federate. The federator was Washington. But all that could be changed. The authority of the

198

Community resided in the Council of Ministers. When it had examined and settled all the problems, the Commission would establish its own indispensable joint bureau.

De Gaulle was not speaking as an economist. He had no fixed ideas about business, but unlike the Anglo-Saxons, he did not accept free trade in principle. For the moment he did not even see a way, through the Common Market, to arouse a spirit of competition. This was to be Pompidou's idea. French industry had been asleep at the switch during an entire century of protectionism.

He was determined to give a structure to the deep-seated sense of unity that prevailed in the Old World, which had been divided and dominated by the two rival superpowers. De Gaulle would reendow it with its historic importance, its independence, its position of primacy in modern civilization. "I intend to organize Europe," he said to Couve. "Before taking you on as Foreign Minister, I would like to know if my policies correspond to your feelings."

Couve de Murville felt himself to be the man to implement this grandiose policy, which must be achieved quietly, without further ado. At one of the first meetings of the cabinet (which was composed of the principal party leaders of the Fourth Republic who had had a hand in drafting the new constitution), he outlined the major features of the foreign policy that would be pursued. "France will participate actively in the organization of the Common Market," he said. "The Common Market will be inaugurated by the end of this year, 1958, by a 10 percent reduction in all tariffs."

This came as a surprise. No one expected de Gaulle to accept the Common Market, since he had torpedoed the EDC and opposed the ECSC. A few days before, on May 20, 1958, Maurice Faure, the Undersecretary of State and negotiator of the Treaty of Rome, warned the Council of Ministers of the Six at Brussels that his country would be forced to invoke the safeguard clauses. The financial and monetary situation of France would not enable her to accept the first lowering of tariffs on January 1, 1959.

At the cabinet meeting in the Matignon hotel, several voices advocating caution were raised. The franc was catastrophically weak; industry was virtually at a standstill. Exports would be jeopardized. A tidal flood of foreign goods would be disastrous. Only the Finance Minister, Antoine Pinay, rallied to the position taken by Couve de Murville. At the Quai d'Orsay it was Pinay who had given the signal for the initiation of the negotiations that led to the formation of the Economic Community. He was certain that confidence would be reestablished, that the situation would right itself.

Then de Gaulle spoke. France would participate actively, from the very beginning, in the construction of a Common Market. With this in mind, Pinay prepared 300 ordinances to stabilize the situation and launch a program of austerity. Pompidou, chief of staff in de Gaulle's cabinet, arranged for a devaluation of 17.50 percent to promote exports. The reduction of national tariffs would slow down the rise in prices that inevitably follows devaluation.

Meanwhile, de Gaulle's return to power aroused mixed feelings in Brussels. Because the signatories of the Treaty of Rome had not been able to agree on a capital for Economic Europe, the institutions of the Common Market had to seek furnished quarters in buildings on the Avenue de la Joyeuse Entrée, where much had to be done to make them habitable.

As the adversary of supranational bodies, it was feared that de Gaulle would stifle the Economic Community before it could get started. So when Couve announced that France would fulfill her commitments, he surprised the entire world.

"De Gaulle did not arrive at this decision in order to support the Common Market," people in Brussels commented suspiciously. "He only did it to extricate French industry from the protectionism in which it had been floundering."

Once the new French constitution had been drafted, de Gaulle immediately concentrated on creating a politically unified Europe. Its foundation would be the Franco-German entente. "There will or will not be such a Europe depending on whether an agreement without intermediaries will or will not be possible between Germans and Gauls," de Gaulle had said in Bordeaux on September 25, 1949.

"I have always said and I have always believed that the basis for a unified Europe is a direct agreement, without intermediaries, between the French and the German peoples, provided, of course, that such an agreement is possible," he had reiterated in a press conference at the Palais d'Orsay on November 14, 1949.

Four months later, on March 16, 1950, on the eve of the London Conference, he had alluded to the suggestion made by Adenauer of a merger of the German and French nations, then went on to restate his position. "If one were not constrained to look at things coldly,

200

one would be almost dazzled by the prospect of combining the assets of Germany and France, especially if the latter were extended to include Africa. . . . The fate of Europe depends on the future of Franco-German relations."

Three months after his resumption of power, on September 14, 1958, General de Gaulle received Chancellor Adenauer at Colombey. De Gaulle had honored Adenauer in a speech in 1950 by calling him "the good German," a man whose initiative he had been following for a long time. The "good German" undertook the trip to France confirmed in the suspicions that he, as the architect of Europe and the number one ally of the United States, might well harbor. Monnet felt warm friendship for the old man, and strongly encouraged him in his dreams of a unified Europe. It was up to Adenauer, Monnet said, to win de Gaulle over to the idea of a European union, and to urge him to head it. If anyone could offer de Gaulle the presidency of the future United States of Europe, it was certainly Adenauer, the Rhenish champion who, ever since 1923, had dreamed of reconciliation, of a Franco-German entente.

De Gaulle and Adenauer met, each having a single end in mind. De Gaulle wanted to offer Adenauer the presidency of the political union he was planning. This would be a spectacular gesture, a sign that Western Europe had been metamorphosed. Besides, Adenauer was de Gaulle's senior.

Seated near the hearth, the two men conversed like direct descendants of Charlemagne. Each expressed the desire to confer on the other the honor of the crown. As soon as the general uttered his first words of greeting, the fears and suspicions of Adenauer vanished. The Frenchman's extreme courtesy touched Adenauer to the quick. He was deeply impressed by the rhetoric so dear to de Gaulle—allusions to notions viewed from a global perspective, a cosmic conception of history.

De Gaulle declared that a Franco-German understanding could constitute the basis of European unity. What was more reasonable? The general envisaged a political union that would be called upon to rally all the people of Western, Central, and Eastern Europe. This would be effected gradually. It implied the reunification of Germany and eventually, some day—who knew—the establishment of a United States of the Old World. Nothing seemed more reasonable than this. De Gaulle suggested that the first steps toward European union might

201

be periodic consultations among heads and ministers of governments or states. They would discuss all the major issues. What could be more logical? De Gaulle said he would accept the existing institutions until something better took their place; he would not ask for their dissolution.

He told his visitor that he was going to create a nuclear striking force because it was essential to European security. Adenauer approved, saying that he found it difficult to put up with "American omnipotence." Although neither man explicitly offered the other the presidency of the union they were contemplating, they parted as very old friends, completely charmed by one another.

This secret conversation pleased Monnet but shocked many Europeanists. De Gaulle was employing the tactics of a traditional outmoded diplomacy with all its ineffectual bipartisan negotiations. Instead of creating joint bodies or setting up federal conferences, the general resorted to all the old tricks, to two-party ententes which only served to alienate those nations that were excluded. He was trying to impose a Franco-German hegemony on Western Europe. And he was trying to turn Germany away from America.

Having formed a personal alliance with Adenauer and laid the foundations for an autonomous and political Europe, de Gaulle turned toward the United States and England three days after Adenauer's visit to Colombey. On September 24, 1958, he sent a memorandum to Washington and London. Allied world policy, atomic strategy, the fate of a divided Europe—all could be settled by the Big Three: the United States, England, and France. But France must have as much access as England to secrets, techniques, and nuclear materials.

For de Gaulle the most important factor was the bomb. Only those who had the bomb could speak with authority. He would have his own homemade bomb. When he formed his government, he assigned the Ministry of the Armies to Pierre Guillaumat, the director of the Atomic Energy Commission. According to the MacMahon Law as modified by Eisenhower, France had every right to secret information from the United States. She was on an equal footing with England. French atomic scientists in 1940 had sent to London the results of their experiments and their patents for heavy water which played an important part in the British contribution to the explosion at Hiroshima.

When de Gaulle possessed nuclear power, with or without American assistance, he would be admitted into the British *sanctum sanctorum*. Then he could participate as an equal in Atlantic arrangements and the reorganization of NATO. The defense of Europe was first and foremost a European affair: the existence of rockets that threatened the United States on its own territory might force it to impose a second Munich on Europe. A European general should head the European armies, supported by the presence of American troops. De Gaulle declared himself prepared to withdraw from NATO, to break off with NATO, if his demands were not met.

But he hoped, he said, to get what he wanted. Eisenhower was a good man, an honest man, a friend. He had obtained a good many things from Eisenhower years before, although he had had to put some pressure on him. Paris had been liberated by Leclerc and Strasbourg had been defended by de Lattre. It was time to begin.

De Gaulle's memorandum was shocking because of its incongruities. The men at the White House and the Atlanticists in Europe could never accept a three-power directorate to solve the world's problems. There was NATO. In any case, a directorate with France, which was not a great power, was unthinkable. So far as Washington and London were concerned, it would be even more unthinkable with de Gaulle, the infernal ally of the 1940's. It would be foolish to give him a share of nuclear power because it would make him the leader of Europe. The number one ally of the United States on the Continent was not France but Germany, and because of the Soviets Germany could not be given the supreme weapon.

Meanwhile, Adenauer was not in the least offended by the Elysée's demands on the White House and 10 Downing Street. The elderly Rhinelander was having a honeymoon with de Gaulle. If his ally, his French friend, obtained a place in the Atlantic summit meetings, he would practically share it with him.

A month went by during which time there were consultations in Washington. On October 20, 1958, Eisenhower stated that no fundamental changes could be made in NATO's structure. He said not a word about the bomb.

"I asked for the moon," de Gaulle remarked later. "I could not withdraw from NATO without first having asked for what we wanted. But there was nothing doing."

After this refusal to meet his demands, de Gaulle began to escalate his attacks on the "American hegemony." He announced a gradual withdrawal from NATO, demanded the eviction of American troops from France, and finally broke with NATO, which was forced to move to Belgium.

After the general was elected President of the Fifth Republic, he chose Michel Debré as his prime minister. This distressed the integrationists. Debré had at first warmly supported a unified Europe. He had been President of the Social Section of the European Movement, the eloquent champion of an Atlantic Community that would include all the free nations and thus buttress Western Europe against the weight of Germany—"the most populous and industrialized European nation." While the EDC treaty was being debated, Debré had discussed in Strasbourg a plan for a political Europe to be presented to the various parliaments. Then, when in his opinion the EDC had gone bad, he spoke out against integration, supranationality, a small, leaderless Europe led by Washington via telecommunication. He attacked Monnet personally and violently, accusing him of using the funds of the High Authority, at America's urging, to propagandize for integration.

Debré denounced the Brussels Commission as a Trojan horse. Whence came the real inspiration for a European commercial union, for which the Europeanists were but a façade? From the White House, of course, for the benefit of the big American companies and the political leaders of the United States, although the pretext was the need for greater efficiency. Debré alluded to two provisions that might be interpreted as limiting the degree of sovereignty to be sacrificed.

But de Gaulle, again to everyone's surprise, did not blame the technocrats in Brussels, about whom Paris had no cause for complaint. The Commission was a model of impartiality. This was due to the quality of the men who had been chosen, and probably, too, to Monnet's idea that work done in common changes men, makes them forget their self-interest for the sake of a common good. The influence of French economists, of French inspectors of finance, was considerable. Hallstein listened to Marjolin. France would not suffer from the initiatives taken by the Europeanists. For Paris the overriding question was whether or not there would be a political council of the Six.

Unlike many Europeanists, Monnet was not opposed to de Gaulle. He voted yes in the referendum. Although he thought the political

Europe de Gaulle had had in mind would be feeble, still it was better than none at all. In 1959, at all the international meetings, Couve de Murville would say, "When it comes to the question of political union, we're takers."

The European concert advocated by de Gaulle was beginning to take shape. The ministers of the Six decided to hold meetings every three months. On July 29, 1960, a major conference took place at Rambouillet. De Gaulle made the following proposals to Adenauer: a political treaty; a popular referendum to be held in the six countries; a permanent political commission; a defense commission and periodic meetings with chiefs of state, heads of government, foreign ministers, defense and finance ministers; the unification of all existing communities under the leadership of the political council; periodic consultation with the Strasbourg Assembly.

Mention of a defense commission brought a frown to the Chancellor's face. It would compete with NATO. Furthermore, de Gaulle's plan was designed to oust England and the United States from the military affairs of the Community. The Americans were in the midst of reexamining their strategy in Europe. The new rockets had changed their concepts of self-defense.

"America is about to pull its atomic arms out of Europe. It is therefore essential that the Six collaborate on all questions that arise in connection with the creation of a common front within NATO," de Gaulle urged.

In Brussels people were distrustful of, but not categorically opposed to, de Gaulle's project. The political organization that he was suggesting might merely take the form of a group of chairs placed in a circle. All decisions would have to be reached by a majority vote. "There's not a grain of supranationality in all of it." But after all, a European political union was not something that people had the courage or the strength to attack. It was a beginning, perhaps not a negligible one. What must be thwarted was any attempt by de Gaulle to use it in order to submerge existing institutions and deprive them of their supranationality. On the other hand, if the supranational communities were maintained under the new union's flag, one could still hope that the political union, transcending mere Gaullism, might become an additional element of integrated Europe.

Meanwhile, on Adenauer's return to Bonn he was taken aside by Erhard and his friends in the cabinet. They were concerned about the proposed defense commission, regarding it as an attempt to undercut NATO.

Ludwig Erhard had spent his early years in Bavaria as a student and a budding politician. He did not have a Rhinelander's feeling for the French. He owed his miraculous halo to the Americans. For him the Common Market was merely a stepping-stone. German prosperity, like German reunification, would have to come from the United States. He watched Adenauer closely in order to restrain him and overthrow him as quickly as possible. The majority of the Bundestag were ardent Atlanticists. A week after he had said good-bye to de Gaulle, after he had signed the communiqué that was intended to launch a European political union, Adenauer sent the general a letter full of reservations.

De Gaulle, however, was not discouraged by this partial retraction. In a press conference on September 5, 1960, he again alluded to a European political union: "In time, we may move gradually toward European unity," he promised. But the remarks that followed angered the champions and architects of an integrated Europe.

"Actually, the states are the only entities that have the right to give orders and the authority to act. To believe that it is possible to build something efficacious in terms of action, and which will be approved by peoples as distinguished from states, is an illusion. To be sure, in the course of our efforts to come to grips with the problem of Europe as a whole, . . . certain bodies have been constituted that are more or less extranational. Such bodies have a certain technical value; but they do not have, they cannot have authority and consequently political efficacy. As long as nothing serious occurs, they function without much ado, but if something dramatic happens, or if there is a major problem to resolve, then it becomes apparent that a certain 'High Authority' has no authority at all over the various national categories and that only the states have such authority."

There was an outcry in Brussels and Luxembourg. The thrust had hit home because the coal crisis had pitted the High Authority of the Coal and Steel Community against the states. The High Authority had advocated quotas for the production of coal which the various governments, at grips with their coal miners, could not accept. The High Authority had to give subsidies to everyone. Never were so many subsidies granted to the coal mines. In short, the High Authority had survived only by allowing the Treaty of Paris to be constantly violated.

The result of de Gaulle's remarks was that Adenauer got the grippe and Erhard wrote some surly articles. But the general did not allow a little thing like that to bother him. The day after the barricades were surrendered in Algiers, he summoned the German ambassador to the Elysée: "We have just lived through a very hectic week, Mr. Ambassador. Let's get back to more serious matters. Let's talk about Europe."

The first summit meeting of chiefs of state and heads of government took place in Paris on February 10, 1961; the second was held in Bonn, on July 18. A French minister summarized the conversations as follows:

"Let's talk politics."

"We can't talk about politics without the United States and England."

"Let's talk about joint defense."

"We can't talk about defense outside the framework of NATO and in the absence of the fourteen other Atlantic Alliance nations."

"Let's talk about a common currency, oil imports, foreign investments."

"We can talk about economic affairs only in Brussels and at the instance of the Common Market Commission."

The French plan for association and confederation was shredding like an artichoke. In Paris the reform of the communities was abandoned. Bonn rejected the idea of a European referendum. Thereupon, the periodic consultations between the Defense Ministers were allowed to lapse. There remained, however, the core of the project: the treaty of political union and the commission of diplomatic experts who were to draft it.

"De Gaulle was skeptical about its chances of success, but he became more enthusiastic," said Christian Fouchet.

The general had appointed Fouchet to the commission of experts to draft the treaty. A dynamic ambassador to Denmark, one of the oldest of the Gaullist faithful, Fouchet was an imperturbable colossus, impervious to the most violent attacks. The first French chargé d'affaires to Stalin in 1944, Minister of Information under Mendès-France, negotiator of the accords with Tunis, Fouchet was Algeria's last Delegate General during the dark hours of the Rocher Noir. He was the most severely criticized minister of the Fifth Republic when he handled national education and questions of educational reform. For twenty years his predecessors had worn themselves out at this task. As president of the commission to draft the treaty for European political union, he gave his name to a series of projects.

At that time, England wanted to join the Common Market.

"She's only trying to torpedo it," the Parisians said. "When Great Britain is afraid of something in Europe, she seeks to become European."

De Gaulle closed his eyes. In two months the project was ready: a lasting union of states that would retain their sovereignty; a council of chiefs of state and heads of government that would meet every three months to outline joint foreign, defense, cultural, and research policies. De Gaulle said nothing about economic policy. (This silence endowed the Common Market Commission with the sole initiative in economic affairs.) The general advocated majority rule, but said that the abstention of one national would not prevent the others from arriving at decisions among themselves. The commission for political union was to be permanent and quartered in Paris.

The supranational communities would remain intact; but at the end of three years, the treaty could be revised to strengthen unity and effect centralization. The British, who requested admission, were told that the union would be open to the 17 member states of the somnolent Council of Europe. The Strasbourg Assembly might serve temporarily as the assembly of the union.

"An executive branch is missing in this political union—a permanent commission that can take the initiative," Monnet objected. "There's every chance in the world that this union will become just another congress, ineffectual as a federation, unless General de Gaulle thinks he can impose his views on his partners. But they don't agree with him. So the union could become a dead end. There's only one good thing about it: the three supranational communities will continue, according to de Gaulle. But at the end of three years their existence might be threatened."

Nonetheless, Monnet and his friends supported the Fouchet Plan. After all, the beginning of a European political union was a step toward integration.

Whatever seemed good to Monnet appeared to be exactly the opposite in the eyes of de Gaulle. The communities, whose jurisdiction was superior to that of the governments, were a thorn in his side, and he was determined to eliminate them as soon as his political union—if it worked—brought about the concerted and quasi-permanent action by the heads of the participating governments.

The general found it difficult to accept the fact that officials, nonelective commissioners responsible only to the consultative Assembly of Strasbourg, could dictate to the communities' Councils of Ministers what they should discuss at their meetings. They monopolized the right to initiate proposals. In his opinion this situation could not continue when the chiefs of state and the heads of government met as a European power.

The draft treaty—Fouchet I as it was dubbed—was presented on November 2, 1961. France's partners objected, but de Gaulle believed that it was extremely important for the union to assume responsibility for its own defense. Defense, the others insisted, must remain NATO's affair. Otherwise, America would lose interest. Rejecting the idea of an administrative commission to serve the states, they proposed the appointment of a permanent secretary-general who would be independent of the states. It was this supranational Europe to which the general objected. The Belgians and Dutch demanded British membership in both the political union and the Common Market.

But the major conflict was over the merger and transformation of the communities that was scheduled for three years hence and would put an end to the supranational Europe of Brussels. This Europe, the Europe of Jean Monnet—of the Eurocrats, as the Gaullists called them—was headed by a strong personality, Walter Hallstein. He was president of the Economic Commission which spoke in the name of the Six, something that no single member state could do.

When someone asked Hallstein if he considered himself to be the government of Europe, he answered: "No. A government is elected. But I am unquestionably a European statesman. When we draft the text of a decision, it immediately becomes the common law. The Council of Ministers answers with a yes or no. But we alone have the right to draft the text. We are therefore the European statesmen."

A short man, his face framed by white hair combed back in stiff locks, Hallstein was a professor of international law. He had become a statesman without first having been a politician. He was a bachelor and a theorist. He had taught at Berlin and Rostock. During the war he was Rector of the University of Frankfurt, a position he left in 1944. After a two-year holiday, he went to the United States to teach. He was as rigid in his concepts as he was subtle in dialectics. Because of his fine reputation as an international lawyer, Adenauer appointed him to head the German delegation in the debate over the Schuman Plan. It was then that he espoused the Europeanist philosophy. For seven years he served in Bonn as Secretary of State for Foreign Affairs. It was he who authored the doctrine of nonrecognition of East Germany—the occupied zone. He refused to carry on a dialogue with the Pankov regime or with the states that recognized it.

As soon as Monnet pronounced the words "economic community," Hallstein made the idea his own. This would be a good thing for Germany and a great historical endeavor to which to attach his name.

At Val Duchesse, Monnet's venturesome ideas baffled the French lawyers, who had been brought up on Roman law. But Monnet was a businessman, a creator of international institutions who had never gone to law school. Professor Hallstein, the theorist of Germanic "progressive" law, played a considerable role in the construction of these institutions. The experts at the Quai d'Orsay thought he was unrealistic.

"The Common Market seemed secondary to the French delegation of which I was a member," said one of the Brussels Commission members. "It was the price we had to pay for Euratom. We had to shut our eyes to many things. . . ."

The Germans attached a good deal of importance to the Common Market, more than the French did. This is why Hallstein became the President Designate of the Commission, the driving force of Economic Europe.

From the very outset, in 1958, Hallstein brought to the Commission, which he had helped to create and of which he was the moving spirit, a persistence and passion for reform which won him the title of "the Martin Luther of Europe." He organized it like a government, with finance, industry, and foreign affairs commissioners. He structured its services very cleverly, arranging them in the form of a pyramid. Every commissioner had two assistants, each of whom in turn had two assistants, and so on. Among this wealth of assistants, the top man had the title of president. On the Avenue de la Joyeuse Entrée, everyone was a president.

Hallstein's deference to the Strasbourg Assembly—which had the right to reverse the decisions of the Commission—won him warm acclaim on the Avenue de la Robertsau.

Hallstein was a hard worker. Under his rule, the Commission became a regular factory for research and projects of all kinds. He lived for his work, a work in which the various governments played only the roles of supervisors and endorsers. His firmness led him to take a position that was at times thought too bold by his colleagues. A professor rather than a diplomat, he was a lonely man. One evening, as he was going home, he told his chauffeur to stop in front of a shop that still had its lights on, and said, "I want to buy a bottle of Bordeaux. It's my birthday today, but no one knows it."

"It was his view that a unified Europe will be created through action taken in common rather than through the institutions themselves," one of his friends commented. "He believes that an idea can become part of a person. He himself, identified as he is with an economic Europe, represents a new Europe in the making. Extremely conscientious, he is scrupulously careful not to serve the interests of any one country, not even his own, to the detriment of the others. Because he is deeply devoted to the ideal of supranationality, he would like to undergo a metamorphosis in relation to his institutional duties; at any rate, to become a true European rather than just a German."

Hallstein was quite willing to accept de Gaulle's political union as well as a merger of the three communities into a confederation if there were a secretary-general with special prerogatives: total independence of the various governments; the right to make proposals to the Council of States, an executive body with powers similar to those of the Economic Community. The secretary-general would then personify the spirit of European cooperation in contrast to the government heads and ministers, who symbolize all that is purely national.

"Let's look at things practically," Hallstein would say. "When do ministers and government heads have the time to 'think in common'? Which of the men around them fails to think as a 'national'? The strict duty of statesmen and high officials is to work for the national interest.

"Should the political union become a reality, it must have a joint body that thinks in terms of collaboration; otherwise it could not represent the Six."

"But why can't the Six designate a joint foreign minister, a joint economics minister, a joint minister of defense?" he was asked.

"Can you tell me the name of a single member of the Council of Foreign Ministers in Brussels who might be empowered in one way or another to represent the other five? There isn't one.

"Besides, supranationality is not a shocking concept. Bavaria dates from the sixth century. It is one of the oldest states in the world. But for centuries the Bavarians have learned to live in the Germanic community. As Bavarians, they have their national laws; as Germans, they have their federal laws. The same is true of the United States."

If Paris had accepted the supranational secretary-general that Hallstein and Monnet were suggesting, the opponents of the political union would undoubtedly have been reassured and the idea of such a union would have been accepted.

"Especially," said one sly native of Brussels, "if Walter Hallstein had been appointed secretary-general of the union."

But de Gaulle, as chief of state, could not abide the idea of being dependent on a community official. Paris was already in open conflict with "Europe incarnate."

Hallstein gave precedence to the Commission over which he presided, rather than to the Council of Ministers. Ambassadors posted to the Community presented their credentials to him before making an official call on the President of the Council of Ministers.

Acting on his own initiative, Hallstein engaged in negotiations involving the free-trade area, the British rival of the Common Market. Couve de Murville had expressed his indignation at a meeting of the Council of Ministers, claiming that the Commission had no right to become involved in international transactions. The negotiations were broken off.

But Hallstein was not discouraged. In 1960, he informed the Council that he intended, as President of the Commission, to establish diplomatic relations with six capitals outside the Common Market—Washington and London, to begin with.

"The Commission is not a state. It has no juridical, international character. It cannot have ambassadors," the French minister ruled.

On May 16, 1961, Hallstein went to the United States anyway, even though he had been deprived of ambassadors. In Washington he was received with the honors accorded the head of a government. He returned in April, 1962, to discuss an Atlantic Organization with

John Kennedy. It was the same idea that Monnet had presented to the young American President; it stressed equal powers for Europe and America.

In Paris this was regarded as a deliberate provocation. De Gaulle's object in proposing political union was to define and promote the policy of the Six in this kind of intergovernmental negotiation.

"There is quite a difference between a Commission dealing directly with the United States or England on behalf of the common interests of the Six, and the six ambassadors of these countries informing the United States of the position taken by the political union," Hallstein observed.

On November 16, 1961, two weeks after the final drafting of the Fouchet Plan, Hallstein was received by de Gaulle at the Elysée Palace. He had come to plead the cause of the supranational system, hoping he might persuade the general that it was in no way incompatible with the political union and the federal institutions that were expected to come later.

De Gaulle clearly defined the general policy of his country as it was applied by his government. As President of the European Union, General de Gaulle could, in collaboration with the other national leaders, establish the policy of the Six; the Six could delegate the implementation of the policy to a secretary-general representing the union.

Monnet had high hopes for the outcome of Hallstein's visit. His innate optimism made him forget such details as the exclusive right to initiate proposals and the other powers of the European executive bodies which were so intolerable to de Gaulle. The fact that de Gaulle was de Gaulle, and Hallstein, Walter Hallstein, two men to whom history had assigned very different roles, two emperors in the grand style, made each uncompromising in the exercise of his powers.

Hallstein's visit to de Gaulle raised a perplexing problem of protocol. What kind of reception should be accorded the president of a supranational commission whose quasi-sovereignty was being challenged in France?

The Gaullist ceremony at the Elysée Palace was full of subtleties. Military honors comprise an entire hierarchy, from the fanfare given to the top brass down to the mere deployment of a company platoon. Hallstein was entitled to the simple honors accorded the president of an international organization.

"Well, Monsieur Hallstein, you are already in charge of our economic affairs. Do you also want to be the Foreign Minister, the Defense Minister, the Prime Minister of Europe? In other words, the European Union would be you!"

The President of the Economic Commission denied this vehemently. He explained that the secretary-general of the union could act only with the consent of the states. All decisions would be made by the individual governments.

Hallstein departed with the conviction that in de Gaulle's opinion, the Brussels institutions were but a temporary *modus vivendi,* that he really wanted to destroy European unification.

"Later on I realized that de Gaulle was a Europeanist in his own fashion," Hallstein recounted.

For the time being, however, the French head of state seemed to Hallstein a man bent on destruction. Although the Fouchet Plan envisaged the unification and reorganization of the three communities within three years, Hallstein thought its real intention was to stifle them. In four years, the principle of unanimity, which the Council of Ministers had scrupulously followed, would no longer be obligatory. But if decisions were made by the majority, the communities would be saved. Among the Six there would always be a majority to oppose any separate, concerted, or individual move to deprive the Six of their powers, their unifying supranational attributes, or their leaders. That was why de Gaulle hurried to rally support for his campaign to undermine them. Averse to a supranational political secretariat, he had no intention of unifying Europe!

For Hallstein a life-and-death struggle was about to begin over the Europe of Brussels. Even Monnet was discouraged. It was impossible to reason with the general. "De Gaulle talks of Europe but he does nothing," Monnet said. "He is a pessimist. He's willing to accept things as they are instead of trying to change them."

The Europeans, isolated as they were from one another, were more and more impressed by American superiority. The Americans, on the other hand, were increasingly impressed by Europe's weakness. Unable to find large groups of Europeans who knew what they wanted, the Americans would become more and more impossible. This was Monnet's opinion.

Meanwhile, the intergovernmental discussions on the Fouchet I draft were progressing better than had been expected. Several solutions seemed possible. After all, there was nothing to prevent the Six from discussing their own defense problems and making suggestions to NATO. It was possible to conceive of a secretariat for the Council of the Union that would be permanent but not necessarily supranational. Hallstein was a very good man. But there were qualified Italians who would certainly be less rigid. Spaak's name was also mentioned.

The next summit meeting should produce some sort of understanding, people thought.

But a clap of thunder was heard in Strasbourg on December 21, 1961. René Pleven, Monnet's former collaborator and faithful friend, presented a sensational report which he managed to get the Assembly to accept. The political union should not now or later challenge in any way the validity of supranational institutions. The joint organism of the political union should itself be supranational.

"Does he take us for Merovingians?" was the angry response from Paris. "Are we going to allow chiefs of state and government heads to surrender the powers of a union to a Mayor of the Palace who will be able to do as he pleases in the domain of international politics?"

It was Hallstein and his technocrats, people said, who were obstructing European unification. They wanted to maintain a vacuum of their own making and conduct themselves as regents, as agents of the United States! Strasbourg criticism abounded. Hallstein's ill-advised maneuvers and the actions of Monnet were regarded as a sly trick on the part of the smaller nations to obtain England's participation.

General de Gaulle was exasperated. Negotiations were dragging on. He felt that his partners were ready to settle for any questionable, illegitimate arrangement. De Gaulle decided to end the mess once and for all—enough of supranationality, of "Frankensteins," of Monnet's diabolic automatons. He would play his hand as if he were in a poker game, double or nothing. To René Mayer, who questioned him, he answered:

"I'm tearing everything to pieces and beginning all over again."

On January 18, 1962, he staged a theatrical gesture in the green-carpet room. The French delegation laid a new text on the table. Supposedly simplified, it was weighed down with a new word: "economics." In this new project, "Fouchet II," economics became one of the union's paramount concerns, along with defense, foreign affairs, and cultural relations.

215

This meant that the Brussels Commission would be stripped of its privileges, its power to take action, its right to speak in the name of the Six. It meant overthrowing Hallstein. For the Elysée, this was simply a matter of common sense. The six government heads could not discuss industrial production, oil imports, or agricultural problems without a mandate from their representatives.

In Brussels a revolt broke out. The campaign for integration was gravely compromised. England, getting ready to intervene, planned to ask permission to participate in the negotiations on April 10, 1962, for a political union.

During the entire crisis, de Gaulle had one ally whose word carried considerable weight: Adenauer. For the German Chancellor a political union based on a Franco-German understanding was more important than the privileges of the communities. The latter would be submerged if a confederation were established that would eventually lead to the formation of a federation.

On February 15, 1962, de Gaulle and Adenauer met in Baden-Baden. Here they proclaimed their determination to accelerate the creation of the European Political Union. But a month later, on March 20, in a speech to the other foreign ministers in Luxembourg, Paul Henri Spaak and his Dutch colleagues led an attack against "Fouchet II."

They maintained that joint defense must be discussed within the framework of the Atlantic Pact and that it should contribute to the development of the Atlantic Pact; that the Commissions of the communities, charged with defining the common interest impartially and determining what transactions were necessary, must retain all these powers; the Secretary-General of the Union must be independent of the governments; the Strasbourg Assembly should become a European parliament, elected on the basis of universal suffrage; majority rule should be established for the Council of Ministers.

Couve de Murville remained adamant. The conference adjourned. Then de Gaulle resumed the offensive. By telephone, he obtained Adenauer's consent to the second point, which empowered the government heads to discuss economic matters without any prior invitation to do so from the Commission. In other words, there was to be an end to the privileges reserved for the Hallstein Commission.

Adenauer was furious with Spaak because of the difficulties he was causing. But France and Germany were not the only countries involved. De Gaulle arranged to meet the President of the Council, Amintore Fanfani, in Turin. The Italians were quite willing to play the role of honest brokers for the Benelux countries.

The meeting took place on April 4, 1962, at the Castello de La Mandria. Fanfani spent all morning in a tête-à-tête with de Gaulle. He pleaded for a combination of political union and supranational communities.

"I will do my utmost to meet your ideas," de Gaulle promised. The two men resumed their discussion after lunch. Also present were Couve de Murville, the Foreign Minister, Segni, and the Italian delegate to the treaty draft, Attilio Cattani. De Gaulle professed himself willing to mention the Atlantic Alliance in the preamble. The political union would therefore not be anti-American. He also agreed that nothing should be changed in the structure of the supranational communities.

"Victory!" his interlocutors exclaimed.

Attilio Cattani again urged the establishment, three years hence, of an elected European parliament. It would represent a real melting pot and be conducive to the future unity of the Six.

"There can be no true parliament without a European government," the French said. "Let's be reasonable. Let's set up a confederation first. After an interval of adjustment, a confederation always develops into a federal state with a central government and a parliament. But let's not put the cart before the horse. A parliament without a European government would be but a center of vituperation against the various national governments—an assembly of critics and angry men. Hasn't each government enough to do already in its own parliament without seeking the grievances of Württemberg deputies against Rome, Sicilian deputies against The Hague or Dutch deputies against Paris?"

In the end, the Italians were fairly well satisfied. But de Gaulle was displeased because he had yielded. And the Dutch were impossible, crying out for England like children asking for their mother.

"It's been knocked to pieces," said Fouchet, brandishing fire and sword as he left for Algeria, where he had been appointed Deputy-General.

Adenauer, however, was not willing to give up his plan for a political union. He frowned when he learned that de Gaulle had agreed to give the Hallstein Commission the exclusive right to take the initiative. He thought this would be a source of future complications. Now it was Adenauer's turn to meet with Fanfani. He did so on April 7, 1962, at Cadenabbia.

"If de Gaulle thinks it's acceptable, I, too, will accept it," Adenauer concluded.

An attempt was made to pick up the pieces of "Fouchet II." A counterproposal made by the Five was handed around and converted by the experts into "Fouchet III." It was to be discussed in Paris on April 17. A week before this meeting took place, England officially requested admission to the political union.

From the opening of the Conference of the Six at the Quai d'Orsay, Spaak and the Dutch minister, Luns, complained bitterly about the conversations that had taken place between the three major European powers. According to them, the political union was not sufficiently integrated. Belgium and the Netherlands were ready to join a federation in which they would have their representatives and their votes. But if the big powers demanded a political union in which they would be dominant, Belgium and the Netherlands preferred to wait until England was admitted to the Common Market and to the confederation. She would counterbalance the Franco-German entente.

"Let's draft a text and present it to the British," Couve de Murville suggested.

"That would be premature," Spaak answered, thus finalizing the rupture.

"Spaak was supporting a paradox," one French diplomat said. "He should know better than anyone else that the British are opposed to any surrender of sovereignty. To demand an integrated union plus the participation of England is to burn all the bridges."

Spaak explained the apparent paradox in the following terms: "I favor a supranational, integrated Europe that makes all its decisions by majority rule. There is no other effective way to arrive at decisions. I have demanded the participation of England so that the small countries will have a counterweight against Germany and France. In so doing, I was quite aware, of course, that her presence might seriously jeopardize the realization of a European political union."

A French minister, commenting at length on the question, said: "Europe is merely a topic for discussion. Not a single one of France's partners has suggested a United Europe of the Six. Political union, which is the first genuine step toward organic unity, has been urged by only one person, Konrad Adenauer. He knows that by tying France to the West he is insuring the stability of his own country.

"The state most hostile to unification is Holland, an island imprisoned by the surrounding countries. Rotterdam, the major port of industrial Europe, benefits greatly from the Common Market. Holland strongly favors free trade throughout the Atlantic and for her river navigation. Opposed to regulations and tariffs, she is demanding nonpolitical integration. The customers of neighboring lands might impose a tax on transport. She is therefore lobbying against it from within the Common Market. In demanding British participation, the Dutch are seeking support for a nation that shares their interest. They will torpedo political union because they want the United States to assume political responsibility for Europe and to pay for the cost of arming the continent.

"Belgium, on the other hand, and especially Spaak, has often manifested a desire for European unification. But the Belgians are tied to the other Benelux countries. And Spaak does not want the big countries to organize a political Europe without him."

The Italians, more than anyone else, were disappointed by the failure of European political union. They had worked very hard to promote it. President Segni confided in Cattani, the Italian expert on the Fouchet Commission. "I am deeply distressed," he said, "to see that General de Gaulle's efforts have been unsuccessful. I regret this for the sake of the entire world."

Cattani traveled all over Europe in an effort to restore broken ties. In Bonn he saw the aging Chancellor, who had nothing but sarcastic comments to make about "that torpedoer," Spaak. In Brussels, Spaak said he needed "time to reflect." Luns, the Dutchman at The Hague, said he was very satisfied by the turn of events, meaning the adjournment. In Paris, Couve de Murville was courteous and encouraging, but de Gaulle was evasive and expressed great anger against the Dutch and Belgian press, which had accused him of wanting to become the dictator of Europe.

On May 15, 1962, a month after the failure of the political union, de Gaulle scrapped his plan. At a stormy press conference, he ridiculed the Strasbourg Assembly integrationists as well as "integrated

Volapuk"; he denounced Monnet—although he did not mention him by name—as being to blame for the opposition he had encountered; he attacked the United States, calling it the disguised federator of a Europe made up of technocrats without a country. "If that's what they want, let them say so!"

The five MRP ministers in Pompidou's cabinet, who had plumped for a European Assembly, resigned that very night. Their action came after a lengthy telephone conversation between Pflimlin and the general. At the Palais Bourbon the champions of an integrated Europe rebelled. The press throughout the country condemned de Gaulle almost unanimously.

Meanwhile, Spaak was wondering if he had made a mistake. The fiery partisan of a federated Europe was too shrewd a politician not to realize that he might be held responsible for the failure of the European political union. It had been almost within reach. Now all hope for it was dashed perhaps forever. But de Gaulle was not immortal. Had the confederation proposed by France been a unique opportunity to lay the foundations for a European state? Since sooner or later confederations evolved and became federations, would not Spaak himself have had a considerable role to play in the political union? Spaak's powerful personality had for a long time transcended in importance the small country he represented. As one of the founders of the Common Market, as Secretary-General of NATO for many years, he might have been called upon to assume important responsibilities on the Continent.

Following this train of thought, Spaak now suggested a fresh attempt to launch a political union, even if at first it were to be limited in scope. The Dutch were furious. The rupture that occurred on April 17 had been a victory for Luns. But the others were rather favorable to Spaak's proposal. So he wrote to de Gaulle saying he was ready to discuss his project again, "taking into account the long delays which England's entry into the European communities would entail." And he saw to it that people knew about his letter. De Gaulle merely answered that he had never doubted that Belgium would ultimately adopt such an attitude, because after all it "accorded with realities and common sense."

Blocked by the small countries that took alarm at the prospect of a Franco-German entente, opposed by Monnet, Hallstein, and the integrationists (who would not tolerate the idea that the community institutions might be threatened), de Gaulle turned his attention to a different enterprise. He would forge a Franco-German European polity, flanked by an Anglo-French scientific, nuclear, military, and economic partnership.

XV

Stalemate Between the
Two Europes

EVER since John Kennedy's election on November 8, 1960, Monnet had been besieging the young President in Washington. Monnet wanted two things: American recognition of the European Community in order to lend it the authority and the international character of which de Gaulle was attempting to deprive it; an equal partnership between the United States and the European Community, the two pillars of the Atlantic, that would open an era of prosperity to 400,000,000 people. It would be the world's largest industrial association.

Such a plan, according to Monnet, was bound to inspire both sides of the ocean so that Europe, in spite of de Gaulle, would flourish.

"Partnership?" Couve de Murville said, as if he had never heard the word.

George Ball, part of the business world familiar to the White House, was a friend of Monnet's. They had become acquainted in Washington during the war. Ball had become a European adviser after Eisenhower left office. It was Ball who introduced Monnet to the new President. The two men had a long conversation.

Kennedy was opposed to a united Europe when he first assumed office. He felt it would threaten American leadership in the West; in addition, a large market might be closed to American exports and investments. The European Community could eventually become such

222

a powerful area that it might be able to compete successfully with American industry throughout the world.

Kennedy then detailed his New Frontier policy, which was at once generous and commercially selfish; he planned to expand the foreign markets for American goods, instead of perpetuating the old isolationism. He was involved in negotiations, enormous in scope, for lowering national trade barriers. In order to further his aim, he revived a world trade and tariff organization, GAAT, that had been created in the wake of a conference held at Havana in 1947. It would comprise about fifty countries, including the European Community, England, the Commonwealth, Switzerland, the Scandinavian countries, and Japan.

"An affair of big business, tariffs, big money," Monnet said to George Ball. "But besides this, an important undertaking of an entirely different nature should be promoted: a political, economic, and military partnership between the United States and the European Community."

On January 25, 1962, in a message to Congress, the President of the United States advocated "an open commercial association between the United States and the European Community."

This was a serious disappointment to Monnet. But he returned to the White House to urge the initiation of negotiations for the most important treaty in the world, with both sides of the Atlantic dealing with one another as equals.

"The Schuman Plan," said Monnet, "has had important repercussions because it called for collaboration on the basis of equality between victors and vanquished. A similar gesture must be made by the world's most powerful nation and the European Community."

Walter Hallstein had been present at some of these conversations. He was welcomed by Kennedy as a head of government. U Thant also received him at the United Nations as a world-renowned figure.

Monnet's project directly challenged the political union that de Gaulle was negotiating with his partners for a European Europe that was basically autonomous.

"The Atlantic partnership merely gives official status to a governmentless Europe," said Couve du Murville. "An association such as this with the United States will have only one capital, Washington. It is an attempt to block the political union that will give unity to the Six and enable them to pursue a definite policy. Jean Monnet," the

223

minister went on to say, "does not propose to constitute an authentic power in Europe, one that will have its own policy. What he is suggesting is designed merely to influence American policy within the framework of an association."

"The Europeans will not be able to discuss matters with the Americans until they have acquired strength through unification," Monnet said. "They should not be deprived of American cooperation. But an equal partnership would make Europeans invaluable to the Americans as partners who will save them from many mistakes."

At the Quai d'Orsay, people said: "The Americans, thinking they are acting for the general good, like to surround themselves with allies and supporters. This blinds them to the more or less colonial nature of their undertakings. The Americans exert tremendous pressure on England and on France's partners in order to paralyze any real attempt at European unity."

On May 15, 1962, de Gaulle held a press conference in which he gave free rein to his fury following the failure of the political union. In veiled terms he directly assailed the architect of the communities, accusing him of having "inspired" the opposition to the union. He also attacked the United States as the unwanted federator of an integrated Europe.

"A so-called integrated Europe, in which there would be no fixed policy, was therefore bound to be dependent on outsiders who would certainly have a fixed policy. Perhaps there would be a 'federator,' but it would not be European. . . . And perhaps it is this which, to some extent and from time to time, inspires certain remarks by this or that champion of European integration."

Touched to the quick, Monnet pressed Kennedy. The White House must make some significant gesture to refute the charge that the Atlanticists were asking for an impossible Europe and were destroying a possible one in order to maintain a vacuum in which American authority would have full sway. He wanted Kennedy to make some statement that would consecrate the Economic Community as a world power. The President promised that he would comply.

Monnet immediately drafted a motion for the Action Committee of the United States of Europe. Over the telephone he procured the promise of signatures from European political and union leaders. It was an answer to de Gaulle, published on June 26, 1962: "The only possible federator of Europe is not America; it cannot be a

country or a man, but a method of work: communitarian action. . . .
This method, which is altogether new, does not include the establishment of a central government. Rather, it will facilitate joint decisions
within the framework of the Council of Ministers. . . .

"Cooperation between the United States and the countries of
Europe," the declaration continued, "must take the form of relations between partners, of two entities having equal power. . . . These
relations are not only economic but will extend to the military and
political domain."

The motion voiced the hope that England would join the Common
Market and that a treaty would be drafted to initiate a political union
that respected existing regulations and organizations relating to economic integration.

On July 4, 1962, John Kennedy delivered a speech in Philadelphia
that satisfied the wishes of Monnet and Hallstein. He called for a
viable Atlantic association among equals; a joint declaration of interdependence; an alliance "between the new union that is forming in
Europe and the old union founded in Philadelphia almost two centuries ago."

On October 11, 1962, Kennedy obtained from Congress the Trade
Expansion Act. It authorized him to negotiate new customs agreements in an Atlantic area of free trade that extended to Japan. These
agreements affected 80 percent of the imports and exports. It was
hoped that eventually all duties would be cut by about 50 percent.

At the time of the Kennedy Round, American recognition of an
integrated Europe was dramatically heralded: the Europe-America
negotiations were to be undertaken by a Commissioner of the Community, Jean Rey, acting as the Foreign Minister of Europe with the
consent of the Six.

In June, 1963, during a trip to Europe, Kennedy made a speech
in the Saint Paul's Church of Frankfurt, the cradle of Germanic unity.
He alluded to Monnet's ideas when he expressed his satisfaction at
the thought of a united Europe. It would be a world power, he said,
capable of dealing with the United States on an equal footing in every
domain. Impelled by the flamboyant American chief of state, the
Atlantic partnership might have gone rather far had Kennedy not
been assassinated five months later in Dallas.

An international conference had been called to set up the Atlantic
Community, that huge bridge between the United States and Canada

225

on one side, the Six and England on the other. Hopefully, it would break down the political barriers that still hindered the emergence of this gigantic political, economic, and military entity.

The principal obstacle to the partnership would probably have been the France of General de Gaulle. But the combined strength of the two great movements on either side of the ocean, moving toward union in a great upsurge, would have been so powerful that the man in the Elysée would have gone under or France would have become an isolated island unable to resist for long. President Johnson had neither such grandiose designs nor the fervor necessary to impose them. On the day of Kennedy's assassination, Monnet lost the most powerful and brilliant ally he could have found for the most ambitious of all his plans.

Meanwhile, de Gaulle had not given up the idea of reconstructing Europe. Blackballed by the small nations, he reached an understanding with the big ones. He based his political regime on a direct entente with the Germany of Adenauer, his personal ally. It was a bipartisan agreement, but it was open to the other nations. Italy was the first country invited to join. After that, the Benelux countries were more or less obliged to follow. The general's initiative fulfilled all of Adenauer's hopes. It was still the Chancellor's aim to tie Germany to France in order to anchor his country in the West before he died. He aso wanted the United States to realize that Germany was independent; Kennedy's attitude toward the U.S.S.R. had not been at all reassuring.

Preparations were made in the summer for developments between Paris and Bonn that were to have resounding repercussions. But first de Gaulle had to disarm England. It was as difficult to reconstruct Europe without her as with her. Eight times the British had refused association with the Continent. They had prevented the OEEC from becoming a truly effective Organization for European Economic Cooperation, over and above the Marshall Plan. They had rejected a customs union with France and the neighboring countries that Monnet had proposed. Although England had been invited to join the European Coal and Steel Community and the European Defense Community, she had remained isolated. She had emasculated the Council of Europe and converted it into a puppet. Remaining aloof from the debates on the Common Market and Euratom, she had organized the AELE and the free trade area with the object of ruining the Economic Community. Ever since July 31, 1961, when Prime Minister Macmillan announced his intention of opening negotiations in Brussels, the representative of His Majesty's Government, Edward Heath, had daily drawn from his briefcase requests for special concessions. Lord of the Privy Seal, and a seductive, skillful debator, Heath gave the impression that what he was seeking above all was England's entry into the Common Market. Britain's intervention during the final days of the Fouchet Plan, which had been blocked by her Belgian and Dutch protégés, was merely, in the opinion of Paris, an exercise in pyrotechnics instigated by Washington. "England is an island," de Gaulle was wont to say.

The French President believed that England was closer to conversion than she seemed to be. Her situation as America's poor cousin grew more obvious after the advent of Kennedy, who advanced into the twentieth century with the radiant self-assurance of a Botticelli figure.

Macmillan was in difficulties in Washington. England had atomic missiles—she even had the H-bomb—but she had no delivery system. Her nuclear bombers, the Victor and the Vulcan, were very vulnerable to the new Soviet missiles. Skybolt rockets and air-to-ground missiles could be released by these bombers far from their targets without endangering the planes that carried them, which would not have to enter the enemy's airspace. But the RAF had neither the technical means nor, above all, the financial means to make these rockets. The London cabinet asked Washington to manufacture them for England. But McNamara, the American Defense Secretary, was reluctant. Kennedy had embarked on a policy aimed at appeasing the Soviet Union. American atomic strategy was being reviewed, and Polaris missiles were being built. Rockets like the Skybolt, and bombers like the Victor and the Vulcan were obsolete, as was England's desire to have a nuclear force of her own.

After the advent of intercontinental missiles, the United States could no longer give help to any other nation in the acquisition of an atomic force. This was the ultimate result of the atom, with its life-and-death-giving powers that no longer could be shared. It was impossible for America to permit England to embark on a course that could lead to a conflict which would have to be met within a matter of minutes. De Gaulle, more than anyone else, sympathized with the British cabinet and sensed the hurt that all the American

227

shilly-shallying had inflicted on England's national pride. The British were reduced to the same humiliating situation in which the French found themselves. Since France had to acquire a nuclear force of her own, why shouldn't the two nations join forces? De Gaulle invited Harold Macmillan to the Château de Champs. He had known the Prime Minister in London and in Algiers, where Macmillan had been Churchill's representative. Macmillan was a fine, cultivated publisher, related to the great families of the English gentry, a gentleman and a gallant one. The general rather liked the British Prime Minister. On August 2, 1961, Macmillan requested that England be admitted into the Common Market, declaring, "What General de Gaulle has referred to as the Europe of Nations seems more suitable to the national traditions of European countries, and in particular to our own. It is a conception to which we willingly and wholeheartedly subscribe."

Macmillan was no "Monnetist," no "maniac of integration." If he managed to disengage himself from the American orbit, if he accepted the common agricultural market, he would be an appropriate partner, provided he succeeded in overcoming the indecisiveness and the hesitations of his compatriots on the subject of Europe.

Cooperation with Great Britain was desirable for France because of England's headstart in atomic science and technology. France only had the A-bomb—the "little bomb"—which made the experts on both sides of the Atlantic poke fun at her. But Pierrelatte ("that joke," as the Pentagon said) was under way and a French striking force seemed imminent. Pierrelatte was the equivalent of England's Capenhurst.

De Gaulle had no illusions about the British. He knew that they would not share American atomic secrets with France. Nor did he expect Washington to allow France direct access to atomic information, although this would have been possible under the terms of the modified MacMahon Law. The Americans, he was sure, would refuse. Nevertheless, General Lavaud, the chief of the French land forces, hoped, through personal contacts, to obtain some information about tooling from the Americans. "You won't get anything, but go ahead and try," de Gaulle told him.

Lavaud returned empty-handed. Perhaps some form of military collaboration with the British should be sought. The June 2, 1962, meeting at the Château de Champs was a trial balloon to test the intentions of the Conservative Party. De Gaulle spoke in general terms of the great things the two nations could accomplish together, far from the United States—things that would not be possible were each country to attempt to do them separately: missiles, atomic power stations, supersonic intercontinental planes, electronic research, a joint deterrent force. (The difficulties the Comet had encountered were devastating for an island that ruled the seas and yet was forced to yield to the United States a monopoly of long-range cruisers.)

Macmillan shook his long gray locks in assent. His hair, mournful expression, and gentle eyes gave him the melancholy appearance of an Irish setter. When he left the Château de Champs he seemed convinced. A cordial entente was apparently a probability. The French experts went to work to set up a program of joint aeronautic activity —the plans for the Concorde, to begin with.

The aeronautic engineers grumbled. "De Gaulle has put himself out. The cost of building the Concorde and all the other planes he is planning in combination with the English will be three times greater than the cost of building them by ourselves at home. British construction costs are excessive, while the profits of British companies are unlimited. On the other side of the Channel the union regulations require a specialist for everything you do and every worker has to have an assistant. But the main problem is that with two administrations you get contradictory instructions, and you have to begin over again constantly."

Later, it was said that Macmillan went back to London without having understood the full import of his conversation with de Gaulle. Perhaps this was due to the British tendency to take time to think things over. In any case, on his return the Prime Minister alluded to "a revamping of British policy" and a "rapprochement with Europe." But he met with more reservations than approval. The entire Labour Party was opposed. The Conservatives were divided. As for the Americans, they were shocked.

De Gaulle's attempt to win over England, plus his successful seduction of Adenauer, aroused anger in Washington. For a time, after the war in Algeria was over and during the Évian Accords, "the man who regards himself as Joan of Arc" had recovered a certain popularity in the United States. But all this changed when the political union failed. The Château de Champs meeting had not been taken seriously by the brain trust in the White House. But the overall rapprochement between de Gaulle and Macmillan gave rise to many exasperated transatlantic telephone calls that nonplussed the British Prime Minister.

On July 4, 1962, when John Kennedy spoke about the union of the Unions in Philadelphia, Konrad Adenauer was being welcomed in Paris (July 2-8) as the quasi-legendary ally. A general accord between the two countries was under consideration. But this was not enough for the old Rhinelander. He wanted a treaty that was political, economic, cultural, and military in scope. It would unite Germany closely with France; and his successors, so the Chancellor thought, would be obliged to honor it.

From September 4 to 9, 1962, de Gaulle was Adenauer's guest. The visit was a triumph. The acclaim the general received might have led one to believe that all the Germans were Gaullists. At the military academy of Hamburg, de Gaulle delivered a resounding speech. "Nothing great has occurred in the relations between France and Germany unless weapons were involved. . . ."

"He is suggesting a direct military alliance," people exclaimed.

Actually, the treaty under consideration provided for strategic cooperation, joint research in construction materials, exchanges of officers and personnel. With this prospect in view, French atomic weaponry could be used for European defense, but there was no question of a Franco-German striking force.

Nonetheless, what had been accomplished was important enough in the eyes of shocked observers. If a Franco-German Europe came into being and was joined by the Italians, the Benelux countries, and even the British, a small European NATO would be created, distinct from the existing one. Military plans would be determined by the Europeans before they were submitted to the Atlantic allies. The planes and armored divisions of the national armies would no longer be purchased from America but constructed on the Continent. A French general would head the European general staff. This would soon signal the end of NATO, or at least it would mean that the organization would be drastically changed and "de-Americanized."

De Gaulle's visit and speech caused a stir throughout the world. There were angry outbursts in Washington and London. Fascinated by the general, Adenauer had betrayed America's protective friendship. De Gaulle was attempting to revive Germanic nationalism.

230

According to French diplomats, representatives of the Federal Republic in Washington and London were given a bad time.

No sooner had de Gaulle departed for Paris than Adenauer was deluged with reproaches from his own party. Erhard and Schroeder, the pro-Atlantic ministers, repeatedly suggested to the Bundestag and the Christian Socialist Party that the Chancellor be retired. But the tough old man was determined to procure a Franco-German treaty. Official negotiations began in October. De Gaulle, for his part, was accused of offering the Germans atomic weapons.

For a long time storms had been brewing within NATO. Ever since 1959, General Norstad, NATO's commander in chief, had vainly demanded an effective deterrent force for Europe. Controlled from Washington, America's atomic arsenal encircled the U.S.S.R. Only the American President could press the atomic button. The progress made in the production of rockets and ballistic missiles increased the danger of a Soviet attack on American soil. Would the button be pressed if the Soviets invaded Europe? Or would Europe be the victim of a nuclear Munich? The cold war over Berlin persisted. To circumvent the threat of an Eastern bloc, the Secretary of State, John Foster Dulles, pursued a policy of brinkmanship. Egged on by the Europeans, Norstad asked for entire batteries of atomic rockets aimed at the U.S.S.R. This would facilitate automatic retaliation in case of invasion, thereby deterring the Kremlin and the Red Army.

"The Europeans want rockets and ballistic missiles as an automatic deterrent? Very well. Are they willing to pay for them?" asked the Pentagon and the White House. De Gaulle had no intention of buying American atomic weapons. He had refused to allow American rockets on French soil unless they were under French command. But the *Bundeswehr* was very resentful at being deprived of nuclear missiles, of having an army that was one war too late. The ministers in Bonn were worried about the terrifying progress of Soviet armaments. They asked to be included in decisions about atomic strategy and the handling of American weapons.

On September 6, 1960, Adenauer was vacationing at Cadenabbia. He was bowling when Spaak, the Secretary-General of NATO, and General Norstad arrived on the terrace. At that time the American Assistant Secretary of State, Herter, was about to ask the Atlantic Council for "European rockets" to be paid for by the Europeans. Norstad addressed a similar request to NATO. The answer, of course, was that America would retain control of any such weapons. The request foreshadowed an attempt to organize a multilateral nuclear force. The situation was a bitter paradox: America's allies could purchase atomic arms, but the President of the United States alone would control their use.

After the question of payment was raised, Norstad's missiles had no takers, with the exception of Germany. This placed Germany's allies in an embarrassing position.

As soon as Kennedy was elected, he put a damper on the sale of rockets to European nations. He was seeking a détente with the East. On June 3-4, 1961, he met Khrushchev in Vienna. The master of the Kremlin demanded a lessening of nuclear threats to the Soviet Union, the removal of the Thor and Jupiter missiles pointed at Russia from Turkey and Europe, and a cessation of the flights of giant bombers that encircled the U.S.S.R. day and night.

Secretary of Defense McNamara was perfecting a new strategy. He told NATO that should Europe be invaded and should nuclear reprisals be global, immediate and automatic, the U.S.S.R. would be virtually wiped out, but so would be the United States and Europe. There would have to be a pause to provide time for negotiation. During this interval, the Europeans, aided by American forces in Europe, would defend themselves with conventional weapons.

The French experts rebelled against this strategy. They claimed that it would deprive nuclear weapons of their deterrent effect. If the Red Army reached Brest, it would be too late to send antiballistic missiles or rockets across the iron curtain. The strategy amounted to a desertion of Europe. Because he was opposed to "the pause," General Norstad was relieved of his command on July 25, 1962. During the debates, de Gaulle urged Adenauer and his ministers to resist the temptation of asking for nuclear arms. France, he said, could never accept a direct German-American military alliance.

On October 23, 1962, the Cuban crisis erupted. When the anti-Castro landing in the Bay of Pigs failed, Fidel Castro sent Moscow an SOS. His island was about to be invaded by the Americans, he claimed. Washington had failed to respond to Khrushchev's request to call off American bombers flying over Russia. Behind in the missile race, the Soviets seized upon the Cuban crisis as an opportunity to improve the balance of nuclear power. Soviet missiles were stationed in Cuba, close to American territory.

Kennedy sent Khrushchev an ultimatum. Ambassador Bohlen called on de Gaulle. For the latter's benefit, Bohlen extracted from his briefcase a packet of photographs of the Russian rockets in Cuba. "I don't want to see them," said the French President. "America is in danger. Its ally, France, will be at its side."

The entire world lived through many anguished hours. Khrushchev withdrew his rockets. But the Kennedy victory was not as complete as it seemed at the time. Castro remained in Cuba. There would be no further military action against him. The United States withdrew from Turkey an entire battery of Jupiter rockets that had been declared obsolete. A hot line was established between the Kremlin and the White House. It marked the beginning of a détente, of tranquil coexistence and atomic peace.

In de Gaulle's eyes this was evidence that although the U.S.S.R. and the United States might bare their teeth at each other, they would never engage in all-out nuclear warfare which was bound to bring mutual annihilation. Suddenly, the world situation was reversed: Cuba had been a turning point in history. Now, if Europe were invaded, it would receive no help in the form of a destructive bombing of the U.S.S.R. Because of the way in which NATO was constituted, with Washington responsible for the defense of the Continent, the Atlantic Alliance could no longer be of assistance to Europe. The flexible defense that McNamara had suggested to the Atlantic Council was significant, according to the French. They pointed out that the Council had expressed no opinion about this "strategy of abandonment" imposed by a mere American decision.

De Gaulle drew his own conclusions: More than ever, Europe must become a European Europe, independent of both West and East. This meant an attempt at détente with the U.S.S.R. and a search for détente "from the Urals to the Atlantic." The treaty with Germany, the keystone of a European political union, was negotiated by Adenauer, in a state of euphoria. Franco-German cooperation was so vast, so general in every domain that in the end it proved an empty shell. The treaty was like a pretty box into which everything could be put.

In order to pry the British loose from Washington, to associate them with Europe, and to allow them membership in European institutions—if they were ready for it—Couve de Murville listened patiently to Edward Heath's arguments in Brussels. During the month of November, 1962, Heath drew from his briefcase his seven hundredth request for a privileged application of the Common Market regulations.

For the last fifteen months, the bargaining had centered around the inflexible concerns of England: the Continent must accept the idea of a free trade area; supranationality was incompatible with British sovereignty; certain Common Market ties must be loosened in order to enable England to preserve her trade relations with the Commonwealth; an agricultural common market was unacceptable to British consumers and farmers; the pound sterling would have to be maintained at its current overvalued level and as a world currency, despite the risks which this entailed for the Six. They might be reimbursed with an unstable currency and find themselves forced in the end to pay the British Empire's monumental war debts.

The experts on the Commission discussed all these matters with the British. There were interminable debates on the size of the duties to be levied on New Zealand beef and butter, Australian wool, Canadian aluminum, Indian jute, and Rhodesian tobacco. "Tonight we come to the turtle soup and kangaroo meat," groaned one delegate.

The experts admitted that delays, alterations, and concessions were in keeping with the regulations. But the solution of each problem depended on the solution of others. The overriding need was for a general agreement.

De Gaulle had no patience with all this bargaining over every dutiable item, nor with the Talmudic controversies over supranationality or internationality. "If England is willing to join Europe, to give up her false kinship with the United States, her illusions about the Commonwealth, then everything will be possible; but if she wants to join the Common Market in order to ruin it, we would do better to break off with her."

At the Elysée Palace there was exasperation at the pressure exerted in Brussels on England, despite her hesitations and hundreds of prior conditions. Monnet and his integrationist friends in the six parliaments, the Atlantic governments, and, behind them, Washington, which was eager to initiate the Kennedy Round negotiations with England included in the European orbit—all these people were doing what they could to encourage England to reach an understanding with the Hallstein Commission. Observers at the Quai d'Orsay contended that Brussels was pushing the wheels of the American Trojan horse.

Late one afternoon, Walter Hallstein announced that Edward Heath had accepted the supranationality of the Community. But he had not agreed to every feature of the agricultural common market. Although many problems had been resolved, things were still up in the air. "We have to be patient," said Monnet. "The British will be forced either to join the Continent or become the fifty-first American state. . . . The longer they put things off, the more they risk a rude awakening, a political shock that might spell the end of their institutions. Public opinion in England is gradually coming around to the idea of a unified Europe. We must help them. They could make enormous contributions of all kinds to an integrated Europe. If they join the Six, Europe will be more solid and cohesive than it has ever been."

General de Gaulle's diagnosis of the situation coincided closely with Monnet's. But he accused Monnet of wanting to tie the Anglo-Saxons to Europe as quickly as possible, of lightheartedly accepting the possibility that the Six would have to assume, through the Common Market, the war debts of the Bank of England. The Germans were likewise not eager to take a chance on the value of the pound sterling. Whenever the United States granted London credits to support the pound, it turned the remainder of the debt over to the European national banks.

De Gaulle decided to clarify matters with the amiable Macmillan. The cooperation that had begun so auspiciously at the Château de Champs was not dead. On October 25, General Puget, the director of Sud-Aviation, signed an agreement in London on the Concorde. But de Gaulle wanted to know whether the Conservative cabinet, which was always so hesitant, so divided, and which had done so little to convert public opinion to an acceptance of existing realities and to the idea of a unified Europe, was ready to give up its special ties with America and with its phantom Commonwealth.

De Gaulle had the perfect opportunity. England had just suffered a grave deception in Washington, a psychological shock. On November 8, London was informed by the Pentagon and by the press that no more Skybolts would be built. Two days later, McNamara confirmed this in a communication to the British government, which, however, refused to accept it. The English rockets had been stricken from the American defense budget. They had been rendered obsolete by the advent of intercontinental ballistic missiles. The Pentagon was stopping all construction of the giant bombers, the watchdogs that circled the U.S.S.R.

The British public was indignant. If there were to be no more Skybolts the United Kingdom would cease to have an independent atomic force. The last symbol of British power would disappear. Macmillan appealed to Kennedy via the long-distance telephone. "Meet us in Nassau next month," the young President suggested.

"I cannot return empty-handed, I would be ousted," the Prime Minister said.

Kennedy proposed a possible compensation. The United States was updating its nuclear force with Polaris missiles and atomic submarines similar to the *Nautilus*. The submarines were capable of cruising for a year; they could travel below the ice at the North Pole and keep the U.S.S.R. at bay with their 18 Polaris missiles, each of which carried an H-bomb. This could raze 18 large cities.

Macmillan announced that he would pass through Paris on December 15, 1962, en route to Nassau to see Kennedy. A fine fire was blazing in the large hearth at the Château of Rambouillet when de Gaulle received him. As always, Macmillan had the look of a melancholy setter. His red-rimmed eyes seemed more inflamed than usual. During the first hour the meeting was cordial. De Gaulle said that the Skybolt affair proved that the United States would never allow England to play the part of a first-rate power. America was about to deprive the British of the benefits promised her in the Roosevelt-Churchill wartime agreements. England would not be given atomic aid. But if she united with 180 million Europeans, she would resume her great position in Europe. She could join the Common Market and cooperate with France whenever she so decided. A European political union was currently being promoted by Paris and Bonn. The leadership of this movement could be shared with England. Macmillan thus had a chance to negotiate from strength in the Bahamas. He had only to acquiesce.

Macmillan made one significant remark, "Were I at England's head, I could do anything!"

The rest of the visit went badly. Macmillan said he did not know precisely what he would say in Nassau. Kennedy had mentioned something that might compensate England for the loss of the Skybolts, but he, Macmillan, had no idea what that "something" was.

"The only acceptable compensation for Great Britain is Europe," de Gaulle cut in. He suspected Macmillan of not telling him all that he knew. He was also afraid that the Prime Minister was going to America hat in hand. He said, in effect, that England's special ties with the United States were a guarantee of dollar aid but that such assistance would destroy England's political sovereignty, paralyze her economic and monetary recovery, and even prevent her from acquiring adequate national defense. Like France in 1958, England could pull herself out of the rut she was in, recover her freedom, and become once again a great European power.

"One must look at things from the point of view of Atlantic interdependence," Macmillan sighed. How could he emasculate the pound sterling, deprive it of its status as a world currency, abandon the Commonwealth, and break off ties with America? No British government could do that. The public would rebel. As for a rapprochement with France, it would have to be limited in scope. The previous June, when he, Macmillan, had returned to London from France, the American Secretary of State had remonstrated with him on the transatlantic telephone.

Much later, Macmillan reported, "Then de Gaulle threw Churchill's famous phrase at me: 'If you ask me to choose between you and the United States, between the big open spaces and the Continent, I will always choose the big open spaces!' "

The general said quite a few other things, too. He had some magnificent, almost tender words to say about England; but he also spoke critically. Macmillan left Rambouillet greatly distressed.

In December, 1962, Macmillan conferred with Kennedy in Nassau. The American President had the bounce and vigor engendered by the elation of his triumph over the Soviets in Cuba. Upon his shoulders rested the overwhelming responsibility for the peace of the free world. His country was assuming most of the costs as well as the deadly risks. He had to rally his allies and counter de Gaulle's attempts at subversion in Europe. He offered Macmillan far more than obsolete rockets; he offered him Polaris submarines, the pride of the United States Navy.

"But they will be American submarines," the Englishman sighed. "Great Britain would not have an independent force. The British public will not consider this an adequate compensation for the loss of the Skybolts."

237

"Of course, they will," Kennedy replied. England would buy the Polaris submarines and they would belong to her. The nuclear warheads would be British. Kennedy would give Macmillan the blueprints for these nuclear warheads, and they could then be manufactured in England.

But there was one small condition: England would naturally lend this nuclear force to NATO. If the United Kingdom alone were attacked, the submarines could be returned to her. Since such an eventuality was highly improbable, it seemed that the British nuclear force would have to be ceded to NATO. But British pride would be salvaged.

Within forty-eight hours Macmillan had capitulated, abandoning all thought of an independent power. He requested, however, that an analogous offer should be made to France. Kennedy agreed, but with reservations. "Something analogous is impossible, since in our eyes France is not a nuclear power. But I will do something 'parallel.' " He would also have to do something for the other allies of the United States.

Norstad and the Assistant Secretary of State, Herter, had promised Germany many things. She was eager to participate in the establishment of an atomic force. In the absence of the White House strategic brain trust and the American general staff, a solution was improvised that was more or less inspired by Norstad's earlier proposal to NATO. A complicated formula that alluded to a collective nuclear force was included in the final communiqué issued by the conference. This was the famous MLF, the multilateral nuclear force, open to all the members of NATO that wanted to share the cost of buying from America Polaris submarines for NATO. These vessels would be staffed by teams drawn from several different nations and would naturally remain under United States command.

On January 4, 1963, in accordance with Kennedy's offer to the Europeans, Ambassador Charles Bohlen came to the Elysée Palace to suggest in roundabout fashion the possibility of buying one or more Polaris submarines. The vessels would naturally be integrated with the forces of NATO, under the supreme command of the United States. But France would be free to use them should her vital interests be challenged. The dialogue was confined to the essentials: "Who would have control of the missiles? A French or an American officer?"

"The submarine will be under French command since France will

238

have purchased it," Bohlen replied. "If France acquires nuclear warheads of her own for the Polaris missiles a French officer will decide when to push the button. If the United States furnishes the nuclear warheads, then an American officer will make that decision."

At least this was what he seemed to be saying. Diplomatic circumlocutions were hardly intended to make things crystal clear. De Gaulle asked for time to make inquiries. French atomic scientists were consulted. They answered, "We haven't got the H-bomb to put in the Polaris. All we have at present is the bomb used at Hiroshima. We're still a long way off from producing the H-bomb."

Kennedy's suggestion would have seemed attractive to de Gaulle if the MacMahon Law, which was modified in 1954 for the benefit of the British, could also have been used to benefit France; or if England had been authorized to share the blueprints for the nuclear warheads which America had offered Macmillan. But President de Gaulle had no reason to be optimistic. Three times he had asked for further clarification on this point, but Washington had not been encouraging. Kennedy had no intention of helping France to become a nuclear power. His gesture was merely a symbolic courtesy.

The British press, however, was shocked by America's proposal to France. Apparently, it was identical with the one that had been made to Macmillan. Great Britain was no longer the privileged ally of the United States.

But the French chief of state was given one additional item. "France will have the right to veto any use of arms if the battle is being waged under her colors."

"This means that France, although authorized to refuse to use these arms, will not have the right to use them."

On January 11, 1963, de Gaulle rejected the American offer. He felt he had been tricked. He had offered England a chance to take her place in Europe, where she would have an important political and military position. But Macmillan had yielded to American pressure. Great Britain was the least independent country of Europe. She could not say no to the United States. She was not mature enough to join Europe in any capacity save that of America's representative in Europe. At least this was the view that prevailed at the Elysée Palace.

The multilateral nuclear force—five Polaris submarines, each armed with 18 rockets—represented 2 to 3 percent of the American nuclear arsenal. It would be purchased for $500,000,000. France was slated to pay 20 percent of the cost. This was not expensive for a nuclear submarine with Polaris missiles.

"But if we can't use it if we're attacked, it's a lot of cash for very fancy equipment," was the dry comment at the Quai d'Orsay. "We are offered a toy with a supervisor to watch over it—we're forbidden to use it without the permission of the seller. It's just a showcase piece to keep the French quiet."

"The Polaris offer is a trick to take back from the British the bomb they had been given, and to deter them from forming an Anglo-French alliance," Pompidou charged. "The Americans are determined to have a monopoly of atomic weapons in the West."

George Ball, one of Kennedy's collaborators, came to Bonn to suggest that the Federal Republic participate in the creation of the multinational nuclear force. The proposal was received with great interest. Konrad Adenauer felt very torn. His friend de Gaulle was categorically opposed to any German acquisition of atomic arms. It would arouse fear in the West and frustrate any plans for a détente with the Eastern bloc. But Erhard, Schroeder, and von Hassel were putting pressure on him to accept. By sharing in America's nuclear power, German naval officers and crews would be able, under American supervision, to familiarize themselves with the handling of missiles and rockets.

Although this possibility denuded a political and military treaty with France of much of its purpose, the Chancellor longed for such a pact more than ever. In his opinion, a close alliance with France was far more valuable than the illusory possession of nuclear arms.

De Gaulle apprised the Chancellor of his decision to reject England's request for entry into the Common Market. Adenauer was deeply distressed. Such a refusal would give rise to a great deal of criticism. He would not be forgiven for not having opposed it. But he had chosen to side with France. At the same time he could scarcely control the tremendous desire of his ministers and of his political party to share in the atomic enterprise. He had no choice but to accept the American offer.

On January 14, 1963, de Gaulle held his most newsworthy press conference. He rejected the multilateral nuclear force. He slammed the door of the Common Market in Britain's face, making it impossible for her to enter. At the very same time, Chancellor Adenauer told George Ball that the Federal Republic would participate in the creation of the multilateral nuclear force.

But this gesture was not enough to win back the very numerous champions of an Atlantic Europe in his cabinet, in his party, and in his country. Heretofore, the integrationists commented, the Chancellor had done nothing to oppose the Common Market. But now he had taken a position. "Beguiled by de Gaulle, he has acquiesced in France's rejection of England's bid to enter the Common Market," Monnet's friends said. "He is leading his country toward anti-Americanism. He has discredited himself in the eyes of his party and lost the esteem of international public opinion."

One week later, Adenauer went to Paris to sign the Franco-German alliance. But his political agony was just beginning. His "dauphin," Ludwig Erhard, openly demanded his retirement.

The Atlanticist leaders of the Christian Democratic Union staged quite a fanfare for the signing of the treaty. A unilateral preamble was presented to the Bundestag. It stated that the purpose of the alliance was to achieve the integration of European troops within NATO, to follow the path that would lead to the establishment of international communities, and to welcome England to Western Europe.

This text, which reflected the outlook of Monnet's committee, turned out to be a complete contradiction of the official version of the treaty. The preface of the official version included the de Gaulle-Adenauer plan for a Union of the Six or Seven who favored Franco-German unity of action, independent of the United States.

The German ministers besieged the White House and NATO in order to urge a swift realization of the multilateral nuclear force. But the President of the United States withdrew his offer of atomic submarines. Admiral Rickover, the father of the Polaris missiles, was categorically opposed to allowing foreign crews to come aboard the submarines, which were still top secret. This was an opportune veto as far as Kennedy was concerned. The Soviets had become alarmed at the idea of Germans cruising around the U.S.S.R. on submarines that were impossible to capture yet capable of wiping out 18 Russian cities. Khrushchev did not mince words in alluding to the sword of Damocles suspended over his head. In his opinion, the atomic submarines were more dangerous than the Thor and Jupiter missiles which the United States had withdrawn from Turkey.

NATO announced the substitution of camouflaged atomic cargo

ships for the atomic submarines. These phantom cruisers, which were to be manned by multinational crews, stirred up enormous controversy among members of the various Atlantic general staffs. How could surface ships—even camouflaged ones—elude Soviet reconnaissance? German journalists rained questions on American spokesmen in Germany and poked fun at the "masked ball" fleet.

Two messengers from Washington, Merchant and Gerard Smith, came to urge European membership in this international fleet. But most of the NATO countries were unenthusiastic about purchasing missiles that would obey only Washington's orders. The multilateral nuclear force seemed inadequate to meet the requirements of an increasingly complex strategy.

The Germans alone fought hard to obtain a nuclear force, which they were quite willing to share with the Americans. Ludwig Erhard, who succeeded Adenauer on October 16, 1963, went to Washington to plead with Kennedy and McNamara. The possibility of a German-American nuclear force caused tempers to flare in the U.S.S.R. and aroused indignation in Paris. With the advent of Erhard, there was no longer any reason for the French government to deal tactfully with the Germans.

In November, 1964, Pompidou, addressing the Assembly, furiously attacked the idea of a German-American atomic force. It was incompatible with the European system and a constant provocation for France, he said. It would destroy the European Community and endanger both the Common Market and the Kennedy Round. After Kennedy's assassination, President Johnson threw cold water on the project. Despite Erhard's impatience, he decided to abandon the idea altogether.

De Gaulle turned his back on the Continent. He left for a trip to Mexico and South America, preparing at the same time to implement his policy of détente and cooperation with the East. Two of his projects had failed. His European political union was thwarted by the Dutch and the Belgians, who opposed any European confederation that failed to include England. His dream of a Europe based on Franco-German cooperation vanished with Adenauer. In both instances, it was England who had prevented the creation of a politically united Europe.

"The general is his own worst enemy," his opponents claimed. "It was his determination to impose his conception of a European Europe on unwilling partners that led to the failure of both his projects. He should have allowed Europe to constitute itself gradually."

It was also true, of course, that it had proved very difficult to sell England the idea of a European partnership. "You were perfectly right to shut the Common Market door on England in 1963," Harold Wilson told General de Gaulle at Buckingham Palace, at the time of Churchill's funeral in January, 1965. "The British were not ready."

XVI

General de Gaulle's Fairy Tales

"WE are the country that has forged an economic Europe," Couve de Murville was wont to say. "For a long time no one believed it would be possible. We accelerated the various stages envisaged in the Treaty of Rome. We integrated the agricultural market, almost by force. Without it, the Common Market would have had little interest for France. No government has worked more persistently than that of de Gaulle for an economic Europe. No one has been as zealous in Brussels as the French Foreign Minister."

"It's quite true that de Gaulle was very helpful in implementing the Common Market," Monnet conceded. "But he consistently opposed joint institutions, although they are the backbone of Europe. In so doing, he slowed up considerably the integration of Europe."

The Common Market began in an atmosphere of euphoria. By December, 1961, it was a year ahead of schedule for the first stage, according to all industrial indications. Tariffs among the Six had been cut by 40 percent—10 percent more than the estimate in the treaty provisions. All the partners were satisfied. French industry proved to be more competitive than employers had predicted. The 17.50 percent devaluation of the Pinay Plan facilitated exports. In short, everything was going well in Brussels.

General de Gaulle, who was pushing for an economic Europe in order to get a European agricultural and political organization under way, was on the best of terms with the Hallstein Commission. He was delighted that the Commission, contrary to predictions, had never

244

expounded any dogmatic theories on the supranational characteristics of the communities. Marjolin and Lemaignen, the French members of the Commission, did all they could to cooperate with their colleagues. The French experts were regarded as brilliant men.

In 1960 Maurice Couve de Murville asked the Six to express their willingness to accept the principle of an agricultural market. The treaty allusion to it contained a few paragraphs of a general nature that had been hastily added at the last minute.

At the close of 1961 the Commission proposed, with the approval of the Germans, that the market pass from the preparatory phase to the second stage. This meant that within five years there would be complete freedom of trade. As a precaution, the treaty provided for a pause of one or two years before passing to the second stage.

"I'm willing, provided the agricultural market gets under way at the same time," Couve de Murville said. Eager to gain two years for his industrial exports, Erhard agreed. After July 1, 1967, the tariff walls between the Six would be lowered.

For France, the fruit and vegetable market was the big thing. The pegging of farm prices, which had attenuated the 1952 crisis, was prohibited by the Pinay Plan. French peasants were being ruined by overproduction, low prices, mechanization, and technological progress. In the countryside there were fresh disturbances. Tractors blocked many of the roads and highways.

Europe became the long-awaited administrator for surpluses in wheat, milk, butter, and French wines which were being undersold, at great cost to the state. Acceleration of the Common Market stages and the sudden lowering of tariffs endangered the interests of industry for the sake of a distressed agriculture.

Fortunately, everything had gone well so far. The experts in France's agricultural ministry were pleased. Europe was buying French foodstuffs. As soon as the tariff barriers were removed, France's silos, vats, and overflowing granaries would be emptied. The budget would be freed of an overwhelming burden.

But experts from the other countries voiced certain reservations. "Nothing is as simple as it appears in the field of agriculture."

And it was true that if industrial production were to flourish, tariff barriers within the Community would have to be reduced and eventually eliminated, whereas agricultural products were subject to a mass of regulations and protected by national subsidies.

245

French wheat could not enter Germany without creating havoc. The German farmers, who produced relatively little, made the state pay high prices for their cereals. On the other hand, Germany imported wheat surpluses cheaply from America, Canada, and the U.S.S.R. The consumer was the gainer: the price of flour was low. The German peasants were prosperous and the "Green Front" had consistently backed Adenauer's government. Inasmuch as the agricultural market established a common price policy, all subsidies were eliminated. Yet the French, German, and Italian farmers could not be abandoned. An infinite number of regulations were needed. The foreign experts cursed "the French fetichism of cultivating the land."

"Prosperous nations are those that have allowed their land to become depopulated and have recruited their farmers for industry," people said. "In Germany, the farmers represent only 9 percent of the population; in the United States, 8 percent; in England, 5 percent. Before World War I, France, with Italy, was Europe's most backward country, so far as industrialization was concerned. Fifty percent of her population was agrarian. Now her peasant population has decreased by half. But instead of accelerating industrialization and modernizing factories, transportation, commerce, and public services by bringing peasants to the cities, the French government helps to maintain its rural population on farms that are too small to feed a single family. Yet a rational, mechanized cultivation of the land would immeasurably increase the output of vast areas and require fewer and fewer farmhands."

"Whenever a big farmer in the Beauce unfortunately takes it into his head to produce 100 kilograms of wheat, it costs the French national budget 1,500 francs because the wealthy grain-growers are paid at the same rate as the poor ones," groaned one Dutchman. "And now the Europeans are going to have to pay for this economic aberration. We're even encouraging it. Expensive wheat will be grown at an ever-increasing rate. This will affect profits and swell the surpluses. And we will have to pay for it."

Representatives of each country enumerated their objections. Germany obtained cereals from the countries of Eastern Europe in exchange for tools and machinery. These imports thus guaranteed reliable outlets for her products.

French wheat would ruin the grain market in Rotterdam, Antwerp, and Hamburg. Rice from Camargue and Piedmont threatened the

246

grain business, especially the hulling factories in the east, along the banks of the North Sea.

Italy, who bought part of her grain from the United States and Eastern Europe, was alarmed at the thought that she would have to buy wheat from the Beauce at twice the price she had been paying. The agricultural market would not bring her new buyers. Her fruits and vegetables were bought in advance by Germany, Austria, and Scandinavia.

The cereal market—the first to be organized—was to go into operation no later than January 1, 1962. This was a commitment. And it was already the end of 1961. Nothing had been accomplished at Brussels despite the efforts of the Commission and of the Dutch Minister of Agriculture, Sicco Mansholt. The agricultural crisis provoked a peasant uprising in France. Farmers besieged the prefecture. The minister, Pisani, was kidnapped on the highway, locked up at a farm and forced to drink a good deal more milk than he wanted.

De Gaulle had an additional reason for organizing the agricultural market as quickly as possible. Great Britain, reluctant to join the Common Market, would certainly reject an agricultural market; it would be a disaster for her consumers and farmers and for the Commonwealth. But the agricultural market was not yet a reality. England's allies among the Six were applying the brakes in the hope that by stopping it, or at least reducing its scope, they would make England more willing to join the Common Market. Paris, on the other hand, hoped that by speeding things up, the British would soon have to say yes or no.

"We'll try to settle it in time for Christmas," said the optimistic head of the German delegation to Brussels.

But by December 25, 1961, nothing had been accomplished. Everyone continued to bargain endlessly, on every floor of the building. The Dutch and the Belgians demanded that the French agree to England's membership in the Common Market. Couve de Murville refused to make any deals. He offered to accept, in principle, the arrangements made by the Commission and which the British were still debating. But he issued an ultimatum: the industrial market would be obstructed unless the agricultural market began to operate according to schedule, by January 1, 1962.

On December 31 a rupture seemed imminent. But someone stopped the clock. December 31 was to last fourteen days and nights.

Meanwhile, discussions continued unabated. The experts stood in for the exhausted delegates, who were collapsing for want of sleep. The fantastic negotiations resembled marathon dances in which for days and nights on end staggering couples kept moving around the dance floor. This was the first of the Brussels marathons.

The man who won the record for physical endurance was the French Minister of Agriculture, Edgard Pisani, a bearded giant, the youngest prefect of France and also her youngest senator.

All around him the ministers were falling asleep at the table; the experts, constantly harassed in the corridors, were collapsing. But Pisani, that jovial monster, a sandwich in his hand, mouthing arguments, suggesting compromises and solutions, seemed indestructible.

It was agreed that the question of cereals would be dealt with first. The regulations were especially advantageous to the French. Each country was seeking promises and guarantees for its products. Dutch pork, German poultry, Sicilian oranges, Piedmontese chestnuts—they were all tossed at Pisani's head.

Slowly and painfully, an agreement was reached. A common price policy for wheat would have to be worked out. The establishment of some amount midway between the French price of 35 francs for 100 kilograms and the German price of 55 francs seemed out of the question. Erhard could not afford to make the slightest move that might hurt the deputies representing the fruit and vegetable farmers, who provided a majority for the Adenauer cabinet. It was finally decided that each government would fix new prices in its own country that would gradually equal the average price fixed for the Community as a whole.

At the gates of this "little Europe," incoming cereals would pay a levy, the difference between the world price and the prices that prevailed in each country. There would be a penalty of sorts for any state that purchased commodities outside the Common Market. Provisionally, additional tariffs would be levied by the national customs offices within the Community: they would amount to the difference between prices in the importing countries and those prevailing in the exporting countries.

France would profit considerably from this arrangement. The French wheat bureau would sell its grain in Germany for 35 francs per 100 kilograms. At the German frontier, the tariff would amount to the difference between the current prices in the two countries—

35 francs in France, 55 francs in Germany. But American or Soviet wheat arriving in Hamburg would be assessed 30 francs—the difference between the world price (25 francs) and the German price. The money derived from the tariffs would be deposited in a common account for subsequent distribution to the states. France would collect approximately 80 percent.

The French emerged triumphant from "Marathon I." Not a single one of the exhausted experts who left Brussels in the wake of Edgard Pisani wondered about the consequences of these disparate prices. Nor did they wonder about Ludwig Erhard, the great boss of the German economy, who must have had some reason for the lordly manner in which he treated the claims of his farmers. In the eyes of France's diplomats, officials, and economic planners, the outcome of the negotiations would be binding for the next twenty years. Apparently no changes were expected. France would continue to produce abundantly while German agricultural production would remain inadequate.

But the "miracle man" of Germany had other ideas. The price of wheat fixed in Brussels should, he thought, stimulate the German farmers to produce more. The Federal Republic must undergo an agricultural revolution. Aided by new fertilizers, research, and better machinery, Germany within a few years should be able to harvest enough grain to meet her own domestic requirements. The agricultural market should not benefit the French peasant alone but should also serve to stimulate German prosperity.

Without realizing it, the French seekers of a European agricultural Eldorado were making conquests that in some cases would ultimately prove illusory.

A year later, on January 14, 1963, General de Gaulle blocked all negotiations for England's entry into the Common Market. Although the British had been trying for a year and a half to secure membership, the general said no, offering England only the status of an associate.

The Dutch, Belgians, and German Atlanticists were indignant. They claimed they had agreed to the French agricultural demands only in order to facilitate England's entry into the market. They had been tricked. Their press lashed out against de Gaulle, profoundly shocking the Elysée. Meanwhile, Couve de Murville quickly let his partners know that cereals were not the only agricultural commodity. They turned a deaf ear.

"If, by December 31, 1963, the regulations that still remain to be determined have not been adopted, the Common Market will probably not survive," de Gaulle said. He repeated the warning in a press conference on July 29, 1963: "There is no use of speaking of the European Economic Community if Europe will be unable to rely for its food supply mainly on its own agricultural production, which is entirely adequate. And one wonders how France will fare under a system from which tariffs will soon be eliminated, save for the duties levied on her wheat, her meat, her milk, her wine and her fruits."

The general's statement irritated France's partners. He had used a whip to impose the agricultural market, dealt a blow at England by rejecting her entry, and dragged Adenauer down the path of anti-Americanism. He had just announced that if Germany acquired American atomic weapons through the multilateral nuclear force, he would blow up the Common Market. Now he issued a fresh ultimatum about the agricultural regulations.

The German Foreign Minister, Gerhard Schroeder, was intent on showing that "we have had enough of the general's authoritarian Europe." He was an ardent Atlanticist and anti-Gaullist. And he was ready for battle. Chancellor Adenauer still clung to power, but he was losing all authority. He resigned on October 11, 1963. Schroeder was free to follow his own policy, which was also that of the "dauphin," Erhard.

In the meetings of the Council of Ministers from April to May, 1963, Schroeder had only one thing to say: "Synchronization." In other words, "We'll make a deal." For every agricultural concession to France, the French must not only make a concession in regard to products that were important to Germany, they must also give way in the negotiations that Kennedy proposed to open with Europe.

Erhard and Schroeder could safely take a firm stand because campaigns were being waged throughout Germany against the Common Market. The Federal Republic was not benefiting sufficiently from it. The country's most important outlets by far lay outside of the Community. Adenauer's opponents were triumphant: "We told you so! There's nothing in it for us."

In Brussels, Schroeder, a skillful debater, expounded his theory of "synchronization" in such a way as to show that the honeymoon with Adenauer was over. His manner surprised even the most anti-Gaullist delegates. "Before he appeared in Brussels," a Luxembourg Europeanist recounted, "no one questioned the common interest when it was defined. Schroeder refuses to open a file until he has obtained concessions on two or three important points. Then he is willing to turn the first page. During the reading of the preamble, he extorts a few additional concessions. By the time we reach Article I, he is making fresh claims. He trades the accumulated concessions already secured against the paragraphs that follow. This endless bargaining destroys the honest atmosphere of the Community."

For their part, the Germans criticized Couve de Murville and de Gaulle for their ultimatums, their *Diktats,* their threats of rupture. Somewhat later, the French minister admitted, "We got nothing without exerting pressure."

Once again, in 1963, the discussions on the Common Market dragged on interminably. Reinforcements for the French President and his ministers came from an unexpected quarter: from John Kennedy and Jean Monnet.

Early in 1963 a poultry war broke out between the United States and Germany. The Germans were enormous consumers of eggs and chickens. Their main source of supply was America. But mechanized modern poultry farms were developing in Germany. By 1966, the country had 40 firms producing a million chickens annually and 10 firms raising twice that number. Hamburg was closed to overseas shipments of poultry.

"If the Germans refuse to eat American chickens," the explosive Fulbright thundered, "they'll have to do without the security that our G.I.'s give them."

In June, 1963, Kennedy came to Europe to campaign for a European-American partnership. He also wanted to reassure the NATO countries. They were worried about America's concessions to Khrushchev in the area of defense. In addition, the President wished to launch discussions of the Kennedy Round that would open up Europe to American products. The European agricultural market worried Kennedy. It threatened to close an important outlet for America's enormous food surpluses. The problem of marketing them preoccupied the White House constantly.

Lobbyists for agricultural interests harassed Kennedy. Monnet was forever lecturing the President personally and through his friend, George Ball. "Why should you care if the creation of an agricultural market is accompanied by a few protectionist measures?" Monnet would say. "If this venture should fail, if the Common Market were to collapse, you would be forced to enter into interminable negotiations with each of the six countries. Each maintains high tariff barriers and pursues different national interests. But if, on the other hand, the agricultural market came quickly into being, you would have to deal with only one agency, the Brussels Commission. The largest market in the world would be open to America. Global negotiation, covering both farm and industrial commodities, would overcome French resistance and eliminate the opposition of the smaller countries, which are preoccupied with trivial local concerns. Besides, the inevitable entry of England will introduce a spirit of commercial liberalism into the old citadel of protectionism. This would mean greater prosperity for everyone."

In this way, Monnet attempted to persuade Kennedy to guarantee the agricultural Common Market, so dear to France, in return for a freeing of trade between the Old World and the New. "A stroke of genius," said his admirers. In spite of de Gaulle, it paved the way for Eur-America.

Kennedy, who had encouraged the British to join the Common Market, called no less vigorously upon the Germans to accept the agricultural market by linking its inauguration with the start of the Kennedy Round negotiations. Ludwig Erhard, who, upon his assumption of power on October 16, 1963, might otherwise have been tempted to abandon the European economic union, was thus brought to accept the Gaullist demands, although he did so with ill grace.

"Your General de Gaulle has no luck in his resentments," said one German diplomat to French friends. "Schroeder was washed up politically. But when de Gaulle attacked the Community, Erhard couldn't give the impression he was yielding to him. So he had to keep Schroeder as his Foreign Minister."

"Marathon II" began in December, 1963. Schroeder opened fire with his plan for synchronization. He laid down two conditions for the resumption of the agricultural debates: a promise to begin Kennedy Round discussions as soon as possible—he called it "the common commercial policy"; a pledge that the agricultural market would not get under way until after the industrial market had begun to operate. The latter was particularly important to the Germans.

The battle cry had been sounded. Each delegation "synchronized" its demands. France's "scandalous advantages" in the grain market were denounced. France, Germany, and Italy were each to pay 28 percent of the costs. France would receive 86 percent of the levies, Germany 6 percent and Italy 3.

"It's not our fault that the agricultural market has so far established regulations only for cereals," the French answered. "France is the only big grain producer."

Thereupon it was decided that to launch the agricultural market, 50 percent of the production of the Six would be operational by December 31: cereal by-products, eggs, poultry, and pork; milk products, rice, meat, and fats. The delegates fought over every item. In the argument over olive oil versus tropical fats, the Italians insisted on preferential treatment for the former.

"Cultivation of the olive tree is as old as our civilization," Saragat pleaded.

"Margarine means Unilever," the Dutch replied. "And Unilever means Holland. Give every product a chance!"

The French had to answer both Schroeder and America about the Kennedy Round. A balance sheet was drawn up by the Elysée, the Quai d'Orsay and the finance ministry. Together they calculated how much the massive accumulation of American imports would cost industry and the French customs. Then they figured how much exports to America might increase, and estimated the extent of the concessions they might reasonably expect in the agricultural market.

Butter and milk proved the deciding factor. The butter currently in stock was unsalable. Milk flowed in France like a river; it was shipped to India and elsewhere for the cost of transportation. Dairy products were as important an industry as steel and coal. The unrelenting policy of de Gaulle toward the United States was submerged in a sea of milk.

Meanwhile, the negotiations in Brussels were bogging down.

"If we haven't finished by December 31, we'll have to readjust the schedule," Pisani said.

But during the morning of December 23, 1963, the greatest package deal of the Common Market took place. On May 4, 1964, the preliminaries of the Kennedy Round began in Geneva. The Brussels

Community sent one representative: Jean Rey, a former Belgian minister who now served as the Foreign Minister of the Six.

Monnet and Hallstein had triumphed. Not only was the Community of Europe recognized by the United States as an international entity, it was also acknowledged as such by General de Gaulle. But Monnet's victory was cut short, at least for the moment. President Kennedy was assassinated in Dallas, on November 22, 1963.

Jean Rey was shrewd about not flaunting his supranational duties. He had agreed to represent each government separately as well as the Six as a whole. Like Couve de Murville, a Protestant, a lover of football, discreet, a good diplomat, Rey decided to begin by listing the tariff demands of each state—there were thousands of them. He would then contrast these claims with the wishes and opposing views of the Americans. These were equally numerous and had been itemized in Geneva by the Assistant Secretary of State, Herter. He would have time to prepare compromise and middle positions, since the Kennedy Round discussions would not begin until final plans for the agricultural market had been made.

"Marathon III" began in December, 1964, with a long lamentation from Schroeder. A gradual annual adjustment to the target price for cereals was equivalent to asking the German government to tear away a pound of flesh from her wheat growers, thereby prolonging the agony as long as possible. For Chancellor Erhard it meant running a deadly risk. The majority of ministers in his cabinet were dependent on the "fruit and vegetable front."

Sicco Mansholt, the "European Minister of Agriculture" and vice-president of the Commission, was charged with finding a solution. Mansholt was a dynamic, "supranational Eurocrat." Even before a unified Europe had been created, he was very conscious of being a European with a capital E.

"I am not a European official, contrary to what people in Paris say," he contended. "I am a European politician."

Mansholt had been a planter in Indonesia. There he had created a model plantation. During his twelve years at The Hague as Minister of Agriculture, his concerns had ranged from cheese to tulips. He was a favorite at the Royal Palace.

Mansholt's bald head was a good barometer of the European Economic Community. When it was pink, Mansholt looked like an athletic, bouncing gentleman farmer, happy to be a permanent member of a European administrative body. Like everyone at Brussels, he spoke French, with no compunction whatsoever about massacring the language. In the heat of debate, his bald head turned red. Then the gentleman from Zuiderzee answered his opponents in four or five different tongues, emulating most of the delegates of the Six. Should Mansholt's pate turn purple, one could expect him to bellow in Dutch. This was a certain portent of crisis.

No one disputed his right to call himself a European politician. As such, he could put pressure on his own parliament and campaign at the Strasbourg Assembly, where, however, he was not always successful. Agriculture was his special domain, his personal department in Brussels. Theoretically, the Commission's power was shared. But Mansholt was an exception.

The most logical method of determining the price rate for European cereals was to average out the current prices in each of the six states. But this would not have appeased the electoral anxieties of Chancellor Erhard, or those of his minister, Schroeder. Mansholt therefore suggested instead that the price should be fixed at 50 francs per 100 kilograms, a figure closer to the German price but considerably higher than the French, which was approximately 35 francs. The world price was significantly less than the French.

The proposal caused an outcry. The Italians raged; the experts decried it as madness. The inevitable call for an expansion of land cultivation would merely add to the existing surpluses. It would break the bank, the FEOGA, which distributed the duties collected. Europeans would pay a high price for Germany's willingness to join the agricultural economic market.

Mansholt hit upon a shrewd idea: Europe should pay. The subsidies which heretofore had been provided by the various governments would gradually become the responsibility of the Community. Europe would pay. But who would pay Europe?

The discussions became increasingly sharp and biting, lasting long into the night. The experts introduced contractual expedients to balance the responsibilities of the member states. These mental gyrations were so complicated that most of the ministers were unable to follow the calculations of the financiers. Two ministers worked until dawn, giving proof not only of their physical endurance but also of their ingenuity in finding solutions. They were Italy's Minister of Agricul-

255

ture, the Calabrian, Emilio Colombo, and his French opposite number, Edgard Pisani.

Public opinion was at a loss. Any minute, it was feared, there would be a catastrophe, the Common Market would be bankrupt. Finally, however, an agreement was reached. Mansholt had saved the day. In Paris, it seemed like the end of a nightmare. At long last there would be an end to peasant insurrections, the hemorrhaging of subsidies, the ruinous rummage sale of surpluses. All the cares and responsibilities could be shoved upstairs. . . .

Germans, Dutch, Belgians, and Italians were going to eat French food. They had agreed to pay tariffs at their frontiers for the privilege of cheap food imports. The complaining French peasants had uncovered a gold mine. France had apparently become, for all eternity, the granary of Europe.

No one seemed aware of the striking progress in biology and chemistry. Agricultural output, regardless of the quality of the soil, was about to increase from 35 to 70 quintal (100 kilograms) per hectare. One hectare of wheat sowed required only six hours of labor per year. The owner of a motorized farm was becoming a high-powered industrialist who had to survey his land only three times a year to see that it was properly cultivated, that the reaping and harvesting were being carried out correctly. No one apparently realized that because of this breakthrough, and with wheat at 50 francs per 100 kilograms, German farmers could make sizable profits.

Amid the ensuing euphoria, Frenchmen seemed unconcerned about the food imports that were arriving from outside the Common Market. The taxes levied against outsiders, it was thought, would automatically discourage exports. Yet countries that exported industrial goods often found it advantageous to import cereals or meat—even if they had to pay taxes—in order to preserve a profitable trade.

Three years after Marathon III, Germany doubled her wheat production; she provided 80 percent of the flour for her bread and pastries. In spite of the levies, or because of temporary concessions, she purchased outside the Community large quantities of cereals for which she exchanged her industrial goods.

Italy was considered a country that had no choice but to comply with Common Market regulations. Yet a young industry sprang up there that boldly and brilliantly succeeded in finding a market in both Eastern and Western Europe. By 1967 she had not yet bought a single kilogram of French wheat. The moving tones in which the Roman negotiators had pleaded trans-Alpine poverty won for their country the right to close its frontiers to French sacks of grain until 1972. As a consequence, the Milanese and Turin industrialists were able to trade factories for cereals in deals with the Eastern European countries. Not only was French wheat not being sold, but Renault and Michelin could not obtain from the U.S.S.R. or its satellites the contracts granted to Fiat or Pirelli. The same paradoxical situation prevailed in regard to pork, poultry, and eggs. The optimism of the French ministers was such that they could not imagine that there would be any European competition in the poultry industry. They therefore reserved this business for small family establishments. No encouragement was given to the mechanization of poultry farming. Chickens and eggs are traditionally the personal preserve of the farmer's wife, her special treasures. Subsidies for the establishment of modern poultry farms were limited. It never occurred to anyone that poultry farms were no longer the special privilege of peasants but a business enterprise for industrialists, aided by veterinarians, biologists, and engineers.

All along the labyrinth of docks that extended from Rotterdam to Antwerp, Dutch farmers were building kilometers of refrigerators for the storaging of pork, ham, and sausage. Food for pigs imported at low cost from overseas was poured almost directly from the cargo ships into the troughs. This required virtually no administrative offices and a minimum number of employees because automation had been developed to a maximum.

On July 1, 1967, pork became prevalent in Europe. On July 2, in the famous Paris Halles, Dutch pork arrived at 2.50 francs per kilogram. The Breton peasants, who had their cereals brought from the Beauce, their corn from the Pyrenees, who were much farther away from small towns than the Dutch farmers, held angry meetings. Their pigsties were costing them money. They could not make ends meet unless they sold their pork for at least 3.50 to 4 francs a kilogram. They besieged the prefectures.

The European free market prohibited subsidies or state aid, as a matter of principle. But the minister, Edgar Fauré, argued vehemently against his Scandinavian partners in Brussels to obtain the right to intervene and make the SIBEV buy the pigs should the pork market collapse. The SIBEV was therefore prepared to make massive

257

purchases in order to prevent peasant insurrections. But the mere prospect of such purchases sent the Dutch and the Germans scurrying to dispatch their pigs to Brittany. It was not only Breton pigs that would be overpriced but European pigs. They were amassing in the province like ants.

The French government went wild. Would they ever emerge from this agricultural nightmare? While the agencies were shuffling their papers, searching their drawers and closets, the price of pigs rose unexpectedly. The influx of European pigs into France had caused the market price to rise in Holland. The increase spread from Holland to the small towns, thence to Brittany. "There's nothing simple about farm problems," the surprised experts said.

By 1967 Germany's industrialized poultry farms took care of 85 percent of the domestic consumption. They might soon be able to export to France.

But in 1964 people had not yet begun to wonder whether the agricultural common market was merely an illusion. Everyone was jubilant. The grain growers, especially those living on large fertile lands like the Beauce, were delighted with the European prices. The peasants in other parts of France were green with envy and expressed their jealousy. "Your turn will come," they were told.

One small problem remained in the cereal market. It had been decided that Europe would pay, but no one knew where Europe would find the resources. Of course, there would be time. The deadline for financing the agricultural common market would not expire until June 30, 1965. The Hallstein Commission was charged with the solution of this problem.

No one foresaw that this simple budgetary matter would give rise to a revolutionary plan that would pit General de Gaulle against the European Community. The great crisis of 1965 was brewing.

XVII

The Great Crisis of 1965

ON March 24, 1965, an atmosphere like that of a bullfight prevailed at the Palais de la Robertsau in Strasbourg. There were brief feverish conversation in the corridors of the Assembly.

"This time de Gaulle's jig is up. . . . De Gaulle has been caught. . . . He'll never get out of this one. . . . He'll have to give in or he'll be beaten at the polls."

The great battle for a supranational Europe had begun. In Strasbourg the Hallstein Commission dropped a bomb: a revolutionary plan to establish an integrated Europe. The President of the French Republic would have to accept it or be beaten by his electors.

The initiative sprang from a disappointment. De Gaulle had just foiled Monnet's offensive to create a European power independent of the various governments, similar to the High Authority for the Coal and Steel Community.

Ever since 1960, the Action Committee for the United States of Europe had been demanding the merger of Euratom, the Coal and Steel Community and the Common Market into a High Commission endowed with the sovereign attributes of the ECSC. With powers theoretically like those of a federal government, the Commission was to be controlled by the Council of Ministers of the Six, which would play the role of a senate of sorts.

This arrangement would have fulfilled the hopes of Walter Hallstein, President of the European Economic Commission. De Gaulle, however, refused to regard Hallstein as the head of the European executive body. Rather, the general thought of him as an international official merely carrying out the wishes of the Council of Ministers.

Ever since 1960, the Gaullists, especially people like Alain Peyrefitte who championed a European political union, had favored another type of unification, that of the communities. They preferred a merger of the three "technocratic robots," the "Frankensteins," which the general had denounced long ago.

"Actually, they want to take advantage of a merger in order to destroy the three supranational institutions and replace them with a permanent secretariat of the Council of Ministers," Monnet's friends claimed.

Holland's Lower House, which actively supported Monnet, launched discussions in Brussels on a merger of the executive bodies. For three years this question had been debated by the Council of Ministers, which examined the principle of supranationality. As the debate continued, the question of a merger of the three executive branches became increasingly momentous for the integrationists.

This was in 1965. Beginning on January 1, 1966, decisions of the Council of Ministers of the Six could, according to the terms of the Treaty of Rome, be reached "by a qualified majority." France, Germany, and Italy each had 4 votes; the Netherlands and Belgium each had 2, and Luxembourg only 1 vote. There were 17 votes in all; the requisite majority consisted of 12. This meant that a big country like France could not block the Commission's proposals unless it had the support of Germany, Italy, Holland, or Belgium.

"This marks the end of vetoes, challenges, marathons, threats to ruin the Common Market, and de Gaulle's ultimatums," people in Brussels and Strasbourg said.

In Paris, the comment was, "The idea of a qualified majority vote is Monnet's diabolical invention. It enables a community that is not organized as a federation or confederation, that lacks unity, has neither a common policy nor a desire for unification, to institute and perpetuate (since the Commission alone can initiate measures) a government of nonelected technocrats who are not directly responsible to the electorate. Such a government would represent a disunited Europe cleverly held together by certain ties and whose capital would be Washington."

General de Gaulle, Georges Pompidou, and Couve de Murville all kept repeating that in matters of major importance, France would not submit to majority rule.

"It is unthinkable," they maintained, "that five nations should impose their unacceptable decisions on a sixth nation regarding any question of the latter's vital national interests."

"Majority rule is a practical necessity," Monnet's friends retorted. If Europe were to become integrated, there must be constant dialogue between the Commission—which represents the common interests—and the various parliaments. In the United Nations nothing could be accomplished because the delegates voted on the proposals of a nation or a group that represented purely national interests. In Brussels, an impartial Commission presented proposals that were designed to serve the general interest. Under a system of majority rule, the Commission could circumvent a coalition acting against the interests of any single nation.

Be that as it may, the advent of majority rule, plus the merger of the executive bodies, gave the Hallstein Commission—now called the High Commission—a quasi-governmental power over economic questions, especially metallurgy and atomic science which today comprise two-thirds of the concerns of all economic policy.

The High Commission could be overthrown only by the Strasbourg Assembly. But since the Assembly was made up largely of integrationists, the High Commission would have the power to dictate to the various parliaments; or so, at any rate, Paris claimed. The Council of Ministers could deliberate only on proposals made by the High Commission.

On March 2, 1965, the Six finally reached a compromise. A treaty would be drafted establishing a single 14-member Commission. It would meet alternately at the ECSC, Euratom, and the Common Market and would enjoy the powers heretofore accorded the executive bodies of each of these institutions. The Dutch no longer recognized their godchild, the High Commission. But they acquiesced. Another offensive was in the offing, one that had even more important objectives: the immediate establishment of a supranational Europe.

At the close of 1964, the Six empowered the Hallstein Commission to draft a plan for the definitive financing of the market in grain and cereals. Theoretically, decisions applying to all other agricultural products would also be reached by the Commission.

The provisional period established in 1962 came to an end on

July 1, 1965. Tariffs were to be collected from each of the member states according to its size and importance. The question of how much each state should contribute provoked dramatic outbursts and led to sordid arguments.

"What we need is a joint treasury, joint receipts," the Commission decided.

The new formula, "Europe will pay," was to be based on the resources of the Community: the taxes levied on cereal imports—that was France's suggestion—which would gradually increase when the temporary concessions granted to importing states were eliminated. But these levies alone were insufficient. The high-priced production guaranteed for every kilogram of grain harvested by the Six would be so expensive that the taxes on imported grain would cover only a part of the sales cost. There would be surpluses, spoilage, and so on.

Immediately a new source of income was considered: Community duties. National duties no longer made sense in a Common Market. Merchandise shipped from Bordeaux, Rotterdam, or Hamburg was no longer unloaded in France, Holland, or Germany. It was delivered to the Europe of the Six. The Community not the states would henceforward levy taxes. In the center of Europe the port of Rotterdam, the turnstile for Continental traffic, had developed spectacularly. It had become the largest port in the world. It was unthinkable that taxes on merchandise destined for the Six should be collected exclusively by the Netherlands.

All the tariffs collected throughout Europe would be paid into the treasury of the European Community. The Dutch were quite reluctant. They felt they were being gulled. Hallstein explained that tariffs were no longer a part of national budgets nor were they controlled by national parliaments. Henceforth they would be included in a European budget by the Council of Ministers and would be controlled by a European parliament, that of Strasbourg.

The Treaty of Rome endowed the Assembly of the Community with only limited powers: although it could reject the Commission's reports, it was merely a consultative body. It did not have a decisive vote on the budget of the European Community; heretofore, the budget had been limited to supplying funds for operations regulated by the Council of Ministers. Otherwise, the Strasbourg Assembly's functions had virtually no practical implications and its decisions were scarcely heeded in Brussels. Its amendments received little attention from the Council of Ministers.

The Hallstein Commission decided that if the Treaty of Rome were amended, the Assembly could be empowered to revise the budget. But the commissioners immediately realized that such a change would lead to all kinds of dissension between the Assembly, the Council and the Commission.

In order to achieve some progress toward European integration, it was necessary to strengthen not the powers of the Assembly (the various governments would always be hostile to the creation of a real European parliament), but those of the Commission itself. In an attempt to unravel the intricacies of the situation, Walter Hallstein and his colleagues hit upon an extremely ingenious expedient—in Paris it was called "satanic." This arrangement enabled the Commission, with the help of the Assembly, to surmount virtually all the obstacles that one or several countries, acting through the Council of Ministers, might place in its way.

The Assembly could offer only advisory amendments to the Hallstein proposal. But if any of these were approved by the majority of the Commission, they would have the force of parliamentary decisions, even if they did not satisfy the Council of Ministers. Provision had to be made for some sort of liaison between the three bodies of the communities as well as for some method of settling conflicts.

This method, devised by the majority of the Council of Ministers, featured the allocation of one vote to each country. It had already been applied by the representatives of the Six in regard to less important questions involving no real complications. It facilitated compromise and accommodation. But The Hague refused to increase the number of its officials. A change in the retirement policy for European officials had been suggested. The Dutch minister had refused to approve it. An affirmative decision reached by the majority relieved him of all embarrassment.

Hallstein explained that if an amendment proposed by a parliamentary majority were approved by a majority of the Commission, four out of six votes would suffice for ratification by the Council of Ministers. (It would therefore be possible to circumvent possible French opposition, even if Germany or Italy supported France.) Five out of six votes would be required for rejection of an amendment. In other words, if the Commission, backed by the Assembly, had the approval of Holland and Luxembourg, together they could thwart France, Germany, Belgium, and Italy, should the latter be opposed.

This revolutionary plan called for several modifications of the Treaty of Rome. The supranational powers of the Commission would have to be greater than Monnet had anticipated but the result would still be in keeping with his principles.

Hallstein, with the invaluable assistance of Sicco Mansholt, had worked this out with painstaking care, as if it were clockwork. The French vice-president, Robert Marjolin, was kept out of it because he was afraid it might have catastrophic consequences.

In the beginning, the former German Secretary of State had no idea of the mechanisms involved. But little by little, after examining budget regulations and tariffs, he hit upon this method which made him the economic sovereign of Europe. "Do you really think the governments will accept this?" he was asked. "Do you think de Gaulle will let you have your way?"

For the integrationists, this was an opportunity to take a big gamble to end Gaullist tyranny, with the backing of the Five, who were exasperated by the antics of the Elysée and the Quai d'Orsay.

De Gaulle was trapped. He had wrested the agricultural market from his partners, but the essential was still lacking: a way to finance it. Paris was waiting impatiently for this gold mine that had been promised its farmers. Its impatience was intensified because of the end-of-the-year elections.

The time was ripe for a showdown: de Gaulle would either accept supranationality, qualified majority rule as stipulated in the Treaty of Rome, the European budget (in other words, the programming by the Commission of all Community activities), and the amendments voted by the Council of Ministers. Or he would refuse, and the agricultural market would not be financed. Six million rural electors were rebelling in France. De Gaulle would be defeated in the elections.

A bombshell of this nature cannot be planned in complete secrecy. "This is madness," Couve told Hallstein on several different occasions. "You'll precipitate a constitutional crisis and ruin the Common Market. Some of the governments are probably encouraging you in order to embarrass de Gaulle. But no government wants to see the Council of Ministers become just an extra piece of furniture."

"Ruin the Common Market? De Gaulle's the one who'll be ruined in the election," several people in Hallstein's camp said.

Protocol as well as custom required that the secret proposal be submitted to the Council of Ministers. But the veto of one government would suffice to doom it. Even if the proposal were debated behind closed doors, it would be slashed to pieces before the public had a chance to pronounce on it. Hallstein therefore decided to make a grandstand play. On the occasion of his annual report to the Strasbourg Assembly, he put the proposal before the public.

Usually, this sort of thing is of no historical moment. But on that day, March 24, 1965, the Palais de la Robertsau attracted a huge crowd. Twenty-four hours earlier, the Hallstein Commission, which customarily met in Brussels, had gathered in Strasbourg to put the finishing touches to the plan. All the important integrationist leaders were present to consult with one another. The atmosphere was taut with tension. A few of the delegates of the Six offered opinions. A rumor spread throughout the capitals of Europe that a coup d'état was about to take place. The excitement was immense.

Like the Eurocrats of Brussels, the Strasbourg parliamentarians were the target of de Gaulle's sarcasm. They all suffered from the same disease, he said. The Constituent Assembly was trying to become a legislative body entitled to full powers. It was proclaiming itself to be the parliament of Europe. The commissioners saw themselves as European politicians and expected to be accorded specialized ministries for a union that had never been constituted.

Couve de Murville passed through the corridors, silent. All whispering ceased at his approach.

"We were breathing the atmosphere of the Estates General on the eve of revolution," one participant recalled.

No sooner had Hallstein mounted the podium than cries went up in the hall.

"Rumors are spreading. Don't keep us waiting any longer! Tell us your plan!"

Walter Hallstein spoke frankly. He outlined the program he planned to submit six days later to the Council of Ministers. But his explanations gave rise to more objections and coolness than to applause. The Assembly was disappointed. Hallstein had been too cautious. He was not offering the Assembly a chance to become a real European parliament. It would merely pass on the budget. It

265

would only propose amendments in an advisory capacity and intervene as a mere auxiliary of the Commission in the event of conflict within the Council of Ministers. What a timid proposal!

One orator after another stood up to urge that the Strasbourg Assembly be given real legislative powers, including the right of veto.

Hallstein walked through the corridors in search of Couve de Murville. He wanted to apologize.

"I would have preferred to put this before the Council of Ministers first. But the secret had leaked out. There was nothing I could do." The French minister's answer was a frigid smile.

The Commission had not exceeded its rights by revealing the plan at Strasbourg. It had the exclusive power to take the initiative. Nevertheless, to make public a plan to revise the Treaty of Rome without prior consultation with the major governments was tantamount to defying the Council of Ministers. Above all, it was a challenge to de Gaulle, the champion of absolute power for the Council of Ministers in all matters concerning the Community, and the firm opponent of majority rule.

The proposal shocked Paris. "Hallstein is having a fit of megalomania," a French minister declared. "For a long time he has been acting as if he were the government of Europe. He has been negotiating with foreign states without bothering to consult the Council of Ministers. He almost annexed Afghanistan. Now he claims the right to impose his decisions on the Council."

The European budget envisaged by Hallstein, swollen with the tariff revenues of the Six and with other "levies," was in fact considerable, although Brussels' estimate of its size was below that of Paris. It far exceeded the requirements of the grain market. The Commission planned to utilize the surplus for various Community projects, including the agricultural structural reforms that Sicco Mansholt proposed for regions in distress—notably Brittany, Normandy, southern Italy.

Hallstein's proposal had no chance of being readily accepted by the Six. The governments of the big countries were by no means prepared to cede their powers to a Commission-Assembly coalition. The most ardent partisans of the European cause, assuming responsibilities in their respective capitals and coming to grips with existing realities, tended to behave like fierce nationalists.

In their criticism of the Assembly, the colleagues of Couve de

Murville, so prone to stigmatize him as antiparliamentarian, were just as outspoken as he. Besides, the governments were scarcely inclined to give up all their tariff revenues in order to enable the Hallstein Commission to play the role of Santa Claus with their money on their soil. To some of them, the idea of recasting the Treaty of Rome seemed foolish. Would not General de Gaulle try to exploit such an opportunity?

Nevertheless, the Hallstein proposal aroused keen interest among the champions of European integration. The extremists among them argued that even the most daring clauses could be imposed on de Gaulle because he simply had to have his agricultural market. As for the reluctant governments that were waging an offensive against de Gaulle, they would be inclined to accept solutions which at other moments they would have rejected. The eagerness of the Europeanists to open a discussion of the Hallstein proposal was intensified by the expectation that industrial rivalry would become very keen after the removal of tariff frontiers on January 1, 1967. The Common Market might become unpopular in certain countries. It was therefore imperative to push the states toward supranationality before such hostile campaigns were begun.

The Action Committee for a United States of Europe met in Berlin on May 9 to commemorate the anniversary of the Schuman Plan. It adopted a motion demanding further steps toward the creation of a unified Europe. However, the signatories did not undertake to obtain the support of their respective parliaments for the Hallstein proposal, which some of them regarded as too daring.

Holland's Lower Chamber, which needed no encouragement for this sort of thing, called upon the Dutch government to defend not only the Hallstein proposal but also the supplementary claims formulated in Strasbourg. Sicco Mansholt, who wielded a good deal of influence in his country, was largely responsible for this action. The Dutch had not forgiven de Gaulle for refusing the candidature of Great Britain. The conversion of Holland's Socialists to the doctrine of supranationality and their recent entry into the Dutch government reinforced the appeal addressed to The Hague by the Lower Chamber.

The Council of Ministers in Brussels was nevertheless slow to come to grips with the Hallstein proposal—the bombshell, as some observers called it. The delegates found plausible reasons for their delaying tactics. Elections were pending in Germany and France.

Political crises were raging in Brussels and Rome where new cabinets had not yet been formed. Above all, however, the matter was highly embarrassing. Professor Reuter later pointed out that the Hallstein proposal was tantamount to saying that the Treaty of Rome could not be implemented unless it was first modified. France's partners gambled on the fact that de Gaulle was a buyer. He needed his cherished agricultural market in order to appease his peasants. He therefore would come around. Couve de Murville fulminated in his muffled way at the Palais Bourbon and elsewhere.

"Some of our partners," he said, "are allowing themselves the luxury of approving irrational proposals, knowing full well that France will not sanction them." He himself was not on bad terms with Hallstein, despite their opposite views on the subject of supranationality, despite the burning faith of Hallstein.

The Commission had continuously backed France's efforts to accelerate the progress of the Common Market and to establish the agricultural market. This may seem paradoxical in retrospect. But in the last analysis, General de Gaulle, abetting the formation of an economic union in order to create his political confederation, had no better ally than his dogmatic adversary, Walter Hallstein. The latter had an extremely difficult time getting the Council of Ministers to meet on June 15, 1965. The Six had formally undertaken to complete, before July 1, the financial arrangements connected with the establishment of the agricultural market. When the Council of Ministers finally convened on June 15, tempers flared. On the eve of the meeting, the Dutch Minister of Economics referred to the current issue as "a theological question." France's five partners would have to accept the risk of seeing the Common Market blocked in order to impose Hallstein's proposal and achieve integration.

"We are here once again because of an ultimatum from General de Gaulle," the Belgians, Italians, and Germans complained. "We are fed up with being the pawns of the Elysée. The French must not think that they'll be able to wear us out once more. . . ."

At the preliminary meeting, each of the five delegations ostentatiously spoke its own national tongue even though French is the customary language of the Community. Matters were complicated by the fortuitous circumstance that the rotating presidency devolved on Couve de Murville, who seemed eager to have it. Luns, the Dutchman, was the first to speak out. He underscored the point that his government had a mandate to support the Hallstein proposal.

"The position of the Netherlands," he warned, "must not be taken lightly." Amintore Fanfani, the Italian minister, issued an even more embarrassing declaration. "The agricultural agreements," he said, "must be regarded as merely tentative." The French delegation was filled with consternation. The very idea of an agricultural market was being challenged by France's Latin sister. Fanfani had been a member of the Monnet Committee. He was a pioneering Europeanist, the only man, except for General de Gaulle, who had proposed the political unification of Europe. In 1960 he had come to Paris with the President of the Italian Republic, Segni, to invite de Gaulle to a summit conference in Venice at which a political confederation was to be established. But de Gaulle had refused. He had found Fanfani too insistent, too imbued with the idea of integration. He preferred, as a first step, that chiefs of states and government heads get together to think about defining common policies. He was opposed to union without unity.

As a consequence, Fanfani felt bitter toward de Gaulle. In addition, he was annoyed by the meteoric rise of his youthful colleague, Colombo, the man who had negotiated the agricultural agreements. He was also having difficulties within his own party: He had perhaps served overlong as President of the United Nations Assembly in New York. The intellectual vivacity of this little man, whose moves were not always adequately thought out in advance, led certain Italian newspapers to describe him as a troublemaker.

On the other hand, the agricultural agreements had been for Rome a very disagreeable surprise. The government that had accepted them was still in office. It comprised 64 ministers and secretaries of state. Economic affairs were divided among five or six separate departments. Only tardily did Italy realize that she would have to make heavy financial sacrifices for the wheat which she imported and for the refrigerated meats which she ordered mainly from the countries of the East.

Couve de Murville's declaration was impatiently awaited. How would he wriggle out of the situation in which he found himself? Would he be willing to accept European integration in exchange for the agricultural market which had been challenged, for the grain subsidies that would benefit France far more than any other country?

Or would he disrupt the Common Market, which for de Gaulle would be an act of political suicide five months before the elections? Tersely and dryly, Couve de Murville stated the French position. In December he had proposed that the levies paid by the importers of foreign grain should be used to subsidize the higher prices promised to the farmers. "As a gesture of conciliation," he said, "France renounces this proposal." What about the transfer of tariff revenues to the Community? "If this should prove necessary, France will not oppose it," he declared. "However, these revenues greatly exceed the requirements in question."

The solution was quite simple: the contribution of the states would continue as before to cover the deficits of the grain market. Taken aback, the Council of Ministers understood very quickly. If the agricultural market was to be financed by contributions from the states, there would no longer be any need for a Community budget. Consequently, parliamentary control would likewise become superfluous. The same would be true not only of increases in the powers of the Strasbourg Assembly but also of the budgetary jockeying that enabled the Commission and the parliament, working together, to prevail over the Council.

"Hence," Couve de Murville innocently concluded, "this theoretical and dogmatic question is not real." The carefully conceived plan of Walter Hallstein was annihilated. It was never again discussed.

There was an outburst of fury in the corridors. An official attached to the Commission exclaimed, "He has pulled the rug out from under the proposal." A Dutchman remarked ironically, "He has presented us with a nice gift. He has returned to us the tariff rights which we had been prepared to surrender!" An Italian had this to say: "By removing one small piece, he has caused the entire edifice of the Commission to collapse. Your Couve de Murville is a very astute diplomat!"

This skill merely intensified the existing ill will. Thirteen days later, when the ministers reassembled in Brussels, the atmosphere was even more tense. Holland declared that she intended as before to link the powers of the Strasbourg parliament to a settlement of the financial question. According to the Italians, nothing could be decided until the hemp, silk, and cotton markets had been organized. The Germans insisted that first of all the price of milk must be fixed at 39 pfennigs

270

and Germany must be guaranteed a sugar production of 1,800,000 tons.

"Isn't this a matter of imposing conditions for the adoption of grain regulations?" Couve de Murville asked.

"No, these are not conditions," was the answer. "But we are referring to the regulations."

The German delegation asked for even more: common fiscal and commercial policies. The powers of the European parliament must be enlarged.

Paul Henri Spaak spoke up. "This is not a serious problem," he said. No one had clashed with de Gaulle more than he over the question of who would be the figurehead of Europe. He sensed that a crisis was about to occur, one that would lead nowhere. "Everything could be settled in the space of one evening," he asserted. "I would be very much surprised if any government could agree to everything that has been suggested today. We must choose between what we can settle now and what should be settled later. Otherwise, the entire day will end in a fiasco."

Couve intervened in order to deliver a final lecture: "We have already made a formal, unconditional commitment. If it is not respected, there can be no more regulations. There will be no Community. I have said this to many people. I am sorry that I have not always been taken seriously."

Until this moment the Commission had said nothing. Would it now offer other suggestions in order to resolve the impasse? A few minutes earlier, Hallstein had consulted Mansholt, his vice-president and agricultural commissioner. At midnight the existing arrangement for financing the grain market could cease to be valid. What would happen if no decision were reached to replace it? "Absolutely nothing," Mansholt informed him. "The member states are always late in sending in their figures. We are still distributing the sums collected in 1963."

Hallstein asked to speak. He said that they should not attribute too much importance to dates and deadlines. He was sure that an agreement could not be reached that very evening, but expressed his conviction that "we can wind this up in a few weeks." The Commission thus let it be known that it would do nothing to disentangle the negotiations. This, at any rate, was the French interpretation of Hallstein's remarks.

271

"The decision we reach will have worldwide implications," a Dutch delegate commented.

In other words, without European integration, there would be no agricultural market. This was the Hallstein formula. The atmosphere of the meeting was marked by a sense of general fatigue. The delegates of the Five were tired of Couve de Murville and Couve was tired of them.

Couve asked for an intermission and telephoned the Elysée. He was up against a solid Dutch-German-Italian front, to say nothing of the Commission. He was particularly disconcerted by the German attitude. Through Wormser he sounded out Lahr, the Secretary of State in the Foreign Ministry at Bonn. Lahr readily replied that his government did not take the Hallstein proposal seriously.

"Do the best you can," President de Gaulle said to Couve de Murville.

At eight o'clock that evening, Schroeder, the German Foreign Minister, arrived to head his delegation. "We've talked a lot about our obligations," he said. "Some of us also have obligations at home. I have just come from Bonn. The Bundestag has unanimously passed a resolution asking the government to support the Commission's proposals."

The Bundestag vote had been inspired by the German political leaders on the Monnet Committee.

"I have instructions not to close negotiations this evening," Schroeder continued. "Tomorrow the Chancellor will confer with the leaders of the government coalition to discuss the matter."

"We were expecting Grouchy and we got Blücher," Jean de Lipkovski quipped when he recalled that day.

Couve de Murville had dinner that night at the French embassy. It has often been said that de Gaulle ordered him to break off the negotiations.

"Our information is just the reverse," a member of the Belgian delegation has recounted. "Brussels is a small town. Even the most secret matters are soon revealed. That evening, while everyone was dining, Couve was distributing instructions to various people for a new battle formation. Edgard Pisani, Valéry Giscard d'Estaing, and the diplomats Wormser and Boegner each had a role to play."

Actually, when the discussions were resumed, Giscard d'Estaing, the Minister of Finance, tried to pry Italy loose from the common front of the Five. Italy profited very little from the grain market. D'Estaing suggested that France pay part of the Italian tariff contributions.

Fanfani reached into his change pocket as if to say, "What kind of a gratuity is this?" But his colleague, the Minister of Agriculture, Ferrari-Aggradi, accepted the suggestion with more subtlety. He said, "What you propose only reinforces our anxiety. The grain market entails so much risk that all regulations should be limited to one or two years."

At midnight, June 30, Couve interrupted the discussion. Nearing the end of his term as president, he offered the chair to his successor, Amintore Fanfani. But Fanfani declined. Protocol required that the retiring president chair the meeting until the end of the last session.

"If I were to take your chair, I would announce that in five minutes the session will be adjourned."

"The Italians can see a crisis coming," the French delegates murmured to each other.

"Not at all," the Italians protested. "We would resume talks the first thing in the morning."

The discussion was resumed. Everyone spoke but no one really said anything. On the question of how long the financial arrangement should last, there were as many opinions as there were delegations. As for the amount Italy should contribute to the common fund, the experts offered a variety of solutions, but this brought no response from the delegations opposed to France. Belgium and Luxembourg suggested compromises but no one seemed to be listening to them. According to Spaak, the Commission, "silent and intransigent," was witnessing what might have been the death throes of the Common Market.

"They didn't even begin to discuss our project," Hallstein said later.

Most of the delegations thought Couve de Murville would yield because of de Gaulle's unwillingness to give up the advantages of the agricultural market.

"I am beginning to wonder whether we ought to acknowledge sadly that no understanding has been reached," said Couve with a bitter smile, "but perhaps the ministers would like to confer with their delegates and the President of the Commission."

At 1 A.M. the Committee, now reduced in size, met in the Hall of

Catastrophes, where the principal agricultural accord had been signed at a time when a rupture seemed imminent.

Hallstein realized that his "little Europe" was about to collapse. "If our project does not meet with your approval we can present a new one in a week, in two days, or even two hours," he said. But Couve remained impassive. "I implored him," Hallstein recounted later.

"Does anyone wish to take the floor?" Couve asked, glancing around the table. There was still time for a minister to say a few words that might open up new perspectives. But the strained silence remained unbroken. The last seconds of the final fifteen minutes were at hand.

"Isn't de Gaulle going to yield?" murmured an attaché who was standing at the door.

Luns, the Dutchman, raised his voice. In private conversations, he was known to give side-splitting imitations of de Gaulle. "I have to return to The Hague," he said. "Let's set a date for another meeting."

"July 25," Schroeder quickly suggested.

The Commission usually went on vacation around that time. July 25 might be the day when they would all be returning.

"I can see," Couve said in his monotonous voice, "that no one wants to finish our business. The meeting is adjourned."

It was 3 A.M., July 1, 1965. In Paris, the cabinet meeting had been postponed for twenty-four hours.

The Foreign Minister returned to the Elysée just in time to give an account of the rupture.

"The negotiations could have been continued," Monnet said. "An agreement would surely have been reached." But it would doubtless not have been the kind of agreement de Gaulle wanted.

"The French seat will remain empty for the time being," the President of the Republic decided.

"De Gaulle has stamped out Europe," the press of the entire world proclaimed. But he might have to pay for the deed in the forthcoming elections.

274

XVIII

The Truce in Luxembourg

GERMAN news analysts, discussing the rupture in Brussels, observed, "De Gaulle decided to break Europe after the failure in mid-January, 1965, of Gaston Deferre's Socialist-Centrist federation, that might have defeated him in the December presidential elections. Deferre was the only candidate who could unite the opposition. Thereafter, the general's hands were free."

International opinion angrily attacked de Gaulle and the quasi-unanimity of the French press. Many Frenchmen were shocked by the curt attitude of the general, by his "ungrateful policy toward the United States and England," and by his sudden rupture with his Common Market partners. Their anger was intensified by his customary habit of explaining nothing to the public.

"The Hallstein Commission and France's five partners need only to hold firm for a few months," people in Brussels said. "De Gaulle will be forced to capitulate because his agricultural market has collapsed. He needs millions of peasant votes if he is to be reelected. He also needs the votes of the partisans of an integrated Europe. He'll either have to swallow an integrated Europe or be blackballed."

On July 26, the foreign ministers of the Five met around Couve de Murville's empty chair. Jean-Marc Boegner, the permanent French representative, returned to Paris. The Five, as the world press pointed out, were in an enviable position. The big bad wolf, the target of the Dutch cartoonists, that nationalist who would never yield to the regulations of a community, had exiled himself from Europe. The

275

Five could do without him; they might even exploit the situation and invite England to take the place of France.

Schroeder bristled at the thought of the "Gaullist tyranny." Luns was very pleased by the unanimous condemnation of the autocrat in Paris. Fanfani declared he would not countenance a compromise, an attitude calculated to produce a rapprochement between the Christian Democrats and the Nenni Socialists, since the latter were ardent anti-Gaullists.

At the meeting of the Five, Spaak merely put in an appearance. "A five-power front is not a realistic alignment," he said. "This battle isn't getting us anywhere. This Commission must get under way, despite what many people say. Its silence has lasted too long."

A Belgian representative then analyzed the situation in a private conversation: The new charter presented by Hallstein was unacceptable not only to de Gaulle but to all the government heads. If only five out of six votes were necessary to reject any budget proposal presented by the Commission and backed by the Strasbourg Assembly, Hallstein would be able to run the Community with the approval of the Netherlands and Luxembourg alone.

Replace France with England? Prime Minister Harold Wilson had shown no inclination to occupy Couve de Murville's chair in Brussels. He had just won his election because of Macmillan's blunder in making overtures to Europe.

Did they really mean to hold out in order to bring de Gaulle to heel or to see that he was defeated by his peasants in the elections? Well, de Gaulle had an unexpected ally who was eager to see the end of the quarrel over the agricultural market. That ally was the United States. The American President's ambassador to the Community instructed his colleagues not to be seen in the corridors and not to express any opinion whatsoever against the French position. The crisis was obstructing the Kennedy Round and blocking American commercial expansion in fifty different countries.

Shortly after Spaak had made his succinct remarks, Hallstein gave up the idea of a new constitution for Economic Europe. He renounced all hope of imposing on de Gaulle a supranational organization reinforced by the financing of an agricultural market. He issued a memorandum that made no allusion to a tariff pool and said nothing about the Strasbourg Assembly's budgetary role.

This gesture had no repercussions in Paris. On the contrary, the

276

French President attacked the Europe of Jean Monnet and Walter Hallstein at a press conference on September 5, 1965. He denounced "the excessive myths that sprang from certain errors or equivocations incorporated in the treaties"; the Hallstein Commission was a "bogus executive body," a "technocratic, irresponsible, nationless apparatus" that sought to arrogate to itself a budget that could total 20 billion new francs. The Commission could become "a great financial power, independent of governments." The Strasbourg Assembly was "an illusory legislature," whose members were not elected to legislate; majority rule "could result in France's hand being forced in all economic questions, and consequently in social and political questions as well. . . . This new voting method . . . might force the member states to yield to the Commission, unless by some miracle they agreed unanimously on an amendment."

"These insults have all the earmarks of a house of correction," one lawyer on the Commission exclaimed as he listened to the bitter words on the Brussels radio.

"He is declaring a personal war on Hallstein," another observer remarked.

At the end of this philippic, de Gaulle proclaimed his willingness to resume negotiations with the governments, stressing, however, that before the Economic Community could be launched, there would be a delay of unforeseeable length.

"Launch the Economic Community?" people in Brussels exclaimed in shocked tones. "De Gaulle must be asking for a complete overhaul of the structure of the Economic Community. It'll be a long time before we have any Common Market."

De Gaulle, in venting his fury, aimed at three main targets. First of all, the new plan elaborated by Hallstein. Reinforcing the powers of the Commission by a fancy voting system was, he believed, designed to obstruct the establishment of a European political union. Hallstein's plan had been conceived with this in mind. The Community, stymied by such impediments, would be governed by economists who would conclude with Washington a union organized by Jean Monnet and whose president would be whoever happened to be in the White House.

The second target was Hallstein, the author of this plan. The former German Secretary of State thought of himself as the master of Europe. He had assumed the right to modify existing institutions

277

in order to increase his personal power, to become "the technocratic Caesar" of Atlantic Europe.

His third target was majority rule which the Treaty of Rome had established and which would be enforced by 1966. In de Gaulle's opinion, majority rule was unacceptable as a way of resolving major problems.

"It is unthinkable that four states with a straight majority, or three states with a qualified majority (that is, allowing four votes for Germany, Italy, and France, two for Belgium and Holland, and one for Luxembourg), should impose their will on one or two others in matters affecting the vital interests of the latter," the diplomats said.

Situations might arise in which a majority vote in Brussels could overthrow a government, create disorders in a country, or pervert the general policy of a nation.

In view of the enthusiasm of several countries for American leadership, the life of any government opposed to American tutelage would be in constant jeopardy, depending on the whims of Washington.

When European integration became increasingly tight-knit, a time might come when it would be almost impossible for a government to break off with the Community without resorting to revolution. This would herald the hegemony of the United States.

"The principle of unanimity," Jean Monnet answered, "is a lure and a delusion. Exercise of the veto power by each and every country will produce paralysis. Look at the Security Council of the United Nations. Majority rule is conducive to harmony. No one need fear a coalition of special interests in Brussels. The Commission is the agency that represents the interests of all. It will not make any proprosals that might jeopardize public order in a given country. . . ."

But the real battle for Europe, in the opinion of partisans of an integrated Community and an Atlantic partnership, was not being waged between Brussels and Paris. It was taking place in France. The outcome would be determined by the electorate on December 5. The hopes of the Europeanists were first focused on Antoine Pinay, one of the originators of the Treaty of Rome. Once the general's Minister of Finance, he had been removed from the cabinet because he favored the American alliance. "The man with the little hat" was very popular. He inspired confidence. Great efforts were made to raise sufficient funds for his electoral campaign.

But despite a few misleading remarks, Pinay, the Mayor of Saint-

278

Chamond, never really wanted to run for the presidency. In *Paris-Match* he wrote an indignant article denouncing an offer of two billion old francs that had been made to him to finance his campaign.

The number one challenger, the leftist candidate, François Mitterand, favored an organized Europe, a Europe, he said, which would not be made up of trusts and monopolies. His convictions seemed beyond reproach in the eyes of the Europeanists, but half of his supporters were Communists who opposed the Atlantic Alliance. Furthermore, a "Europe free of trusts" sounded somewhat disconcerting. To be sure, the Common Market had been created precisely to challenge the big American corporations that had 180 million customers; Monnet had asked for antitrust laws, like those of the Americans. But Europe of the Six was emphatically liberal, opposed to statism and to the conceptions of Mitterand's partisans.

An outsider appeared, Jean Lecanuet, a candidate with charm. He was a member of the Center, he had a dazzling smile and television charisma. He brandished the flag of Europe, the emblem of the American alliance. Jean Monnet, who usually voted Socialist, officially supported him.

The most important question for France and Frenchmen was that of a United States of Europe. But the debate during the elections remained superficial, never going beyond sentimental considerations. The true foundations of a United States of Europe were not discussed throughout the election campaign.

Lecanuet captured 15 percent of the voters; of these, it was difficult to estimate how many were Europeanists and how many were firm anti-Gaullists. Spaak, the most realistic of the Six, did not believe that de Gaulle would be defeated. He therefore began immediately to try to safeguard the institutions of the Community.

General de Gaulle used the Hallstein proposal, which had been rejected by all the governments, to demand a revision of the Treaty of Rome. The changes he had in mind were quite different from those Hallstein advocated. Spaak was anxious to avoid any challenge to the treaty lest it never be signed. He also hoped to rescue Hallstein from the full brunt of the Gaullists' resentment. There were some who regarded the controversy over Hallstein as the main issue of the elections. A Europe with Hallstein would be the Europe of Monnet. This was important because the executive organs of the three institutions were about to be merged into a single body. The treaty of unification had been signed on August 8, 1965. The Dutch parliament delayed its ratification, wanting first to make sure that Hallstein would head the single Commission and that the other members would favor him. The Belgian minister promised his colleagues that he would push the candidacy of Hallstein in Paris. On the other hand, he sided with de Gaulle in the controversy over majority rule. To an editor of *Nation Belge,* Spaak said, "The truth is that when major questions arise, the Community cannot function unless there is unanimity."

On September 25, 1965, Spaak offered Couve de Murville a way out of the impasse. He suggested by letter that the ministers meet without the Commission, an eventuality provided for in the treaty.

Five days later, Couve de Murville answered from the Palais Bourbon. The crisis, he said, resulted from the failure to form a European political union. The various government heads had not cooperated harmoniously. The Brussels negotiations could not be resumed unless the demands of the Hallstein Commission were condemned by the Six.

"We will agree to a meeting of the Six without the Commission, but it must take place in Brussels," the Germans and Dutch replied. Brussels was to be General de Gaulle's Canossa.

The Germans and Dutch addressed themselves to Emilio Colombo, who had succeeded Fanfani as President of the Council of Ministers. Colombo agreed with Spaak. As long as the French did not insist on a revision of the treaty, the reconciliation could take place anywhere. Colombo addressed a letter to Couve de Murville which Ambassador Formani presented to him. It proved very helpful.

The German minister, Schroeder, announced his impending visit to the Quai d'Orsay. The Americans were eager to initiate the Kennedy Round. Moreover, Schroeder was anxious to save Hallstein from the wrath of the Elysée.

These diplomatic moves outside the framework of the Community were a source of concern to Monnet and the integrationists. They indicated a return to the old-fashioned diplomacy which had enabled de Gaulle and Couve de Murville to pull off deals. At the Quai d'Orsay everyone was told something different, whereas the Community round tables literally forced the various governments to come out into the open and to speak with a certain consistency. In order to maintain a united front of the Five against Paris, Monnet and his friends organized a clearinghouse of sorts. It enabled them to say later that no real division had occurred.

On November 17, a communiqué was issued after the cabinet meeting. It stated that Belgium, Italy, and Germany desired a resumption of the discussions, and that therefore a meeting of the Six should be arranged to seek a solution to outstanding problems.

"It's the beginning of wisdom when a man running for office becomes wary," people in Brussels remarked.

But there would be no Canossa. The meeting took place in Luxembourg, not in Brussels. On December 5, 1965, the balloting in France began. The question of European integration affected to a certain degree the way people voted. The 5 percent that de Gaulle failed to get in order to be elected in the first round was probably made up of worried farmers and sincere Europeanists.

On December 8, 1965, the day of the Feast of the Immaculate Conception and four days before the second round, the Protestant Couve de Murville went to Rome for the conclusion of the Vatican Council. He also conferred with his Italian opposite number, Colombo.

Had de Gaulle been blessed by both the "heavenly voices" and those of Europe? On December 12, he was reelected. This marked the end of worldwide suspense. In the second round, he received the needed votes from half of Lecanuet's backers. In Brussels, the feeling was one of defeat. On December 22, after ten days of reflection, Hallstein sent the general his congratulations.

The first spectacular gesture of the French President was to break with NATO. Then he got the American army out of France without further ado. This latter event shocked a large segment of French public opinion and, of course, an even larger segment of opinion in pro-American countries. And it had unexpected repercussions. The general staff of NATO was transferred to Belgium. The Belgian Socialists opposed the move. Spaak, the former Secretary-General of NATO, was forced to retire not only from the government but from public life.

On January 17, 1967, the Six met again in Luxembourg, the Community city and capital of the ECSC as well as of the Grand Duchy over which Prime Minister Werner presided. Everything seemed to go well. No humiliation for France was involved since Couve de Murville did not have to go to Brussels, capital of the Commission.

The delegations were reduced to a minimum in order to avoid theatrical gestures or the spread of rumors. In the ancient building that housed the mayoralty of Luxembourg, the French minister immediately placed the coffin of Hallstein on the table; however, he did so discreetly. No names were mentioned. The unification of the three executive bodies to be accomplished very shortly would decrease the number of commissioners from 27 to 14; there would be a single President instead of three. Schroeder sat in his chair, grumbling. Germany would not favor a summary execution of these plans.

Couve de Murville gave a speech indicting the Hallstein Commission. He enumerated ten different complaints that France wished to register against the Commission and also cautioned the members that the new single Commission must not repeat these mistakes. Without consulting the various governments, the Hallstein Commission had gone to Strasbourg with a proposal to modify the Treaty of Rome. Similarly, it had initiated friendly relations with Afghanistan and published statements that were an affront to the French chief of state.

In acid tones, Schroeder challenged the bases on which the French complaints rested. Couve drew from his briefcase an article published in Holland, sponsored and paid for by the Community, but since withdrawn from circulation. It described de Gaulle as a cockatoo, a penguin, and a parrot.

"That is intolerable," Luns agreed. "And even exaggerated," he added under his breath.

A more or less explicit diminution of the Brussels Commission met with ready approval. Couve de Murville acknowledged that the Treaty of Rome endowed the Commission with a supranational character, but he denied it any sovereign attribute. Accordingly, the red carpet spread out at Hallstein's door for the reception of ambassadors was removed. To be sure, the President of the Commission continued as before to stand next to the President of the Council of Ministers when letters of credence were presented. But because the Commission was no longer regarded as sovereign, ambassadors discarded their morning coats and paid their visits in business suits. This was the end of a long quarrel over supranationality.

It was more difficult to get the Five to accept the execution of Walter Hallstein, although this task could be accomplished if one were patient. For nine years or three successive terms, Hallstein had held the presidency. The Germans insisted that he should be named the first president of the single commission. Couve de Murville looked for a way out. But he encountered fierce resistance when he asked his colleagues to renounce majority rule.

"It is admissible, and we often apply it, when secondary matters are at stake. It is not practicable for vital questions."

"Europe will never come into being if unanimity is always required," the Dutch and the Germans replied. "Majority rule was introduced in order to launch the process of unification."

With an eye on the impending meeting in Luxembourg, the French delegation proposed the following schedule: An agreement to be reached before the end of the month on the question of majority rule; the matter of a single commission (the eviction of Hallstein) and the financing of the agricultural market to be settled by the beginning of February.

Schroeder thundered, "You are tampering with the schedule again. This is a new *Diktat!*" He left the meeting, and it soon became plain what he wanted. The Americans were in a hurry to negotiate the Kennedy Round. The financing of the agricultural market and the question of Atlantic tariffs should be discussed at the same time.

Couve agreed. The Kennedy Round was to be the setoff.

Ten days later the Six reassembled in the old town hall. Spaak offered a compromise on the issue of majority rule. It was a question of interpreting the treaty, not modifying it, he said. If a vital national interest was at stake, the dictates of wisdom required that no unacceptable decision should be imposed upon one or two states.

Schroeder, supported by Luns, rebelled. After the defeat of Hallstein, majority rule was the only means of forcing de Gaulle to accept integration. The following day Spaak, the Sancho Panza of Europe, proclaimed, "The Common Market must be saved. There must be neither victors nor vanquished in Luxembourg."

The Dutch minister dozed. When he awoke from a possibly feigned but certainly conciliatory slumber, the situation was reversed. At the start of the conference, Couve de Murville had stood alone against his five colleagues. Now Gerhard Schroeder was the sole defender of "majority rule at any price." A member of the French delegation had "enjoyed" telling his neighbors what de Gaulle was capable of doing to his partners if majority rule were retained. The majority of the Six thereupon discovered that the very high wheat price granted to Schroeder to satisfy his Green Front was creating intolerable complications. Stockbreeders who were paying too much for their corn declared that they were being penalized for the benefit of the corn-growers. The fantastic surpluses would bankrupt the FEOGA.

283

Suddenly it was Schroeder who demanded that the principle of unanimity be applied without fail when agricultural regulations—that were of particular interest to him—were being considered. The compromise was recorded in a completely equivocal yet sensible communiqué: "When very important interests are at stake, the members of the Council will try to work out with reasonable speed solutions that can be accepted by everyone. . . . The French delegation believes that the discussion should be continued until a unanimous agreement has been reached. The six delegations feel that this divergence should not prevent a resumption of the Community's work."

The financing of cereals as well as of products of special interest to Germans and Italians was to be determined on the basis of priority. Simultaneously, the Kennedy Round negotiations were to be resumed. Nothing is quite as effective as such ambiguity in arranging things.

In two months, that included a little marathon session of twenty-two hours, the grain regulations were adopted at Brussels on May 11 for a period that would terminate on December 31, 1969.

"Is this an unconditional agreement?" the journalists asked. They could not believe their ears.

A large part of the agricultural market was to go into effect on July 24, 1966, with gradual changes, special provisions, and certain items omitted—lamb, wine, tobacco, and so on.

"Ninety percent of all agricultural production is covered by the accords. Seventy-one percent of free trade (10 billions) would be administered by the organizations of the Common Market. This is an international settlement unique in history," Walter Hallstein triumphantly announced.

General de Gaulle was aware of the 5 percent he lacked in order to win the elections in the first round. It was the dissatisfied peasants who had failed him. Edgard Pisani, a dynamic minister in Brussels, an ardent supporter of renovation in France—he was in favor of enlarging and modernizing farms, of organizing them into cooperatives, of instituting improvement in trade—had never succeeded in making himself popular.

There is no real Minister of Agriculture in France, only a Minister of Farmers. His primary assignment is not to organize profitable markets for consumers and farmers, or to modernize production sufficiently to meet the domestic and foreign demands; his job is to insure the survival of two million farms and ten million peasants. Half of the farmers cannot leave their small outmoded farms at a moment's notice, nor can they readily adjust themselves to teamwork under the guidance of experts.

With a certain sense of relief, Edgard Pisani handed his portfolio over to the former Premier, Edgar Fauré. A virtuoso of old-fashioned radical politics, Fauré had prophesied an annual expansion of 5 percent. At the age of fifty-five, to fill his leisure moments, he had resumed his studies and passed his examinations. As the holder of a chair in Roman law, he gave brilliant courses on agrarian reform since the Gracchi.

Now he undertook the well-nigh impossible task of trying to reconcile the rural population to the existing regime and to put the peasants in direct contact with the Common Market. He claimed that small farms should survive and mustered all his skill to help them. He pleaded the cause of the small stockbreeders who were penalized by the high price of cereals and meal.

But he was confronted by a formidable debater, Gerhard Schroeder. The Germans are the apostles of free industrial competition. But in agriculture—France's number one industry—they defended the high prices demanded by the Green Front which guaranteed a majority for Chancellor Erhard. Schroeder obtained satisfaction on three essential items: wheat (kept at 50 francs); milk (raised to 39 pfennigs); sugar, the demand for which was guaranteed within the framework of existing quotas (1,800,000 tons for Germany) by three different price levels.

The high prices secured for the powerfully organized dairy farmers, corn growers, and beet growers satisfied the pressure groups that were most heeded in France. But they also encouraged German agriculture so greatly as to enable the Federal Republic to meet its own main requirements. Germany ceased to be a buyer of France's agricultural products.

The Common Market, with its free competition, opened France to the industrial products of her neighbors. Because of her artificially high agricultural prices, she found it impossible to export. Instead of relieving France of her surpluses, the Common Market thus tended to create new difficulties for her. High European prices encouraged overproduction that had no outlets.

Milk is France's number one problem. In 1967 the Niagara flowing from the cowsheds cost the French taxpayer, apart from the "reimbursements" of the Common Market, 135 billion old francs. Of this amount, 70 billion were used to distribute, more or less free of charge, powdered milk to the starving masses of India and Mexico. In addition, 7 billion francs were spent on machines and refrigerators to augment this ruinous waste. Almost 200,000 tons of butter were unsalable in Europe in 1967; 45,000 tons were distributed with considerable difficulty. European butter, because it lacked the flavor of local butter, was rejected by the starving countries. Tourists of the Mediterranean Club were the beneficiaries: they could buy French butter in Morocco for a franc and a half per kilogram.

In Paris people were saying that the European mechanism for the maintenance of prices had been installed upside down. Community help for exports was diminished when price fluctuations led farmers to reduce their production; it was increased when rising prices caused the cow barns to yield more.

The Dutch and the Germans wanted it thus, on the assumption that there would be a market economy. It made no sense when, instead of a market economy, there were prices guaranteed by the government. Regardless of whether the price of condensed milk and butter rises or falls throughout the world, every French dairy farmer has but a single thought: to sell more and more. When inventories increase, export subsidies must be doubled or tripled, not reduced.

There is an overproduction in milk everywhere except in Italy. The Europeans fight each other with knives in order to sell to the Italians. French cooperatives and exporters outbid each other in the reverse sense of the word. Assistance in the form of exports is practically imposed on the Italian consumer. In the agricultural market it is a mark of good fortune not to be a producer.

The French tried to sell their cheese to Germany. The Sopexa company in charge of opening up foreign outlets for agricultural products waged an intensive publicity campaign beyond the Rhine to sell French camembert. The Germans were repulsed by ripe cheese. But they discovered the delights of tenderly soft camembert, washed down with French wine. Just as the Germans were beginning to enjoy it, a Netherlands corporation, Unilever, introduced a Dutch camembert. It was made with German milk in a Dutch factory located in Germany. It had a German taste to it, naturally, and it did not tend to run like French camembert. Unilever had benefited indirectly from Sopexa's advertising campaign and now proceeded to launch an all-out campaign of its own. It won the Germans over. "The one commodity that can easily outstrip milk is veal," people in Brussels said. "The French should sell a lot of their meat. Steak with fried potatoes is the most popular dish in the world."

But milk, used as electoral ammunition, benefited from the constantly rising prices. Meat was taxed. A healthy cow yielded 2,500 liters per year and at present yields 3,200. The price of veal has not increased proportionately. Milk can be sold as soon as the cow is milked but it takes years before beef is marketable. Animals are vulnerable to epidemics, drafts, and fluctuations of the market.

"Organize Normandy and Brittany like Denmark," was the suggestion made in Brussels. Pisani had already tried this. Small Danish farms are grouped into a cooperative. The agronomist buys the animals, places them on the farms, sells them, supervises the breeding of cattle and farm production, including dairy products, especially cheese. Groups of producers are awarded subsidies, encouraged, and given assistance of every kind. But the planners encountered the stubborn resistance of the French peasants. Individualistic, determined to be their own masters, even though in reality they are the slaves of farms that are usually too small, these peasants lack scientific, technical, and commercial expertise.

Pisani noted that the most strikingly successful stockbreeders were those in cooperatives organized by townspeople and former winegrowers in the Bas-Rhône-Languedoc. There were barns containing 600 to 1,000 calves. Fattened for slaughter in 400 days, these animals were looked after by a specialist and a farmer and supervised by a veterinarian. Fodder, milk, and grain were provided by other members of the cooperative. All sales were made directly to the wholesale butcher. Some of the very young live calves were shipped by plane to Milan, arriving there undamaged. This was one aspect of the Languedoc; the country had been watered and renovated through the efforts of Philippe Lamour, president and founder of Aménagement du Territoire.

As we have said, the trading carried on by Europe with the Eastern European countries competed with the export of French cattle. In 1966 Germany imported 500,000 head of cattle of which only 6,000 were French. In exchange for the meat, the countries on the other side of the iron curtain imported machinery and factories.

287

Fiat and Pirelli became meat importers; in return they installed factories in the U.S.S.R. and in other parts of Eastern Europe. Pierre Dreyfus, a Renault official, had to buy cattle and rugs and go through all kinds of contortions to resell them in order to install factories in . Bulgaria and Rumania.

The anarchy caused by overproduction in France, plus Europe's reluctance to consume French food, threatened the very existence of the Common Market in 1967 and 1968. Half of the French agriculturalists were satisfied with the high price of milk, wheat, and sugar. It was the Eurocrats in Brussels who sounded the alarm. The agencies empowered to grant subsidies were about to go bankrupt. The remaining 50 percent of the farmers, those who did not benefit from the guaranteed high prices, were in a state of muffled or open revolt against the government and the Common Market.

"Those are the people who can ruin everything," one agricultural official said. "We haven't made sufficient allowance for the technical progress of our neighbors. Dutch butter is competing in the market place with butter from Normandy. The Dutch are buying proxies in Rungis. The Germans and Dutch are buying farms in France and reaping surprisingly good harvests. Industry cannot absorb a million workers. Perhaps we are drifting toward peasant uprisings." A group of peasant leaders headed by Debatisse went so far as to demand payments for a million efficient farms doomed to overproduce without being able to make a living.

"We have undertaken the task of governing markets; we are not concerned with people or occupational structures," Sicco Mansholt, the "Minister of European Agriculture," admitted.

He developed regional plans for the rationalization of agriculture. But the German peasants, who obstructed roads in order to obtain the subsidies that had been denied them, rejected his structural reforms. Their leaders likewise rejected this intrusion. In an effort to cope with the tidal wave of milk that was costing the Six 400 billion francs, Mansholt suggested a reduction of prices and the substitution of milk-fed veal for butter. Edgar Fauré raised the question astutely in Strasbourg. The European deputies rejected any tampering with the milk jug which was very much of an electoral issue save in Italy.

All these crises brought the following question to the fore: Were

288

not the French, who continued to believe that they were nurturing
Europe, actually nurturing illusions?

Trapped by de Gaulle, Walter Hallstein continued to struggle. To
keep him his post, the Dutch abstained from ratifying the treaty that
united the three executive bodies.

"If you absolutely insist on keeping Hallstein," Couve de Murville
said, "we will retain the three executive bodies with the understanding
that within three years, the Communities will be united."

The Dutch and the Germans protested. "The fusion should be
effected under the aegis of Hallstein."

"We should decide to rotate the Presidency of the Commission,"
countered the French.

"Fine," said Schroeder, "but Hallstein must be the first President."

Suddenly, everything changed. Chancellor Erhard, Germany's pro-
American leader, was deposed by his party in much the way he had
deposed Adenauer. The Social Democrats formed a coalition with
the CDU in order to promote a reversal of foreign policy. Their
leader, the Socialist mayor of Berlin, Willy Brandt, favored overtures
to the East. Before becoming Germany's Foreign Minister, he had
paid a visit to de Gaulle. The new Chancellor, Kurt Kiesinger, was a
faithful disciple of Adenauer, and a fervent supporter of the Franco-
German rapprochement.

When the Chancellor came to the Elysée to renew Franco-German
collaboration, the case of Walter Hallstein was settled quickly. "This
good fellow, Walter Hallstein. He has been in office ten years," said
General de Gaulle. "He should be allowed to spend his Christmas
holidays at home."

The Dutch clung to the coattails of the man who had been "Europe
incarnate." But the great man of Brussels, disconcerted by the failure
of his plan for rapid integration, realized that he would not be named
head of the Commission. He belonged to an outmoded Europe. Obviously, the rulers of Germany would no longer wage a theological
defense of supranationality, of a technocratic authority standing
above governments; they could cease to struggle for a direct bridge
between Brussels and Washington.

Germany had grown, put on weight, rid herself of her complexes
as a vanquished country. The greatest power in Europe felt entitled
to pursue a policy of its own, detached from American tutelage,

289

which would bring it closer to France (Kiesinger was obsessed by the de Gaulle-Adenauer pact) and also to England. Brandt, a Socialist, felt close to the British Labourites who were now in power.

Hallstein was disheartened by the desertion of Kurt Kiesinger and Willy Brandt. He resigned on March 7, 1967. His friends, who were also Jean Monnet's—the champions of European integration—bid him an emotional farewell. A professor of law, a theoretician of diplomacy, never the holder of an elective office, he lacked political shrewdness; but the Economic Community owed him a great deal.

On June 5, 1967, the Council of Ministers appointed Jean Rey, former member of the Belgian cabinet and negotiator of the Kennedy Round, as President of the executives of the three communities. A lawyer, Rey had conducted the difficult Geneva negotiations with unfailing courtesy, to the entire satisfaction of the Six. He declared that he had been invested with a supranational mission, acknowledged by Couve de Murville in Luxembourg. But his language was discreet, and it reassured the various governments, notably Paris.

When he visited the Elysée, he came as a private citizen, driving his own Jaguar. To his great surprise, an escort of motorcyclists surrounded him. The Garde Républicaine paid him almost sovereign honors, far more elaborate than those formerly paid to Hallstein. The guerrilla war against the Commission was over.

In the meanwhile, the tenth anniversary of the Treaty of Rome had been celebrated. The head of the Italian government, Amintore Fanfani, had decided to exploit the occasion to launch anew the idea of a political union. The Atlanticists had not welcomed this initiative. Fanfani, once a member of the Committee of Action headed by Jean Monnet, was now reprimanded by Monnet. Fanfani neglected to invite him to the ceremonies at the Capitol that were to be attended by the Fathers of Europe.

De Gaulle, accompanied by his partners, was in Rome on April 10, 1967. Jean Monnet was absent. . . . His invitation had gone astray, the Italian Foreign Office explained when the incident was publicized. But Monnet was present in the person of an intermediary. His machine for prefabricating majorities had doomed the Fanfani project. The Dutch Chamber had passed a negative motion. The Italian minister suggested a meeting of the foreign ministers of the Six to reexamine a proposal for the creation of a European confederation.

290

"The Six are a very congenial group," said de Gaulle. "By all means, let's talk."

But the Dutch vetoed the suggestion. "Nothing can be undertaken without England," they said.

For several months, Jean Monnet had been working on Europe and Great Britain in an effort to bring the English into the continental community. A new battle was beginning.

XIX

The Battle of England

BRITISH Prime Minister Harold Wilson marched on the Elysée one morning in June, 1967, smoking his pipe as he walked down the Faubourg Saint-Honoré and looking like a rosy-cheeked Sir Lancelot. His aim, forcing open the gates of the Common Market, disconcerted the leaders of France. "He must not warm up the motor before the expiration of a year," they said.

For almost eighteen months Jean Monnet and his friends had been working on Europe's parliaments and governments and on European public opinion to insure a favorable response to this bid. So far as they were concerned, Wilson's arrival was several months late. Furthermore, he failed to utilize the strategy that had been suggested to him and that he had been implored to adopt. His arrival in France was a false maneuver.

"The question that needs to be answered is whether Harold Wilson will be the great man of the century, the man who will bring together a nation of 240,000,000 people," said Jacques van Helmont. He was the Secretary-General of the Action Committee for a United States of Europe which through the intermediary of political and trade-union leaders, exerted influence on two-thirds of the voters of the Six.

The Europe of the Treaty of Rome was at a low point early in 1966: The defeat of Walter Hallstein and of his plan for the speedy integration of Europe; de Gaulle's successful disruption of the Front of the Five in Luxembourg; the abandonment of majority rule.

292

At the Hôtel Matignon, Jean Monnet was declared out of the running.

At this very moment, in the greatest secrecy, the head of the English government was converted to the European idea. With the feverishness of a youthful militant, Monnet stopped writing his memoirs, contacted the leaders of the Five by telephone, and resumed his trips to the various capitals. "With England on our side, everything will be different," he said. "European union will again become possible."

He had a plan.

No one had been as cruelly disappointed by the British as he, the inventor of the communities. England had rejected all his invitations to participate in his unifying enterprises.

The British Conservatives rejected supranationality. The Labourites refused any kind of association with the Continent.

Countering the Macmillan government's negotiations with Brussels in 1962, Gaitskell, the Labour leader, had elevated to the status of dogma the following prohibitive conditions: Maintenance of the traditional commercial relations with the Commonwealth; protection for the Free Trade Area; continuation of protective tariffs for the benefit of English agriculture; retention of complete freedom of action in determining foreign and economic policies.

When the Labourites regained control of the government in the elections of October, 1964, they did not know why they had triumphed. Did they owe their success mainly to Miss Christine Keeler, wearing a dog collar and walking at the end of a leash by her friend in Conservative circles? Or were they chiefly beholden to the hesitant, unpopular and eventually unsuccessful attempt by Harold Macmillan to obtain admission to the Common Market?

The old guard among the Trade Unions still viewed England's association with the Continent, which the aristocratic Montagu Bank had "maneuvered," as a move on the part of the industrialists to pry the workers loose from their trade-union benefits. The British Socialists, as traditionalist as Indian army colonels, thought European unity was a French hoax whose inevitable failure they had predicted in 1956. To place the affairs of England in the hands of the Continent was mere foolishness. How could anyone take a Brussels international official for a gentleman?

One recalls the confidential remark made by Harold Wilson to

General de Gaulle at the time of the funeral services for Churchill: "You were right to refuse England admission to the Common Market in 1963. At that time we were neither ready nor resolved to join."

In a speech delivered on April 29, 1965, Wilson also said, "We do not have the right to jettison our friends and relatives for the imaginary advantage of selling some washing machines in Düsseldorf."

The cabinet contained only three marketeers (partisans of the Common Market): Brown, Callaghan, and Jenkins, but even they did not pretend to be Europeans according to the criteria of General de Gaulle and Jean Monnet. England could approach Europe only like a flagship rallying a flotilla to be led into vast seas.

"I will never allow anyone in my house to speak ill of the United States," said George Brown, then Minister of Economy.

The Wilson government's program was conventional enough: to modernize England, reinforce the pound sterling, and use the privileged ties with the United States and the U.S.S.R. to try to mediate between East and West, especially in regard to the war in Vietnam. But these pleasing prospects fell apart like election placards under a heavy rain.

When Wilson went to Washington to request financial aid he was received sarcastically by the President. "I can tell that the Labour Party is back in power," Johnson said to him. "The pound sterling is losing ground fast."

"Johnson has gone crazy," the Prime Minister confided to a Downing Street official. "We shall have to find a new ally," the *Sunday Times* reported in an article that analyzed in depth the evolution of the Labour Party.

"De Gaulle?" he was asked.

"That's right!"

But the advances England made to the Russians met with indifference. In the eyes of the Kremlin, the Labourites were no better than the Conservatives. "Disciples of Marx with a touch of Groucho," said Togliatti.

The British economic and financial situation remained most unfortunate. George Brown stuffed the pockets of his colleagues with notes and reports depicting membership in the Common Market as the only way for Great Britain to take care of her chronic deficits. Since this was also the thesis of the Conservatives, he had to be careful in advancing it. Wilson listened to Brown, but he was torn by contradictory advice from others. There was fierce opposition from both the right and left wings of the party.

Con O'Neil, the Undersecretary of State in the Foreign Office, had served as an envoy to the Community. He sounded the alarm. "When de Gaulle disappears, Germany will dominate the Europe of the Six."

Another minister, Stewart, invoked Britain's traditional policy: never to allow any state to dominate the Continent. England must intervene in Europe and reestablish the balance of power.

"Must we take as dogma Gaitskell's five conditions?" the Young Turks of the Labour Party asked the Prime Minister at the close of 1966.

"Things have changed since 1962," Wilson answered noncommittally. "Actually, there are two main problems connected with the Common Market: the rise in prices if we buy commodities on the Continent; the enormous tariffs we will have to pay for our imports from the Commonwealth."

One of the main ambitions of the cabinet was to take the Commonwealth in hand once again. The Conservatives, people said, had not maintained close contact with this immense archipelago of free countries, most of them Socialist. Trade with former colonies and dominions was continually decreasing. Industry, navigation, insurance companies, and British banks were feeling this more and more acutely. Macmillan had sacrificed British participation in the Common Market because of protests from the Commonwealth. Yet he had not been given credit for his loyalty to the former empire.

What was needed was a large, free union. Its revival was unfortunately hindered by the revolt of the Rhodesians who proclaimed their independence but were unwilling to accept black power. In January, 1966, a conference was held in Lagos. Wilson hoped to preserve his world and thereby old England as well. But the Africans were indignant because London would not declare total war on the whites of Rhodesia.

"You don't want to fire on white people? Well, then you're a racist," Zambien Kapwépé shouted at Wilson.

The Dominion leaders showed not the slightest inclination to renew their economic allegiance to dear old England. The plane that

295

brought Wilson back from Lagos was the scene of some bitter reflections and also a conversion.

"George," Wilson said to his economics minister after his return, "I am going to astound you. We're joining it. But don't say a word! We have a good deal of work to do. . . ."

The work was to convince the cabinet, the party (both its right and left wings), the trade unions, parliament, public opinion—something Macmillan had failed to do. In any event, the opposition must be neutralized.

Jean Monnet threw himself into his crusade: to bring the English into the European union.

"In the course of a year," he later recounted, "I saw everyone individually: Nenni, Brandt, Barzel, Rosenberg, Herbert Werner. I talked for hours on end to all the party chiefs and the leaders of the non-Communist trade unions. It was necessary to get the English to make up their minds, to encourage them. It was necessary to create, in support of their admission, unanimous agreement among the Five and a strong party in France."

"But," someone objected, "the English have never sincerely accepted supranationality."

"Supranationality," Monnet replied, "is an outmoded issue. With de Gaulle, we have moved from quarrels over principle to questions of fact.

"British membership," he continued, "represents the last opportunity for Europeans to do something about their growing inferiority to the United States, to escape colonization by the big American corporations. Soon we will be nothing but underdeveloped countries in comparison with the United States.

"Europe has become a great consumers' market. It offers 180,000,000 customers to the industrial giants of America. By making war on the Brussels Commission, by impeding economic, financial, industrial, fiscal and technological integration, de Gaulle has for years prevented the creation of a great producers' market, the establishment of inter-European consortiums powerful enough to resist corporations as large as General Motors and General Electric. His chauvinism has impeded the advance of the Continent. Every year the disparity between America's progress and our backwardness becomes more pronounced.

"Power and wealth depend on research. A European firm that

spends in its laboratories a hundred times less than Dupont de Nemours will not obtain even a thousandth of the results reaped by the latter.

"De Gaulle maintains a juxtaposition of European states. If the United States were merely the juxtaposition of Texas, Pennsylvania, and so on, America would not be what it is.

"Ten years after the signing of the Treaty of Rome, people in Paris are beginning to realize the importance of an inter-European society, the need for legislative, financial, and fiscal unification—in short, they are beginning to see that there must be an economic union. But nothing is being done because de Gaulle refuses to entertain anything except vast strategic plans which are beyond the reach of a disunited Europe.

"A French firm sought to Europeanize itself, to establish ties with enterprises in neighboring countries. Lawyers worked six months to find a pattern for such mergers.

" 'There is only one solution,' the Finance Ministry agreed. 'Liquidate all your assets. Will that mean the ruin of a large French firm? If so, that can't be helped.'

"To defend Europe against American investments, a large European financial market is needed. We have six small markets which, combined, are not comparable to Wall Street.

"None of our countries is capable of providing itself with computers, income-producing atomic reactors, intercontinental airplanes, a satellite system. Because of nationalism, we have not even reached the point of producing color television on a cooperative basis.

"With England in the Common Market, everything will be different.

"She will bring with her the world's second-largest financial market which, when linked with ours, would be in a position to finance big European corporations. She will contribute considerable assets. These include reactors that function, research centers of the first rank, factories specializing in the use of advanced techniques, a network of diplomatic, commercial, and financial ties, and an influence without comparison on this side of the ocean.

"With England, the Common Market of 240,000,000 consumers and producers can become an economic and political union comparable in strength to the United States.

"Thus Europe will be in a position to deal on a basis of equality with the United States, to negotiate as an equal with America for the

297

establishment of the economic, political, and military association of the two Unions desired by John Kennedy—an area in which prosperity will be enjoyed by 440,000,000 people. This Europe will also be in a position to treat with the countries of the East, to regulate in concert with them the problems of peace and peaceful cooperation.

"England is bound to enter the Common Market if she does not want to become the fifty-first American state. Her economy is falling apart. The Commonwealth is breaking up. The pound is burdened with the weight of war debts. But such a great country, the only one in Europe to escape defeat, cannot easily shed its pride and its illusions. We must help the English make up their minds; for the sake of the general interest, we must facilitate their access to the Continent."

To achieve his objective, Monnet advocated a procedure and tactic calculated to foil General de Gaulle. England must join the Common Market unconditionally, without reservations, and accept without restriction the same duties and rights the other countries had accepted. Among the Five, at any rate, there must be unanimous agreement to accept England without discussion.

After this occurred, it would take the Community several years to adjust to the change and to benefit from England's participation. Meanwhile, some of the provisions of the Treaty of Rome would serve to ease this period of adaptation.

Should de Gaulle reject out of hand England's bid for membership, the situation that prevailed in 1962 would be completely reversed. Great Britain would be in agreement with the Five. Should she become a sixth member, Paris, as the sole opponent, would virtually be forced to capitulate. If, in spite of everything, de Gaulle vetoed England's entry, he would find himself in an untenable position during the legislative elections of 1967 because voters would be inclined to express themselves one way or another on the issue. The slightest change in the voting pattern could prove decisive. Were the general robbed of his majority, he would be forced to resign. A new French government would bring France back to Brussels. Then the great Europe of the West could be finally achieved.

Monnet had virtually disappeared from Paris. He waged his campaign elsewhere on the Continent, in London, and in the United States. Whenever he returned to his home on the Avenue Foch he was chained to the telephone. He encountered many difficulties and objections in his efforts to mobilize statesmen, parliamentary leaders and heads of labor unions to blind acceptance of England. Integrationists feared that the British might break up the existing institutions. Monnet no longer attempted to defend supranationality. But the mechanism of these institutions must be preserved.

What the institutions needed was additional power, Monnet said. A European political union would not be feasible for a long time. Therefore the various bodies in Brussels should be awarded political power in order to negotiate with the United States and the Eastern European countries for the kind of understanding that would be perfectly consistent with the aims of the Labour government.

This was one of the advantages to be derived from England's entry. The British would no longer challenge the existing institutions or conclude with France some vague political union, which would in turn be imposed on France's partners.

Objections of all kinds were raised. And the disconcerting truth was that the British were less open to reason than the others. The men in power intended to act on their own behalf. The same was true of the opposition. Neither side was willing to have its hands tied by Gaullist or integrationist formulas. Finally, for all sorts of reasons, no Englishman was a member of the Action Committee for a United States of Europe.

On the other hand, Monnet won the approval of forty-four first-rate European leaders who promised, in the name of their organizations, to support British membership in the Common Market and to see that their parliaments voted in favor of it. The French members, Guy Mollet, Maurice Faure, René Pleven, and others, had to do their best.

"Jean Monnet wants to bring the British to the Continent at any cost," officials at the Quai d'Orsay said. "His purpose is to establish an Atlantic Europe subject to American authority. He is asking for a strongly united Europe, but one without any real capital or political power. He says he wants a Europe strong enough to negotiate on an equal footing with the United States. But his real aim is not to give such a Europe political independence, but rather to influence American policy. The kind of England he is seeking is an American Trojan horse."

Meanwhile, Harold Wilson had still not publicly declared himself in favor of joining the Common Market. He was at pains to keep his formidable task of persuasion from becoming apparent. It must in no way compromise him. Wilson was no boisterous reformer or apostle of revolution. He was a graduate of Oxford, a gifted orator when occasion arose, but primarily a manipulator, as cautious as a Sioux Indian. He began his career as an economist in the secretariat of Churchill's war cabinet; it was then that he first met Jean Monnet. Rising gradually from the Labourite rank and file, he avoided the limelight. A Member of Parliament since 1945, he assumed no special responsibilities. Between two puffs of his pipe, he would mull over an idea and get his colleagues to take the initiative. Then he would give the impression that his hand had been forced.

In the beginning he had only a parliamentary majority of four. But the March, 1966, elections swelled his majority. Among the newly elected M.P.'s were several young pro-marketeers. Jean Monnet and his friends were astounded. During the election campaign he never mentioned the Common Market, save once in Bristol, on the eve of the balloting, when he attacked the opposition.

"Edward Heath turns tail like a spaniel whenever General de Gaulle snaps his fingers," Wilson threw out.

The majority of Labourites were hostile to the Common Market, whereas the Conservatives campaigned for membership in Europe. Wilson wanted to avoid giving the impression that he was following their lead. But he appointed George Brown Foreign Secretary.

"The services will now get to work," announced the ebullient minister. He himself went into action. The first obstacle to British membership in the Common Market was the Free Trade Area. The London Declaration forbade the British to quit the Free Trade Area without the consent of their six partners.

Brown utilized the occasion of an unimportant SELE meeting at Bergen in Norway to announce that a way could be found to break down the Common Market barriers, which had caused difficulties for their exports. "We'll set up a consultative body whose function it will be to establish new relations with the Brussels Community."

The Dane Per Haekkrup quickly realized that Brown was planning a marriage between the Free Trade Area and the Community. His country, which was contiguous to the Europe of the Six, had been a candidate for a long time. "Lengthy betrothals are no good," he said, before his colleagues had had time to react.

In a few bantering tête-à-têtes, George Brown did away with the Free Trade Area. No governmental declaration of intent had as yet been formulated. But on May 9, 1966, Queen Elizabeth, who was visiting Brussels, made a brief statement that her Prime Minister had suggested to her. It concerned "the hope for greater unity between the United Kingdom and all the European countries that desire it."

"Well, now, this looks as if it's becoming something to take more seriously," was the comment in Paris.

On July 7, 1966, Premier Georges Pompidou and Maurice Couve de Murville went to London to take England's pulse. It appeared that de Gaulle had always wanted to "walk hand in hand with that great country," which he had often urged to assume important and broad responsibilities in Europe. But he wanted an independent England liberated from American influence.

Since Great Britain's dependence on the United States was primarily financial, the two French visitors hoped to find out whether the Labour government was prepared to put its house in order and pry itself loose from Washington. They were in no great hurry to welcome England to Brussels. The agricultural market was not yet perfected. The question of how to finance it would be debated once again in 1969. If the British were admitted before this problem had been resolved, it would be very easy for them to ruin the agricultural market in order to avoid paying heavy tariffs. Besides, the industrialists in France were not yet ready to face British competition. Finally, the French government hoped that within two years it would be able to obtain from its partners a common currency based on gold, so that the Six could dispense with a reserve currency—meaning the dollar and the pound. Their respective economies already overlapped so completely that for all practical purposes they constituted a single entity. In Munich the Five reached an agreement with Michel Debré to the effect that all deficits in dollars and pounds would be paid in gold.

If England entered the market before the "Euror" (the word Valéry Giscard d'Estaing gave it) was instituted, the pound sterling, whose true value was always a subject of controversy, would largely be converted into marks, francs, florins, and lire. It would be up to the six state banks on the Continent to absorb Britain's debts and deficits.

And indeed, just as Pompidou and Couve arrived in London, the press announced that the Bank of England was about to go bankrupt. This was an opportune moment for the Frenchmen to mention the

301

sacrifices that Britain would have to make before joining them in Brussels: devaluation of the pound; liberation from the shackles of the Commonwealth; "no more pleas to Uncle Sam for help"; America's exclusion from Europe's affairs.

"Take our word for it," Couve explained. "Joining the Common Market is not like going on a lark."

They mentioned Pinay's 360 ordinances enacted on December 29, 1958, the day before the first lowering of tariff barriers. Pompidou spoke of the 17.50 percent devaluation of the franc, effected to prevent a rise in prices, which had been synchronized with the opening up of imports.

"An elementary course in political economy," the British press commented, echoing the irritation of the Labour ministers.

Wilson replied. The pound would be stabilized within two years. Devaluation would not make any sense in England. Great Britain bought foodstuffs from abroad. The rise in prices would be instantaneous. As for the pound becoming a reserve currency like the dollar, the issue was not a valid one. The amount of pound holdings of the Commonwealth had not fluctuated in the last fifteen years. They served merely as ready cash for sales and purchases in London. This had nothing to do with the inflated dollar or American investments in Europe. It was true, he conceded, that the pound was a worldwide problem that should be discussed at international monetary meetings. But the Common Market had nothing to do with it.

The Frenchmen were not persuaded by Wilson's brilliant ducking of the issues. National banks on the Continent would be asked to underwrite the pound's chronic difficulties. Washington granted subsidies, took full credit, and handed the subsidies over to European institutions, which had to make them good.

The French visitors let it be known that they understood the game. Once England joined the Common Market without first devaluing the pound, it would be too late to debate the matter. British deficits, and also the depreciation of the pound, would be taken care of by the currency of the Six, to the latter's detriment. Thereafter, devaluations would cease to be necessary.

"What Jean Monnet is trying to do," the French delegation said, "is to get the Europeans to absorb the weak English currency in exchange for England's membership in the technocratic Community."

In 1961-62, Heath had asked for 788 special concessions. Now

Wilson would ask for only 47. But he complained about the terrible sacrifice imposed on England in connection with the imports she had to continue buying, especially from New Zealand, to the tune of £ 500,000,000.

"No, much less, at least during the first years," Pompidou answered. "We can arrange for a ceiling."

European political union was also discussed. Certain institutions were envisaged: An executive body composed of ministers delegated by the various government heads; an assembly made up of delegates from the political parties of each country; an economic senate. The British were most reluctant. A political Europe with de Gaulle meant the severance of ties with the United States. It also meant the liquidation of Monnet's communities.

Wilson and Brown asked that Ireland, Denmark, Sweden, and Norway be admitted to the Common Market if England were. The French frowned on this. If England were accompanied by three or four of her AFTA partners and welcomed by her three Benelux protégés, she would not be merely joining the Common Market, she would be preparing to conquer it. The British group would consist of from six to eight countries. France, Germany, and Italy would be the only three truly Continental members. One could already foresee that the European Community would be linked to the Free Trade Area.

Pompidou suggested an accelerated procedure for England's entry into the market, alone and unaccompanied. There would be a period of bilateral discussions, then an interim period of association during which time England would have no voting rights, and finally a settlement entitling the British to participate in the Community balloting.

"An interim association without voting rights?" Wilson protested. "Are you treating Great Britain as if she were Nigeria, Malta, or Cyprus? This is an insult!"

The question of voting rights during the interim period was very important. If England could vote while the discussions relating to her entry were under way, she would have a veto power and could block the Community until all her demands were met. De Gaulle was trapped by the principle of unanimity upon which he himself had insisted. Even if the decisions were to be made by a qualified majority, England's four votes, the five votes of the Benelux countries, plus the four possessed by Italy, which was quite anti-Gaullist, would enable

303

the British to muster thirteen votes against the eight of Germany and France combined.

The visit ended none too cordially. The Prime Minister did not attend the farewell dinner at the French embassy. But, according to the *Sunday Times,* he had told the Frenchmen infinitely more about his intentions than he had confided to his own colleagues in the cabinet.

Pompidou and Couve returned to Paris with the feeling that Wilson would not request entry into the Common Market before the expiration of a two-year interval, the time it would take to convert his friends and stabilize the pound.

On October 22, 1966, Wilson assembled at Chequers (the country house of the head of the government) a number of experts as well as the members of his cabinet. "This is J Day," Londoners commented.

"Is this a good time to consider entry into the Common Market?" the Prime Minister cautiously asked.

No antimarketeer would say no. "It was like asking us if we should pull the shades up in the morning," one minister observed.

On November 10 Wilson made an innocuous announcement to the Commons: The government intended to explore the possibility of joining the Economic Community.

Jean Monnet burned with impatience. He had put all kinds of pressure on five parliaments and had warmed up public opinion in the six countries, only to await the arrival of a tortoise.

But the notion of the Common Market was beginning to take hold in England, as well as in the mind of the Prime Minister. "It is not altogether impossible that I might become the president of a European Union," he told his colleagues.

In Rome on January 13, 1967, Harold Wilson began "to explore the possibilities." He intended to visit all the capitals. This was the first phase of the "accelerated procedure" suggested by Pompidou— that of bilateral discussions.

Monnet's friends were irritated. The strategy that had been suggested to Wilson was to lay down no conditions for membership, which five out of the six parliaments had already accepted. Yet here he was, with a bunch of conditions in his briefcase, going on a tour and raising all kinds of objections.

At 10 Downing Street Monnet's activities had been greatly appreciated. But his tactics were considered simplistic. The unconditional

304

adhesion of England to the Common Market would always be vetoed by de Gaulle, who wanted an England divorced from Washington, rid of her chronic deficits, and willing to eat French food. To accept all the obligations of a member of the Community might prove embarrassing when discussions centered on the essentials: The payments to be made; the question of structural changes in Brussels.

Amintore Fanfani gave the former Oxonian a brief examination on the agricultural market from which Wilson emerged with an honorable mention. The Italian and the Englishman were in total agreement on "the excessive carrying costs." They also agreed that Great Britain's entry would prevent the impending Franco-German alliance from creating a Gaullist hegemony.

A week later, the Prime Minister flew to Strasbourg. He was accompanied by Duncan Sandys. Great Britain's membership in the Common Market thus became officially the concern of both political parties; the country was unanimously supporting the move. Wilson attended a meeting of the Council of Ministers, which another Labour government had rendered impotent. "The Sleeping Assembly"—which included Englishmen—woke up for the occasion. The European enthusiasts who composed it gave Wilson and his companion an ecstatic welcome.

In a grandiloquent speech, the Prime Minister deplored the fact "that a long line of fortifications loomed on the coasts of our maritime Europe."

The next day, on January 24, 1967, he paid a visit to the Elysée. "His itinerary was not very shrewdly planned," said a French diplomat. But as the seeker of the Golden Fleece climbed the staircase of the Elysée there was a certain irresistible spring to his step.

De Gaulle was not offended by Wilson's having first gone to Strasbourg. "It was doubtless a pilgrimage of repentance," he said.

An original supporter of the Council of Europe, de Gaulle had vilified the Labourites for emasculating it. He reposed a great deal of hope in the new Labourites, assuming they would free Great Britain from the humiliating role she had been called upon to play as Washington's poor cousin. But he was worried about Wilson in this connection. The Prime Minister never neglected a chance to proclaim publicly his loyalty to America. A little double talk, however, was perhaps necessary until England's finances had been put in order. The important thing was for Wilson to get started.

305

"I bring you the technological resources of Great Britain," Wilson said, echoing Macmillan's remarks of 1962. "The pound is not a problem."

In the general's opinion, the pound was not one but two problems —England's debts that the Six might have to pay; her predictable inability to free herself of Uncle Sam as long as she believed that the pound sterling was "not a problem."

The next day, at the Hôtel Matignon, the discussion of the agricultural market grew sharp. The British kept insisting on bringing the Danish, Irish, and Norwegians with them into the Common Market. "If the Six become the Ten, with seven on England's side, we might as well hold our meetings in London," Georges Pompidou whispered to the man seated next to him.

Wilson and Brown persisted in their demand for admission to the Common Market with full voting rights. To them, the transitional period of association, an interval without voting rights which would end when Great Britain was in a position to assume Community obligations, seemed an unacceptable arrangement.

The British press noted at a luncheon in the Elysée that de Gaulle drank a toast "to George Brown and to England, our friend, and our old and always cherished ally," but forgot to mention Wilson.

A curious and perhaps significant incident occurred in Brussels on February 1. The two British pilgrims were guests of the Belgian government. They were acquainting themselves with the Community. Walter Hallstein, who was still serving as President of the Commission, invited them to dine at Val Duchesse. "We would prefer to invite you to the embassy," the Prime Minister answered.

But most of the commissioners discovered they had prior engagements. They probably did not wish to draw Paris' ire, the British surmised.

"Not at all," the diplomats corrected them. "This is a matter of protocol. The Commission is supranational. It is up to it to welcome visitors. If the commissioners accepted the invitation they would be denying the Commission's sovereignty."

In the end, Wilson and Brown dined with the three Socialist members of the Commission: Sicco Mansholt, Robert Marjolin, and Lionello Levi-Sandri.

On February 14, leaders in Bonn who had been primed for the discussion were awaiting the two Englishmen. Willy Brandt assured them that they would be supported by the Socialists. But both the Chancellor and his Foreign Minister were anxious to avoid giving the impression that they were taking a position different from that of Paris. They too took the monetary problem very seriously. They also had questions to put to the British officials. "We want equality of rights in matters of atomic defense. We want weapons like those of our allies and of our possible attackers. Will you see that we get them?"

Wilson and Brown were very embarrassed. They hoped to go to Moscow. They had no intention of satisfying their former enemies.

At The Hague on February 24 they were welcomed with open arms by the President of the Council, Zijlstra, and the Foreign Minister, Luns. Sicco Mansholt, who knew every aspect of the agricultural market—he had devised most of it—had studied the price scale for British membership. The cost of agricultural levies would not reach its maximum for seven years. But in 1969 the question of financial regulation would be debated once again. Some arrangement could be made in favor of Great Britain. Wilson took heart.

These tours of consultation were the despair of the integrationists and Atlanticists. The British Prime Minister was wasting precious time. He had allowed the French elections to go by, even though at such a juncture de Gaulle would have shown himself to be most accommodating. The elections took place on March 5 and 12; de Gaulle barely scraped through with a parliamentary majority of two.

Five days later Monnet sent a note to London in the name of his committee, begging the British to join the Common Market unconditionally and immediately. "Within six months," he explained, "the Continent's enthusiasm for England will subside. Wilson will become involved in discussions of secondary importance."

Cautious as he was, Wilson still sought the unanimous approval of his cabinet and party. The antimarketeers were no more than a handful of isolated opponents. It was important to avoid resignations or demonstrations.

Finally, on May 10, after a last meeting at Chequers, Wilson presented the candidacy of Great Britain to the Community. In doing so, he had the approval of the House of Commons. But it was merely a request, not the unconditional acceptance for which the Monnet committee had asked and which the five parliaments expected.

Wilson had abandoned neither his conditions nor his attempts to bargain. A traditional parliamentarian, he had no faith in Monnet's methods of persuasion, in the efficacy of the clandestine gatherings where the advocate of unity mobilized his eminent coconspirators to commit the votes of their parties, in Monnet's capacity to influence public opinion. The situation in Germany constituted a striking vindication of Wilson's attitude. The most powerful political leaders of the strongest country in Europe—the second commercial power in the world, the third industrial power—feared England, her traditional policy of "divide and rule"; the votes she might marshal in a Europe of the Ten; her overwhelming political influence due to American support; the adverse effect of the pound on the mark and on other free currencies; the competition of British industry, which paid comparatively low wages because British food was cheap. But Kurt Kiesinger and Willy Brandt could not take a stand. They hid behind the skirts of General de Gaulle since public opinion in Germany clamored for British participation and American protection.

"A divorce between England and the United States is inevitable," said a former British minister. "Washington's tutelage is resented with increasing bitterness in leading business circles. The American industrial invasion—only one British automobile manufacturer is left in England—is becoming more and more unpopular. No one loves a rich relative. But in Great Britain there is not a single movement, nor a single newspaper that advocates Gaullist neutralism. The ties with America are so numerous that it would take at least ten or fifteen years to break them, even if there were a desire to do so."

On May 16, 1967, six days after the British made their request to Brussels, General de Gaulle held a press conference. For the first time, in reply to a question from an old acquaintance, Harold King, director of the Reuter news agency in Paris, the French President clearly stated his position. "Dear friend, at long last I will answer you about England and the Common Market. . . ." To put it briefly, England and her associates would introduce destructive disturbances in the market. It had taken ten years of "critical confrontation" to achieve the agricultural market, which was so important to France. "The Common Market is a prodigy of sorts." The Six constituted a compact geographical and strategic entity. England was not part of the Continent. Involved with countries across distant seas, she was hostile to the Community and had tried to stifle it. Now she was demanding that fundamental changes be made before she joined it.

308

She realized that "she will have to overcome the obstacles which her very clear-sighted and profoundly experienced Prime Minister has described as formidable."

England could not subject herself to the regulations of the Six. Her balance of trade would be disastrously affected by the levies on her imports. The price of foodstuffs would rise to the level prevalent in Western Europe. England would have to increase wages and the prices of her manufactured goods. If she entered the Common Market without agreeing to participate in the agricultural market, she would eliminate one of France's main reasons for belonging to the Community.

Among the Six, capital flowed freely. There was monetary stability. But the pound was not convertible; it could not be used outside of England. Europeans could not accept an isolated partner living beyond its means. From the very start, de Gaulle went on to say, the Six had united in order to establish a European entity that would be fully capable of taking independent political action. England, like the United States and the Commonwealth, had special commitments. Either the British would recapture their entire freedom of action or the Continentals would have to give up the idea of a European Europe.

England made no secret of the fact that she was demanding many changes in the Common Market. If she had her way, everything accomplished so far would be ruined. In the general's opinion, there were two alternatives: association with the Common Market or profound economic and political changes within Great Britain.

On June 15, Monnet's Action Committee replied by issuing a declaration signed by 44 European leaders. For the first time, two incumbent ministers—Willy Brandt and Wehner, the representatives of Germany's two major political parties—were among the signatories. The declaration demanded England's entry into the Common Market and association of the other candidate countries with the Six; an advisory committee that would work with the Community and the United States and discuss with them on equal footing such things as American investments in Europe, the balance of payments, technological changes, and so on.

Harold Wilson returned to the Elysée on June 17. He favored neither a Gaullist Europe nor the drastic reforms the general demanded. But the Monnet committee and the Dutch had assured him that he had the warm support of the Five. He therefore approached

309

the Elysée with great assurance, totally unprepared for the setback that awaited him.

On June 26, 1967, at a meeting of the Council of Ministers in Brussels, Couve de Murville declared that the Continentals must establish a common policy before entering into direct negotiations with George Brown. Couve argued that a Europe of the Ten would constitute a vast area in no way organized for combat yet vulnerable to any country's desire for conquest. What he feared was an enslavement of Europe by Anglo-Saxon industry and diplomacy.

The Hallstein Commission, now the Jean Rey Commission, was asked for its opinion.

Meanwhile, General de Gaulle was making plans to bring home the message by a trip to Quebec. In his eyes, the province of Quebec was a perfect example of what would become of France and of Europe if they were subjected to Anglo-Saxon hegemony. Canada had all the trappings of a democracy, but business, the bank, construction, oil, wood, the mines—all were Anglo-American. French Canadian lumberjacks felt imprisoned. Quebec doctors, architects, and lawyers were treated on their own soil like specialists from a second-rate zone. Anyone speaking French in a Montreal hotel might very well be told to "speak white."

If the British were to join the Common Market, overnight English would become the official language in Brussels. All official documents would be drafted in English. Even in Paris, English would be used for administration and business.

The great European financial market would be installed in London and would synchronize its activities with those of Wall Street and other centers. In short, London would be "Atlanticized." Of course this would be most convenient for businessmen. Large corporations with headquarters in Paris, London, Frankfurt, and New York would in actuality become, as in Canada, financial consortiums operating under international leadership with American efficiency and drive.

The effects would soon be felt on everyday political life. The authority of large American corporations, mobilizing a huge personnel through their merchandizing subcontractors, would be irresistible. The establishment and development of these corporations would be extremely beneficial to any country, but should they go bankrupt and close down their factories, a national catastrophe would result. It was therefore up to the member states to take the necessary steps to control these tyrannical monsters. In an Atlantic, federated Europe, from which the desire for independence was absent, these Euro-American giants could become uncontrollable. Frenchmen would either be converted to an American way of life or become second-class citizens. Paris would be merely a pleasant meeting place for businessmen.

"Long live a free Quebec," the general had shouted, causing consternation throughout the world. What he really meant was, long live a free France, a free Europe, and a boot in the hindquarters of the London government which was attempting a quick conquest of the Continent.

In its report of September 29, 1967, the Brussels Commission acknowledged the problems raised by the French. Negotiations must commence immediately if these problems were to be resolved, it declared. But the French categorically opposed the opening of negotiations. At a meeting of the Five, the Dutch suggested that negotiations should begin without the French. But the German government was reluctant; Kiesinger and Brandt did not want a rupture with Paris. They needed General de Gaulle to talk to the East. Moreover, the presence of France was necessary to counteract British preponderance.

"England must dominate the Continent," George Brown had told the Germans and the Swiss.

But the Chancellor and his Foreign Minister were opposed by their respective political parties whose leaders, including Brandt, had signed Monnet's declaration. Public opinion, generally, favored England's entry into the Market.

On October 13 in Bonn, Jean Monnet, seated in the place of honor, listened to the Bundestag debate on the declaration of his Action Committee. Kiesinger intervened to say that the Germans must be cautious, they must take into account the objections of the French. But a unanimous parliamentary declaration in favor of Monnet's Europe was being prepared. The Chancellor jumped up and shook hands warmly with Monnet. Then he sat down beside him. The deputies rose and gave the anti-Gaullist an enthusiastic ovation.

The pound was once again in dire straits.

"That's because de Gaulle is attacking it," the British and American journalists charged. For the last two years, ever since Jacques Rueff criticized American inflation and preached a return to gold, de Gaulle had been denounced as a Goldfinger who was depleting the treasure in Fort Knox.

Now look at him, the British and American press exclaimed, pillaging the reserves of the Bank of England, selling the pound sterling on all the world markets to convert the pound into gold. But he was not alone in doing this. Orders for gold, mainly for deposits in foreign banks, were pouring in from the Middle East, from Rome, Zurich, Algiers, and even London. But the general's campaign against the stability of the pound and the dollar unleashed speculation and led many people to expect devaluation.

According to the Quai d'Orsay, official publications proved that in 1967 France had not added a single gram of gold to her reserves. Italy, to name only one country, had increased her gold reserves by $90,000,000.

On November 20, 1967, the British government devalued the pound by 14.30 percent, to achieve a convenient parity with the dollar. Everyone expected a devaluation of 30 percent but Washington, according to financial circles, was opposed. The dollar would have collapsed as well. A proper but inadequate step, people in Paris said.

In Brussels on November 20, 1967, Couve de Murville vetoed a proposal to open negotiations with England. He demanded that the question of England's entry into the Common Market be subordinated to the righting of her balance of payments. And he asked for this in writing. Great Britain's short-term debt amounted to $12,000,000 and she owed the central banks $7 billion. The mere prospect of her acceptance into the Common Market would suffice to save the situation. But Paris claimed that the Europeans would have to foot the bill.

The Belgian minister, Harmel, contended that the negotiations would last for years. During this interval the British might be able to stage a recovery whereas the Europeans would be blocked. These would be terrible years, Couve retorted. England's allies would block the Common Market. The Community would be torn to shreds.

The French veto produced violent explosions. In an adjacent room Sicco Mansholt terminated the meeting of the ministers of agriculture. "No one wants to continue," he said.

The Benelux countries, with Wilson's approval, officially proposed the formation of an association comprising the Five outside of the

Common Market, with England and the EFTA countries, and without France. The Five and the Seven would organize an economic, political, and Atlantic Europe, without France.

But the German government demurred. On February 20, Kiesinger and Brandt arrived in Paris with half of the Bonn cabinet for a meeting on the Franco-German alliance. De Gaulle said that it might be possible to make some arrangement with England. Satisfied, the German ministers departed.

De Gaulle expressed the hope that England would join Europe when she was ready. In the meantime, a "little Kennedy Round" would be offered the British—reductions in tariffs and an exchange of agricultural products.

"De Gaulle seemed to be giving in, but actually he merely accepted something he had been suggesting for the last five years," one diplomatic observer commented.

The British press fulminated. "French predominance in Europe can develop into a Franco-German hegemony." The German press was likewise bitter, as were the parliamentarians. If the German ministers were satisfied, was this not simply because Great Britain's entry had been blocked? They apparently preferred political control of Europe to an economic partnership. "We'll just have to wait for de Gaulle to disappear from the scene," Washington observed.

But the guns had been loaded. The devaluation of the pound unleashed a gold rush. "In the beginning of this gold affair," a Swiss financier explained (a "gnome of Zurich," as the Londoners called him), "the battle was waged by de Gaulle against the dollar and in behalf of a European currency."

Since his return to power in 1958 and Washington's refusal to welcome him as the leader of Europe in a three-power directorate of the free world, the general had availed himself of two weapons against American power: the French striking force (a political instrument employed mainly to convince France's neighbors that the United States could not protect them with atomic weapons) and a European currency. The latter, "Euror," was blocked by Washington. At Bretton Woods, shortly after the war, the United States substituted the dollar and the pound for a universal gold standard.

In the opinion of the French chief of state, the dollar as a reserve currency enabled the United States to print money that was not

313

matched by gold reserves, and to buy or establish with this currency businesses and corporations in Europe without having to open up its purse; to support American policy throughout the world; to finance, in part, the war in Vietnam.

Through the Marshall Plan, this planned dollar inflation made possible the economic recovery of Europe. But de Gaulle felt that the United States had benefited enough from the printing of its "greenbacks." In the general's opinion, American prosperity was due in large part to the profits made at the expense of European economies, to investments made at relatively little cost because of inflation.

Europe did not need the United States to print money, de Gaulle claimed. It had twice as much gold as America and was entitled to have its own currency. It should enjoy whatever benefit it could derive from controlled inflation, as a means of payment, legitimized by the growing needs of an expanding economy. In asking for a return to the gold standard, de Gaulle assumed the posture of an adversary of Anglo-Saxon financial privileges, of a champion of monetary democracy.

Little by little, he established his monetary striking force (a new way of printing money, Jacques Duhamel quipped) by hoarding tons of gold. This hoarding, which many people thought futile, was part of a vast campaign to rid Europe of the dollar, to free the Six from a foreign currency that had been denounced as parasitical, and to establish "Euror," backed by the monetary reserves of the Six that included considerable sums from the Bank of France.

The White House was operating in a reverse sense. It asked the Ten, who were liquid because of the Central Bankers Gold Pool, to guarantee an additional supply of dollars by exercising the right to draw upon the International Monetary Fund. De Gaulle refused to give his signature. He withdrew from the Pool and demanded a revamping of the international monetary system. This would permit Europe to have its own currency, thereby endowing it with a vital instrument of independence.

The British had not been very prudent, the Swiss financier added. They should not have attempted to force themselves upon Europe and de Gaulle. The shakiness of the pound had caused considerable speculation while the discussions were under way. Why climb up a greased pole with a wooden leg?

It was equally imprudent of the Americans to push the English into battle. The war in Vietnam, largely financed by inflation, had dangerously reduced the value of the dollar. No one in Washington was plugging for a reduction of American deficits in order to strengthen the dollar.

One striking paradox was that the Bretton Woods accords had fixed the value of gold at $35 per ounce, yet dollars were worth less and less. The dollar was no longer guaranteed the value of gold; rather, it was gold that was identified with the devalued dollar. It was not difficult to foresee that this precious metal could not for long be allowed to lose its theoretical value in the vaults of Fort Knox. The speculation caused by the devaluation of the pound, the purchase of bullion by stockbrokers, banks, emirs, corporations, and many Eastern European banks, emptied Fort Knox of half of its reserves and cost the nine faithful members of the Gold Pool $3 billion in gold.

The Bank of England capitulated in March, 1968, halting the sale of gold. Washington likewise gave in, exchanging its dollars for the gold held by state banks that would not speculate—in other words, that would make no demands. Although it was a restrained devaluation, the Gold Pool collapsed.

Gold became free. There ensued a period of important developments that was likely to affect, for better or worse, the fate and unity of Europe.

XX

The Elimination of Frontiers

ON July 1, 1968, at zero hour, a great event was scheduled to take place: the elimination of the frontiers that separated the six signatories of the Treaty of Rome. Barriers removed, stakes uprooted, customs offices closed, demobilization of an army of customs officials who henceforward would be needed only along the periphery of the Community, shouts of joy, tourists delivered from an endless amount of red tape, condolences offered to unemployed smugglers—one can imagine the celebration!

The free movement of goods was to become effective that very night with the complete abolition of customs duties. Yet there was no apparent panic among the estimable tax collectors (about 18,000 of them in France alone). Nor was there any apparent excitement among the smugglers. In effect, there was no nocturnal turbulence on that first evening of July save that caused by reporters and cameramen.

Nothing much happened because many things had already occurred during the past ten years. Tariffs, which had been reduced gradually and piecemeal, were by 1968 no more than 15 percent of what they had been in 1958. They had declined from 1.5 to 2 percent for raw materials, 4.5 to 6 percent for automobiles sold between France and Germany, 4.80 percent for cameras, and 3 percent for wool. Trade between the Six had increased 138 percent (compared to 89 percent throughout the world). The result had been a general sense of well-being among the Six. Private consumption had increased 107 percent in Italy (with a 36 percent rise in prices), 99 percent in the Netherlands (with a 37 percent increase in prices), 70 percent in Germany (23 percent rise in prices), 63 percent in Belgium (with a 23 percent increase in prices).

The fateful July 1, 1968, was therefore a symbolic day. But a good deal of work remained for the customs officials who now became tax collectors.

A cheese exported from Holland was freed from Dutch taxes. When it arrived in France, the TVA subsidy for French cheeses had to be paid. Camembert was shipped untaxed to Belgium but a Belgian tax was collected at the frontier. Thus tariff barriers still remained after July 1. So did frontier policemen, who stamped the passports and identity cards of travelers outside the Community and watched for felons eager to breathe the foreign air. Tobacco was liberated that night, but only theoretically. French agents continued to collect duty on cigarettes. As for alcohol, German distillers were paid tariffs by way of reimbursement because they enjoyed a monopoly.

Customs officials continued to collect duties on certain specified industrial products, and sanitary inspectors still examined meat, dairy products, and so on. In the guerrilla warfare of frontiers, there were still very active roles to play.

The Common Market, that cradle of future European fraternity, had indeed begun amid shouts and bad temper. Tricks, ruses, and frauds of all kinds inaugurated the regime of free competition. To encourage exports, the various administrations joined hands.

"The daily Common Market is not going well," Roland Nungesser, Secretary of State for Foreign Commerce, had observed in 1967. "It is being ruined by cheaters."

"Very few saints are to be found among government officials," people in Brussels had said.

A thousand complaints were leveled at the Italians: "They have ruined the household goods industry in the Benelux countries," the Belgians and Dutch lamented. "Their refrigerators, stoves, and washing machines are being sold 20 to 30 percent cheaper than ours. In 1958 Italy produced 15 percent of Europe's refrigerators. In 1968 she is producing approximately 50 percent of Europe's refrigerators. The vacuum-cleaner industry, which is very well organized in Germany and France, was able to compete with the Italians; but we had to close our factories. The Italian cleaners do not meet the standards that are enforced in other countries. Their manufacturers do not pay taxes; they sell without presenting invoices and receive refunds for exports."

"There has been some cheating," the Italian government admitted. "But there are cheaters in every country."

"But you encourage them. You organize the dumping of products!"

The French Minister of Agriculture received endless complaints about his "pig tricks." An outbreak of pestilence among pigs was reported in the Pyrenees. Measures were promptly taken to isolate and slaughter the diseased animals. Trans-Alpine veterinarians forbade the shipment of pigs to one-third of French territory for a period of six months. Brussels was annoyed by these sanitary restrictions. One regulation was applied, supposedly to limit infractions, but it was not always enforceable.

"The Dutch are fairer," the Parisians said. "Very properly, they announce that there is a regional epidemic and guarantee the wholesomeness of the meat in the rest of the country. If they are informed of an isolated epidemic in one part of France, they allow their animals to be shipped elsewhere in our country."

The Dutch were bothered by the tides. Their prices for river transportation were based on the water level, which was usually estimated in a fog and adduced as a reason for increasing shipping rates. They had to be forced to establish rates based on factual, published water levels.

The commencement of this idyll of the Six produced an endless flood of complaints. Leafing through those files, one would think that Europe comprised nothing but rascals and that the most clever and vindictive among them were the government officials. "Reprisals!" the ministers ordered their customs officials. The exports were all-important; imports were barred.

Paris complained that tariffs were too low at the frontiers of the Community, that they did not discourage the import of cattle and cereals from outside the Community. Besides, France's neighbors often forgot to pay the levies, leaving the cost of agricultural surpluses to be paid out of French funds.

Furthermore, each of the national tariffs competed with one another for imports arriving from outside the Common Market. Each country receiving goods retained the revenues from tariffs levied on merchandise that circulated freely among the Six. Frontier customs offices engaged in competition, reduced the tariffs, rebaptized the products in order to give a friendly government special privileges and attract customers. The wall of the Community was riddled with holes. Imported products circulated like the Europeans themselves, without any examination of their port of origin. What was needed was a European customs bureau.

In 1968, the future of the Common Market did not appear rosy to the French.

"What General de Gaulle will be reproached for one day," said one of his ministers, "will not be that he was anti-European, that he impeded European unification. Rather, it will be said that he was too European, that he accelerated the stages of the industrial market in exchange for the agricultural market, that he accepted the Kennedy Round before the French were ready for it. But would we ever have been ready? Europe is not solely a region, it's a thirty-year jump forward. Could we reconcile ourselves to being the kind of country Spain became after the loss of her colonies?"

"Europe is going to bleed," said a group of economists. "Competition in the Common Market has scarcely begun. It will grow more arduous. But competition in the Kennedy Round will be even tougher.

"In the next five years, tariffs will gradually be reduced by half. By then the products of fifty different countries, including the United States, Switzerland, and Japan, will be circulating freely."

In the space of a few years, Japan has quintupled her automobile production. She may also multiply her capacity to manufacture electronic goods, optical instruments, textiles, and all kinds of new items. Japanese prices, from shipbuilding to transistors, are unrivaled, as is her economic dynamism. A battle of giants will ensue between the United States and Japan.

Under the dual impact of the Common Market and the Kennedy Round, thousands of French businesses seemed condemned to disappear. It was thought that by 1971 or 1972 there might be two million or more unemployed, not including the large number of people who would lose their jobs through technological progress.

The entire western section of France was pauperized during the middle of the last century by the elimination of regional frontiers. Prior to this, Brittany had a virtually self-sufficient economy. The French Common Market put an end to activity in the province. The

319

European Common Market may have even more dire consequences for the West.

Industrial geography is changeable. The anxieties that manifest themselves are less the consequences of regions than of certain branches of activity, especially businesses.

Mechanical engineering was prepared for a severe setback. The country's most important sector, it was also the oldest and most diversified. It comprised some powerful export firms, but also a number of outmoded ones, ill-prepared to withstand American or German competition.

An incipient state of panic was brewing in the building industry. In France the construction costs were reputed to be 30 percent higher than those of neighboring countries. Italian and German building contractors expected to be awarded big contracts, to receive large orders, and to build factories, workers' cities, new towns, highways, and airports.

Anxiety was felt in almost every area, especially in big business, in enterprises of considerable importance. Mergers were encouraged. Tottering firms that might have been saved by a new planning team were merged with other companies that were also foundering. They infected one another as if they had a contagious virus. The mergers turned out to be a collection of feeble enterprises.

Regions already affected took fright. The mayor of Bordeaux, Jacques Chaban-Delmas, forecast a very difficult future. Fifty percent of the regional concerns had no trade departments. "It is a shame to see that many employers are totally unaware of the problem," he said. "Public opinion must be alerted."

"France decided in favor of competition [by launching the Common Market]," declared Raymond Barre, French vice-president of the Brussels Commission. "We got off to a late start. Our semi-industrialized country is threatened and may be confronted with a serious situation."

But apparently the largest sector of French production will hold its own, at least long enough to adjust itself. Other segments of the economy, like Michelin's tires, electronics, the tooling industry, may even become the shining lights of the Common Market. Big and small companies have gone to America to find a place for themselves, and they are getting ahead. But for a large number of firms, there is a considerable risk in becoming part of Europe in the twentieth century. They are self-enclosed, steeped in protectionism, accustomed to old-fashioned formulas and imbued with faded pride.

Two things are urgently needed: a school for employers, inspired by or directly imported from the Harvard Business School, staffed by professors of business who ought to be the best paid in France; a corps of economic "surgeons" whose mission it would be to effect at once the requisite liquidations. They would curb unemployment and reduce to a minimum the number of factories about to close by finding efficient buyers for them.

We are on the threshold of a great adventure that comprises all the dangers of war save that of losing lives.

If France, like Italy, succeeds in becoming economically competitive with the aid of imagination, talent, nerve, and the great freedom of action the industrialists enjoy, she will achieve at one bound a thirty-year advance and thus emulate America. This, as General de Gaulle predicted, will probably spell the end of the old leisurely habits, of the peaceful life with "the sky above the roof, so blue, so calm." Frenchmen will doubtless experience the struggle for survival, the vicissitudes of unemployment, the search for jobs and the anxieties about tomorrow, perhaps even the nervous breakdowns that are so characteristic of American life. But France will have caught up with her century.

But should she only half succeed, she may find herself, under the cover of French or international companies, subjected to a growing number of American, German, Dutch, or Japanese employers. That is, unless social upheavals, peasant insurrections, and demonstrations by the unemployed force France to give up the Common Market and the opportunities and risks of the Kennedy Round. This is an improbable but not an impossible eventuality.

But fears about the staying power of the French economy or France's difficulties with her partners may lead the government to break away from the Community and seek other, less restrictive trade relations. This cannot be ruled out.

Conditions in France, especially the country's lack of preparation, are best illustrated by the fishermen's strike along the coasts in February, 1968. The men of the sea have been threatened for many years. The floating factories of the Dutch trust, Unilever, transport and deliver canned fish at prices that cannot be rivaled. The ultra-modern trawlers of France's neighbors sell their cargoes of fish in the ports at prices considerably lower than those of the French; yet French prices are very low for the nation's fishermen. Japanese tuna boats fishing off the coast of Morocco unload thousands of tons of tuna in Rotterdam whose tins carry a Dutch label.

On April 15, 1968, fish became part of the European market. Frenchmen demanded that a minimum price be fixed for fish but the Dutch opposed this. They maintained, "The fishing industry is not like agriculture. If we fix the price of everything we will never have free competition, and that would mean the end of the Common Market."

"Stop importing fish. Outlaw such low prices!" the strikers clamored.

No one along the coasts or anywhere else seemed to have heard of the Common Market. The Economic Community is at once very backward in organization and far more progressive than anyone realizes.

By June 1, 1970, the regulations governing competition are to be made identical among the Six, although this was not stipulated in the treaty. Experience and prevailing realities will determine how the problem should be met. What is needed is identical rates for energy, transportation, direct and indirect taxation; a common social security program and identical regulations for such items as industrial products, wines, and pastry.

The harmonization of indirect tariffs, stipulated in the treaty, has barely begun. The French TVA was adopted in 1968 by the Germans and accepted in principle by the other partners. However, in France and Germany the same rules were applied but the rates differed.

"Theoretically, exports are not affected by these differences," said an automobile tycoon. "The tax on a French car sold in Germany is paid by the Germans; the French tax has been removed. The tax on a German car sold in Belgium is paid by the Belgians; the German tax has been eliminated."

But harmonization is purely theoretical. French cars cost more to manufacture, and the gross profit is less because, to cover state budgetary expenses, several different taxes must be added which other countries do not levy. The French levy these taxes to subsidize agriculture, take care of deficits in nationalized industries, pay for atomic research, and finance a system of economic planning that is ruining healthy, profitable firms and even endangering their very existence in order to aid and encourage companies or regions that are in trouble. The state monopolies in themselves constitute a very heavy burden. The state pays 50 percent of the operating costs of these enterprises, which include electricity, coal, gas, oil, railways, banks, and the telephone system. State taxes in France are higher than elsewhere. The taxpayers still have to pay for the deficits incurred by the nationalized industries. Nevertheless, industry is the state's number one customer as well as its biggest source of tax revenue.

But this is not all. Monopolies paralyze the related sectors. The French railway system is opposed to the modernization and expansion of the country's canals. The Rhineland, Holland, and Belgium owe their prosperity to the waterways that enable them to procure raw materials at a low cost. The Rhine will soon be linked with the Danube. In France, the canals for river barges date from the time of Louis XIV and the Second Empire. A Rhone-Rhine canal is still in the stage of preliminary study. The canal of the Midi, which could spur the economy in France, has never been developed.

The French railway system has also opposed the widening of existing roads, the building of additional industrial highways that could to some extent replace modern canals, the use of 50-ton tank cars and 100-ton trucks. Dump trucks in the Basse-Alpes travel over ancient stagecoach roads. Factories in the Jura have to rely on similar routes. Industrial development in Brittany is seriously handicapped by the absence of large highways.

The telephone system has become a nightmare for many large concerns. Orléans, for example, has become an important industrial center yet it is impossible to telephone to or from the city. Businessmen are obliged to go all the way to Paris every morning to put their calls through.

Raw materials, fuel, transportation, and the communications system are all more expensive in France than elsewhere. They are handicapped by persistent backwardness and additional costs.

In Germany, electricity, coal, gas, oil, and banks are free from interference by the state. Their operating expenses are lower and more flexible. Management is not hampered by a stultifying monopoly. It operates under the free enterprise system. The telephone service is good.

In Brussels the harmonization that is a prerequisite of free competition has been slowed down because of quarrels over integration, to say nothing of crises, breakdowns in communication, and reprisals.

Owing to the absence of any coordinated effort, the 120 ministers of the Six continue each year to issue tens of thousands of regulations. They are totally uninformed about the regulations which their partners are issuing. In 1966 Germany revamped her commercial system without consulting her partners. The French government reformed its social security system with no thought of harmonizing it with that of its partners. The opposition denounced these changes, but nowhere were discussions held on such basic questions as: What is the proportion of welfare expenses hidden in the price of a Peugeot, Fiat, or Volkswagen? How generous should the country's social security provisions be without endangering the economy and increasing unemployment? The Six never thought of getting together to weigh the overall advantages against the cost.

Nevertheless, European unification began in an atmosphere of euphoria. The devaluation of the franc in 1958 aided French exports by lowering the rate of exchange. As soon as the first tariff reductions had been effected, chain stores, occupational groups, and cartels hastened to cross borders to sign nonaggression pacts.

The Common Market was regarded as a paradise for consumers. Everyone was certain that the reduction of frontier duties would lead to a decrease in prices. But what usually happened was that prices were raised. Foreign salesmen who came to France in search of customers found there were barriers: The basic cost of establishing sales offices was high (commercial property exists only in Italy and France). But they also found that some doors were open, mainly those of retail merchants. Out of 755,000 retail stories, 150,000 had scarcely any contact with wholesalers or chain-store buyers. Instead of being obliged to organize a complicated system of distribution, importers simply raised their prices and doubled the profits of the retailer. Salesmen exploited the so-called Mercedes-Benz complex— "It's more expensive but it's better; it's made in Germany"; or, "It's more elegant; it's made in Italy." And they made a lot of money. The cost of household goods and tape recorders increased. In Marmande, a town of 15,000, an official observer noted that 27 shops sold German and Italian goods as profitably as French products and yet did not infringe on one another's business. French factories were forced to close. Their owners did not realize why they had failed on their

324

own soil. Discount shops multiplied since they were able to offer amazing bargains.

In Germany, French salesmen found very few retail shops but many wholesalers anxious to protect themselves against international competition—graduates of business schools, they held firmly to their prices. However, some trade did develop. Battles were not always waged with the sword. There was some fencing.

Worried in the beginning, French industrialists relaxed. They took their time in adapting to a competitive situation. They were also slow to modernize their equipment and negotiate the necessary mergers. Thrown among rivals condemned to unite, each waited for the other to commit hara-kiri, believing that whoever held out for the final quarter of an hour would win. Cabinet ministers sounded the alarm, urging businessmen to lower their prices and organize for the future, but they were voices crying in the wilderness.

"In order to lower prices," businessmen answered, "we would have to invest and make a profit. But taxes eat up our profits. We have to raise our prices because the state doesn't let us keep anything for ourselves."

"If you raise prices you'll be committing suicide," the Minister of Finance warned. "When competition really makes itself felt all of you will disappear."

But the fiscal stranglehold was not loosened for all of that.

"We smelled the roses of the Common Market before we were made to feel their thorns," Albin Chalandon, a banker and financial authority, remarked.

Today the French business situation is very precarious. Hampered by controlled prices, obsolete factories, and scant profits, companies have gone deep into debt in order to make some money on their investments. Out of the 50 largest French concerns, 10 are actually prosperous, 7 lose money, and the rest are content merely to get along. Of a total of 1,000 big businesses, a large proportion never venture beyond dealing in very fine handicraft. And out of 350,000 small concerns, Albin Chalandon added, how many do only odd jobs, how many survive solely by paying subsistence wages?

The average Germany factory is twice as large as the French: 735,000 German firms account for 12,000,000 wage earners, whereas in France 765,000 firms take care of only 6,500,000 employees.

France's foodstuffs are competitive. But most of her industrial commodities are 12, 20, sometimes 50 percent more expensive than comparable German products because of higher production costs. France is exporting less than her competitors, although her imports are increasing more rapidly than her domestic production. The crisis experienced by factories that manufacture synthetic textiles is due less to a lack of consumers than to the fact that 36 percent of the goods sold are imported. As a consequence, the increase in domestic consumption, which can be attributed to higher wages, tends to benefit the foreign exporter more than the French themselves.

What are the reasons for the French industrial lag? Eighty years of protectionism. The French have never had an industrial outlook. Many regard profit as theft. The employer is the enemy. Investment and research are merely ways to conceal profits. Too many employers, sons of archbishops or diplomaed pedants, have no conception of modern management and do not encourage competition within the company. French merchants sell what they produce instead of producing what can be sold. The head of a factory outranks the sales manager.

French firms, it must be said, have higher welfare costs to pay than their counterparts in other countries. Taxes that grow daily more burdensome deprive people of hope that their concerns can become competitive. And a gigantic administrative machinery which, since it governs everything, limits a company's prosperity, forces the profitable industries to subsidize the ones that limp along, and gives the foreign competitor an edge.

"Is it true," someone asked Ambroise Roux, the vice-president of the French Employers' Association, "that too many French business executives are incapable of coping with international competition?"

"The Common Market was organized by sleepwalkers," he answered. "They failed to take into account that for three generations our industry and trade have been autarchic. Many employers have been traumatized by protectionism or are convalescing from its ill effects."

"Is it true that our prices are from 10 to 50 percent higher than those of our neighbors?"

"I have asked that a series of analyses be made comparing French and German prices. The first showed that there was a 30 to 40 percent differential. The second showed the very opposite. The third was so complicated and detailed that one could only draw certain general conclusions from it. The truth is that there is a great disparity between the various occupations, the various regions and the various companies. There is also a great variation in the quality of products and in the cost of transportation and manufacture. Consequently, French prices may vary as much as 50 percent. . . ."

There have also been several studies contrasting the wages paid by French and German firms. In general, German wages are higher. But the fiscal levies and welfare taxes, which have increased 25 percent from 1958 to 1968, are higher in France.

The Common Market no longer results in higher prices, save for certain special items like shoes, for example. Italian models, which are very much in demand, cause prices to rise 25 percent each year. French sales have made remarkable progress. "Prix uniques" (somewhat similar to Woolworth's), supermarkets, and miniature supermarkets have multiplied. Chain stores and cooperatives that originated in the workers' movements of northern France have expanded considerably. One of these cooperatives has toted up as many as 10,000 sales coupons.

Foreign chain stores—British, Dutch, and German—have been established in France. Attracting hundreds of retail buyers of food, hardware, and clothing, these stores soon became "Frenchified" and now place most of their orders locally. Some expanding businesses have achieved striking success by selling at wholesale or even at less than wholesale prices. Organized merchandisers account for almost 50 percent of all national sales. They constitute a barrier against the formidable invasion of German and Dutch merchants. In addition, they provide a channel through which foreign goods enter the country in what amounts to a one-way traffic.

"I am faced with a painful dilemma," remarked Roger Durand, an enterprising merchant who is the spark plug of Sopegros. "I buy in Germany at factory prices that are 10 to 25 percent lower than those charged by French producers of household appliances, canned foods, and baked goods. I can find color television sets at 1,500 francs. I simply have to buy in Germany. The result will be unemployment in France. But if unemployment increases, I'll no longer be able to sell. . . . Faced with German and Dutch prices, we'll have to be ruthless with our French suppliers."

Continuing, Roger Durand said, "The Germans are now waging an offensive in France. Often displaying great ingenuity, they are willing to sell through the intermediary of French firms like that big producer of stockings who has placed his packets in all the tobacco shops. Since 1967 the Germans have been organizing their own chains of stores. Institutes have been established in Cologne and Düsseldorf that sell very careful analyses of the French market. Statistics on who buys what are compiled daily. Brewers in Dortmund buy cafés in order to distribute their beer.

"German owners of supermarkets and miniature supermarkets in France are joining forces with French chains to open new stores. They also offer their French partners shares in new German stores. Frenchmen and Germans thus help one another sell their products. It is a sort of Common Market in action. But these partnerships may become one-way streets. French firms have very modest reserves and cannot obtain at home the kind of loans that German banks offer their customers. These French firms are therefore unable to participate in German enterprises and are sometimes compelled to sell a majority of their own shares to the Germans."

Foreign trade officials frequently say, "All French industrialists have not yet realized that one must employ in the Common Market the same sales techniques that are used in the department of Corrèze. In other words, it is necessary to set up networks of sales outlets and conduct advertising campaigns. One small shoe-manufacturing firm, Eram, in Cholet, that employs 400 workers, has opened 25 stores in Belgium and is doing remarkably well. But 60 percent of our producers operate in the Common Market as they do in South America. They write to the commercial counselor at The Hague or in Bonn to obtain a list of agents. Very good commercial agents are rare and already overburdened; . . . those who agree to represent a new product are not always the best."

Marcel Bleustein-Blanchet has stressed this point: "French firms are the ones that advertise the least in the Common Market. As a consequence, foreign products are often better known in France than their French equivalents."

The sale of products in foreign countries naturally involves serious financial problems. German and Italian industries, having prospered for years, are able to do better than French firms whose profits have long been microscopic.

328

René Sachot, famous since 1930 as a pioneer in the field of industrial mergers, began with a small mustard factory in Dijon and went on to establish the Générale Alimentaire, an enormous consortium of food industries. To open a mustard factory in Germany, he had to put up a billion old francs. He exchanged shares with the big English firm Heitz, which already had a network of sales outlets in Germany. Thus it is the English who are selling his condiments in Germany.

"What we need most," say foreign-trade officials, "are several hundred dynamic export agencies—like those serving Rotterdam, Antwerp, and Hamburg—to assist French firms of moderate size. The 800 French manufacturers of footwear export ten times less than the Italians. They should organize groups of 10 to 40 in order to have a representative in every important sales center. If specialists are not available in France, we must look for Italians, Germans, Dutchmen, or Americans rather than close down."

However, the integration of the Six is further along than it seems. When Germany's economy catches a cold, France begins to sneeze. When the Italian miracle took place, German exports to the peninsula increased 30 percent. France's partners are annoyed by de Gaulle's "maniacal anti-Americanism." The general growls against the German-American alliance with the Common Market. But half of the time the Six join forces against the inflation of the dollar.

On February 2, 1967, the Brussels Commission proposed to the ministers of the Six a four-year plan for monetary, financial, and budgetary unity of action with an eye to attaining an annual growth rate of 4½ percent. Expansion requires stability; stability precludes inflation which spreads like an epidemic from one country to another. Hence, the Commission advocated uniform budgets and joint promotion of investments.

The finance ministers did not accept the plan in its entirety. Had they done so, the six budgets would have been cast in the same mold; the same taxes would have been standardized. The freedom of governments would also have been greatly reduced. But the finance ministers favored common principles and agencies such as a monetary committee, a budgetary committee, a contingency committee, and a central banks committee to place the states under surveillance of each other.

None of the Six can, without breaking its promises, proceed to a

329

devaluation of its currency. The result is a foreign exchange that remains rigid, pending the establishment of a European currency which has been ardently advocated by Valéry Giscard d'Estaing, who wants to become Europe's Finance Minister.

The directors of state banks, who constantly confer in Brussels about what decisions to make, already constitute a sort of Board of Governors that attempts to reduce inflationary pressures and regulate the flow of loans from one country to another. At the time of the inflationary surge in Germany, the Bank of Holland refused loans to German borrowers.

The Treaty of Rome does not obligate the signatories to harmonize their direct taxes. But industrialists are urgently demanding an equalization of fiscal burdens. Negotiations are currently in progress. On January 1, 1970, the free movement of persons, businesses, funds, services, and goods is scheduled to begin. Taxpayers and firms will be able to choose their own tax collectors. If one state should prove voracious, its businesses will flee to its neighbors.

When the European plan goes into effect, the public expenditures and revenues of each state will be strictly limited. National budgets will gradually become mere slices of the European plan. Parliamentary debates on them will become largely a formality.

"We have chosen liberalism," Georges Pompidou announced in September, 1967. The next day prices rose on the Stock Exchange.

Already it seemed that any large-scale Socialist experiment was out of the question in the Europe of the Six. A peaceful revolution undertaken by a government of the extreme left could take place only after a denunciation of the Treaty of Rome, the system of free competition, and a break with the Community.

This explains Communist opposition to the process of economic integration that is already under way. Another consideration justifies the hostility of the French and Italian Communist parties—the only ones in the Europe of the Six—to the establishment of a federation or confederation: They would be throttled. In a European parliament elected by 100,000,000 voters, the Communist votes would produce only a tiny minority of deputies. The latter would do nothing more than echo local resentments. Deprived of all hope of taking over the government, they would fail to secure satisfaction for even a minimum of their demands.

A recent poll has shown that Frenchmen who vote for Communist candidates are for the most part against the nationalization of landed property, the suppression of the right of inheritance, and the dictatorship of the proletariat. In despair they would rejoin Socialist, Social Democratic, or Labor parties that are only nominally Marxist. United, these parties would constitute a considerable force capable of alternating with the great liberal Christian party in forming governmental majorities.

In principle at least, the Treaty of Rome outlaws private or state monopolies. The Charter of the Six has introduced free competition in all areas save where it is excluded by special conventions. The Community's Court of Justice has condemned the private monopoly of banana imports into Italy. It has likewise spoken out against the exclusive selling rights granted by Grundig to a French concessionaire.

Monopolies, not state enterprises, are forbidden. There is no debate over Renault. But theoretically at least, the French government, which has a monopoly of tobacco and matches, should open the French market to all of the Community's producers in these fields. (Besides, it has greatly expanded its sale of foreign tobaccos.) A special regulation is to be drafted on this subject because of the complexity of the problems involved—the monopolistic control of tobacco plantations, the monopoly of sales outlets. In any case, the discussion has not been heated. Importers actually enjoy a certain advantage in dealing with a government monopoly, and their goods will in any case be subject to taxation. Finally, a chain of tobacco shops that operates with a ridiculously small overhead is unbeatable.

A problem has been raised by one item in the electoral program of the Federation of the Left: the nationalization of commercial banks. It is legal for a government to nationalize enterprises as well as to create nationalized enterprises. But foreign banks, which include commercial banks, have been established in France. In 1967 they were given the right to open branches. The practical result of nationalization, then, would be to give a monopoly to foreign banks that could not be nationalized. A vital sector of the French economy would pass into the hands of foreign financial powers.

The most obvious way to make Europe independent or merely prosperous enough to compete with the United States, is to create large inter-European corporations combining talents, funds, enterprises, and research laboratories. Everyone is in agreement on this.

331

"Europeans must combine," says Jean Monnet, "in order to produce know-how, techniques, and new commodities, to catch up with America by creating consortiums controlling the immense resources needed to conduct industrial research."

"Applied research," Alain Peyrefitte, a member of the ministry, has stated, "costs three to ten times more than basic research. It is no longer possible for crumbling industries to carry on research. Consequently, private firms or nationalized industries must unite in all the countries of the Six in order to attain a size comparable to that of American companies."

"Starting with existing European industries," says Oliver Guichard, the Minister of Industry, "it is necessary to create industrial organizations that do not have to become gigantic in order to function effectively. Otherwise, the big American firms will be able to get everything they want from Europe, and they will go on to create branches that will transfer to the other side of the Atlantic the profits earned on this side."

However, Brussels has for years been discussing the status of European firms. Quarrels between jurists enlivened the debates. The Germans recognized only large-scale enterprises as European, whereas the French argued that three businessmen—a German, an Italian, and a Frenchman—could constitute a European firm with a small amount of capital at the start. The Germans, thinking of magnates like Krupp, answered that a single participant could constitute a firm. They thus rejected the French conception. There was also much palaver about installing within the inter-European firms factory committees like those in France or trade-unionist managers like those in Germany.

Rightly or wrongly, the French accused the Americans and the cartelized and often Atlanticized German industrialists of opposing intra-Community mergers. France's partners accused her leaders of blocking the work of the Commission by their dogmatic opposition to integration. Pierre Dreyfus failed in his attempts to effect a merger between the Renault and Volkswagen companies. He was also unsuccessful in his attempts to combine Renault, Fiat, Volkswagen, and British Motors.

Despite joint laboratory work by the two countries, Alain Peyrefitte failed in his efforts to induce Bonn to accept a color television partnership utilizing France's patented formula. German firms associated with American manufacturers preferred the RCA formula, claiming that this would make production less onerous.

Alain Peyrefitte replied: "To purchase manufacturing licenses in order to economize on research is tantamount to renouncing the world market."

Paris ended up by cooperating with the Soviets. Agreements were concluded, nevertheless, by French and German chemical firms, and also by French, Italian, and German pharmaceutical firms, notably in the "affair of the century"—the pill—that resulted from the process of perfecting estrogen. Other arrangements for cooperative action were worked out in different areas, although no plans for a Common Market superfirm were made.

In September, 1967, Georges Pompidou announced that the status of European firms would be seriously studied. The Germans showed an interest because the Euro-American mergers were proving more costly than anticipated. In one typical affair, the American firm agreed to hire out its patents for 1 percent of the volume of business of the company it was joining, whether the license would be used or not. It furnished 10 percent of the capital. The government contributed 30 percent as a form of aid to regions in distress. European investors, with Euro-dollars at their disposal, provided 50 percent. The remainder was supplied by the European firm itself.

Finally, attention was given to the formula coined by Jean-Jacques Servan-Schreiber in his book *The American Challenge:* "Let's pay them so that they can buy from us."

The people on the other side of the Atlantic traded, for all practical purposes, their intelligence, their capacity to manage businesses, their expertise, their inventions. They were assisted by the American government's masterly skill in exploiting the managed inflation, the new John Law system.

But the status of inter-European firms raised many fiscal questions. Should the taxes imposed on consortiums be unified in order to prevent them from automatically establishing their center in Luxembourg where dividends are taxed very lightly? Should the dividends of individual stockholders be taxed only once, when the foreign holders of shares have to pay taxes twice—in the state where the firm is located and in their own country?

This was not all. Multinational companies required for their financing a large money market, a European Stock Exchange. Those in charge of French finances, who had long regarded the Bourse as a reservoir of funds reserved almost exclusively for the government, regarded this sort of thing as quite revolutionary.

The financial departments of the central banks studied the possibility of creating a European Bourse geared to meet the needs of the 30 or 40 giant enterprises that would have to be formed: airplane manufacturing companies comparable to Boeing and Lockheed; public works firms for the construction of superhighways; new European plants plus cities for their employees; electronics companies producing telecommunication satellites; chemical and petrochemical firms, and so on.

This, it was thought, could be a joint Bourse, integrated in the manner of the German stock exchanges that conduct business during the same hours, quote uniform prices thanks to instantaneous coordination, and execute orders without distinction no matter where they have been placed. London, Paris, Frankfurt, Hamburg, Milan, Luxembourg, Brussels, and Amsterdam, equipped with interconnected boards, would constitute but a single "place" for important European and international securities.

Some people prefer to see the integrated Bourse conduct business in the evening, when Wall Street is in session. They want global market sessions, encompassing securities on both sides of the Atlantic.

This could prove an opportunity to activate European and, especially, French savings, stowed away in banks and above all in woolen socks; to mobilize the fabulous accumulation of gold hidden by private individuals in Swiss banks, under mattresses, and in cellars. The era of gold could thus make way for an epoch in which securities would be owned by everyone.

Euro-America is coming into being at the same time as the Common Market, and in some respects even more rapidly.

When the announcement was made that frontiers would be eliminated, industry panicked. An enormous number of business leaders flew to the United States. Some went in search of new outlets. Baron Bich (maker of the Bic pen) took over control of Waterman. Péchiney installed factories in the United States. A shoe manufacturer opened ten stores in New York. But most of these "business tourists" returned thoroughly overwhelmed by the technical progress they discovered in domains that were very familiar to them.

334

"It's impossible to compete with them," was the word passed around in the planes returning to France. "If I don't make some kind of deal with the Americans my nearest competitor will, and then I'll be sunk."

Immediately after the war, and for a long time, American businessmen were the only "Europeans." Their companies knew no frontiers. Their passports were valid in all the Western countries. (They still are.) They did not even need a visa. But the best passport of all was the dollar. They were the only people in Europe who had a European mentality, since for them frontiers were merely incidental. They were the only ones who piloted corporations the size of a continent in a market of 185,000,000 people that was comparable to the American market. They were also the only ones with a currency that was valid in the six countries, that was convertible and at a premium. Above all, they alone really saw the Continent, which was not visible to Frenchmen, Italians, and Germans because of their customs barriers and their age-old hostilities.

"For fifteen years American penetration of Europe had been planned with extraordinary care," Charles de Chambrun recounted when he was Secretary of State in the Ministry of Economics. As a descendant of Lafayette he was a rightful citizen of the United States and had been invited by the Business Council, the 70 executives who advised the White House.

Chambrun had offered to investigate their research facilities. To test them, he gave them the names of two average-size French business firms in the provinces. Two files appeared, listing the characteristics of each enterprise, its activities, assets, administrators, stockholders, and also the abutting properties.

"The Common Market," said a Brussels Commissioner, "was a windfall for American companies in Europe. It facilitated their task. The nationals of the Old World were afraid of one another. They fought over American dollar aid, over the Americans who knew how to make these dollars, over their skill in running businesses, over their methods."

The big American companies were the best equipped, the cleverest in exploiting the gold mines the Marshall Plan created in Europe through the fiction of subsidies. This was the American gold rush in Europe. The 185,000,000 customers in the Old World represented a new Klondike. Business was more profitable east of the Atlantic than west of it. And the prices were higher.

In the space of 15 years, the big corporations of the New World invested almost $20 billion in Europe, but these dollars were for the most part earned in Europe. In 1966 American investments increased 17 percent in the United States, 20 percent in the world, and 40 percent in the Common Market. Germany was considered the best bet. She was back on her feet, thanks to her occupiers, who owned more than half of the Federal Republic's capital. The American role in Germany's economy converted Germany into one of the main satellites of the United States.

Of the 170 Dutch companies that have recently merged, 93 are partly American. France and Italy are the only two countries where American investments are comparatively low. For a long time the Gaullist government discouraged American investors but later on sought to reactivate them for the sake of the distressed areas in France and in order to give French producers the benefit of American know-how. The French government could never make up its mind whether it was more reluctant to see American factories on the soil of France or in rival states. During recent years the government's anti-Americanism has resulted in the loss to France of several very desirable American establishments.

France found herself in a paradoxical situation. On January 1, 1967, capital was allowed to circulate freely within her borders. But just prior to that, in December, 1966, all export of capital had been prohibited. Exceptions were made only if special authorization were given. After the first of the year, the export ban was lifted for currency but not for gold. One restriction remained: capital brought into France for more than a year must have special authorization. The Finance Ministry intended to retain control of foreign and particularly American investments. This situation is to last until 1970, when capital will circulate freely within the Community.

Many Frenchmen are taken aback by the intrusion of foreign capital and foreign companies, at the thought that their employers might be German, Dutch, British, or American. "We won't feel at home in our own land!"

"Europe will be our country. We'll have to get used to the idea," Philippe Lamour has said ruefully. "We already have many foreign employers, and we've come to know them. I recently met a great apostle of Europe who was shocked because residents of Strasbourg had to cross the Rhine to work in Baden. But isn't that what Europe signifies?

"Many business enterprises will be threatened because of the Kennedy Round and the Common Market. The optimists believe that the invasion of foreign executives and capital represents a great opportunity for France. She has neither the manpower nor the means to replace immediately the many firms that are going under. Their replacement or reorganization by European or American companies will introduce a spirit of competition into our country. We will learn more effective business methods."

"Let's not fool ourselves," the pessimists say. "This take-over will not raise our standard of living as much as some people anticipate. The Common Market cannot accomplish everything expected of it. Rescue operations are always undertaken in trying circumstances. In Brazil the standard of living keeps declining under American financial control."

"There's no need for a transatlantic reorganization," the leaders of the French Employers' Association insist. "Industries that are properly managed continue to be entirely competitive. The government should adopt measures to stimulate business. But the necessary rescue operations can be conducted without a generalized American control of our economy. We must not approach the Kennedy Round and the Common Market in a defeatist frame of mind. Dynamic French firms have demonstrated that we too can establish successful business concerns in Belgium and in the United States."

"The Kennedy Round and the Common Market being what they are," said Charles de Chambrun, "we are destined to become part of the Anglo-Saxon world, whether we want to or not. Unlike the Germans, who are more or less internationalized, few Frenchmen are at home in the atmosphere of big business. We are still steeped in an economy of washerwomen and employers who show no interest in public affairs."

Frenchmen are shocked when Americans export dollars in order to invest them in various American businesses and then demand the right to invest more on the basis of subsidy agreements. In France the economy is closely tied to the Finance Ministry and controlled by the treasury. In America, big business serves as the adviser of the

337

economy. Taxes are used primarily to further American industry or to control inflation.

Frenchmen are also shocked to learn that pressure groups are permitted in Washington, that a senator has the right to collect a fee in return for protecting private interests in the Senate, provided he lists his honorarium on his income tax form and pays a tax on it.

Frenchmen are indignant when aeronautics manufacturers block the sales of Caravelles because the noise of their jet engines is unbearable, thus giving themselves enough time to build rival planes; that aeronautic companies ask that supersonic "bangs" be prohibited in order to keep the Concorde away from their internal airlines. This means there will be time to build a giant swing-wing plane that will be subsonic over continents and supersonic over the ocean.

The outlook of Frenchmen is quite out of date. They must adjust themselves to the world of the future. Just as Americans have come to France, so Frenchmen must go to America to protect their position there, using the same weapons. They should organize a French lobby in Washington. Americans are quite willing to listen to very frank, even rather sharp talk, if the overall tone is friendly. It is not at all in the interest of the American government to have Frenchmen regard the West as their enemy and the East as their only ally.

Shortly after the war André Malraux drew a picture of what an Atlantic civilization might become if it were not uniquely a business world but a balanced entity of nations united around the ocean. On occasion he wondered whether General de Gaulle was not the Philopoemen of Europe, the last Greek strategist to attempt to unite the Achaean cities in order to protect Hellenic liberty against Rome.

But today things are more subtle. The Six are really not six at all but seven. Should the Six become the Ten, one more would still remain to be added. Uncle Sam, carrying his atomic umbrella, is seated in every home of the European hamlet, his pockets stuffed with patents. Armed with inventive genius, generous and domineering, clumsy and voracious, he is nonetheless endowed with priceless lessons to bestow on his old, grumbling hosts. At times he attempts to unite them around his person, but he often manages to divide them instead, causing consternation by his abuse of power.

European unity can be achieved with America, who wears the face of the future, or against and outside her. The presence of the United

338

States has enormously complicated the very things it should have facilitated.

Did de Gaulle really kill the Community spirit—as his enemies claim—by putting national before common interests? Or have the "Fathers of Europe" put blinders on their eyes to avoid facing human, political, and economic realities?

One thing is certain: It took the United States of America many long years to find itself at a time when everything was less complicated. Today it is the young people who want European unification. Since they will not always be young, they will achieve it. The dreams of youth become the realities of the mature man.

Index

341

345

347